Ancient Greece on British Television

**Screening Antiquity**

**Series Editors: Monica S. Cyrino and Lloyd Llewellyn-Jones**

Screening Antiquity is a cutting-edge and provocative series of academic monographs and edited volumes focusing on new research on the reception of the ancient world in film and television. Screening Antiquity showcases the work of the best-established and up-and-coming specialists in the field. It provides an important synergy of the latest international scholarly ideas about the conception of antiquity in popular culture and is the only series that focuses exclusively on screened representations of the ancient world.

**Editorial Advisory Board**

Antony Augoustakis, Alastair Blanshard, Robert Burgoyne, Lisa Maurice, Gideon Nisbet, Joanna Paul, Jon Solomon.

**Titles available in the series**

Rome *Season Two: Trial and Triumph*
Edited by Monica S. Cyrino

Ben-Hur: *The Original Blockbuster*
By Jon Solomon

*Cowboy Classics: The Roots of the American Western in the Epic Tradition*
By Kirsten Day

STARZ Spartacus: *Reimagining an Icon on Screen*
Edited by Antony Augoustakis and Monica S. Cyrino

*Ancient Greece on British Television*
Edited by Fiona Hobden and Amanda Wrigley

*Epic Heroes on Screen*
Edited by Antony Augoustakis and Stacie Raucci

**Forthcoming Titles**

*Designs on the Past: How Hollywood Created the Ancient World*
By Lloyd Llewellyn-Jones

*Screening the Golden Ages*
Edited by Meredith E. Safran

*Pontius Pilate on Screen: Soldier, Sinner, Superstar*
By Christopher M. McDonough

*Screening Divinity*
By Lisa Maurice

*Screening Antiquity in the War on Terror*
By Alex McAuley

# Ancient Greece on British Television

Edited by Fiona Hobden and Amanda Wrigley

EDINBURGH
University Press

Edinburgh University Press is one of the leading university presses in the UK. We publish academic books and journals in our selected subject areas across the humanities and social sciences, combining cutting-edge scholarship with high editorial and production values to produce academic works of lasting importance. For more information visit our website: edinburghuniversitypress.com

© editorial matter and organisation Fiona Hobden and Amanda Wrigley, 2018
© the chapters their several authors, 2018

Edinburgh University Press Ltd
The Tun – Holyrood Road
12(2f) Jackson's Entry
Edinburgh EH8 8PJ

Typeset in 11/13 Sabon by
Servis Filmsetting Ltd, Stockport, Cheshire

A CIP record for this book is available from the British Library

ISBN 978 1 4744 1259 9 (hardback)
ISBN 978 1 4744 1260 5 (webready PDF)
ISBN 978 1 4744 1261 2 (epub)

The right of Fiona Hobden and Amanda Wrigley to be identified as the editors of this work has been asserted in accordance with the Copyright, Designs and Patents Act 1988, and the Copyright and Related Rights Regulations 2003 (SI No. 2498).

# Contents

List of Figures and Tables — vii
Series Editors' Preface — ix
Acknowledgements — xi
Contributors — xiii
Abbreviations — xv

Broadcasting Greece: An Introduction to Greek Antiquity on the Small Screen — 1
Fiona Hobden and Amanda Wrigley

1. Are We the Greeks? Understanding Antiquity and Ourselves in Television Documentaries — 24
Fiona Hobden

2. Louis MacNeice and 'The Paragons of Hellas': Ancient Greece as Radio Propaganda — 44
Peter Golphin

3. The Beginnings of *Civilisation*: Television Travels to Greece with Mortimer Wheeler and Compton Mackenzie — 64
John Wyver

4. Tragedy for Teens: Ancient Greek Tragedy on BBC and ITV Schools Television in the 1960s — 84
Amanda Wrigley

5. *The Serpent Son* (1979): A Science Fiction Aesthetic? — 109
Tony Keen

6. Don Taylor, the 'Old-Fashioned Populist'? *The Theban Plays* (1986) and *Iphigenia at Aulis* (1990): Production Choices and Audience Responses — 123
Lynn Fotheringham

| | | |
|---|---|---|
| 7 | The *Odyssey* in the 'Broom Cupboard': *Ulysses 31* and *Odysseus: The Greatest Hero of Them All* on Children's BBC, 1985–1986<br>Sarah Miles | 147 |
| 8 | Greek Myth in the Whoniverse<br>Amanda Potter | 168 |
| 9 | The Digital Aesthetic in 'Atlantis: The Evidence' (2010)<br>Anna Foka | 187 |
| 10 | Greece in the Making: From Intention to Practicalities in Television Documentaries. A Conversation with Michael Scott and David Wilson | 203 |
| Bibliography | | 224 |
| Index | | 246 |

# List of Figures and Tables

## FIGURES

| | | |
|---|---|---|
| I.1 | *The Drinking Party* (1965): former pupils cross the fields to join their old schoolmaster for dinner; 'Phaedrus' (John Fortune) is the first to speak on the topic of love. BBC. | 3 |
| 1.1 | Football crowd scenes in *Ancient Worlds*, episode 3 'The Greek Thing' (2010). BBC Productions. | 30 |
| 1.2 | 'Greek fire burns even here in a valley in the American Midwest': views from a car window, driving through Sparta, Wisconsin, in *Greek Fire*, episode 1 'Source' (1990). Transatlantic Films. | 33 |
| 2.1 | Notice for Louis MacNeice's *The Sacred Band* (1944) in the *Radio Times*, 31 December 1943, p. 16. | 59 |
| 3.1 | Mortimer Wheeler lighting his pipe in silhouette on Delos: *Hellenic Cruise*, episode 3 'Delos to Athens' (1958). BBC. | 67 |
| 4.1 | Philoctetes entrusts Neoptolemus with his prized possession, the bow, in *Philoctetes* (1961). BBC. | 90 |
| 4.2 | Bernard Williams speaking in front of a family tree, with illustrations of characters from *Bacchae* (1962) descending. BBC. | 93 |
| 4.3 | The theatre at Epidaurus on the cover of Associated-Rediffusion's teachers' leaflet for *The Angry Gods* (1961). | 99 |
| 4.4 | Barbara Jefford as Medea. Teachers' leaflet for *Theatre and Temples* (1963). | 101 |
| 5.1 | Diana Rigg as Klytemnestra in *The Serpent Son* (1979) on the cover of *Radio Times*, 1 March 1979. | 111 |
| 5.2 | Aegisthus standing behind chorus members in 'Agamemnon', part 1 of *The Serpent Son* (1979). BBC. | 114 |

| | | |
|---|---|---|
| 6.1 | The Chorus of *Iphigenia at Aulis* (1990). BBC. | 130 |
| 6.2 | Religious figures: Tiresias and Oedipus in *Oedipus the King* (1986); Iphigenia and priestesses in *Iphigenia at Aulis* (1990). BBC. | 131 |
| 6.3 | Chorus movement in *Antigone* (1986): Antigone ascending the staircase, with Chorus below. BBC. | 134 |
| 6.4 | The blinding in *Oedipus the King* (1986): Oedipus in the doorway; close-up on blood stains. BBC. | 142 |
| 7.1 | Yumi, Ulysses, Telemachus and Nono in *Ulysses 31* (1985). DiC Entertainment and Tokyo Movie Shinsha. | 150 |
| 7.2 | Tony Robinson narrates episode 10 of *Odysseus: The Greatest Hero of Them All* (1986). BBC. | 161 |
| 8.1 | The Doctor offers advice to the Greek generals at Troy in 'The Myth Makers' (1965). BBC. | 171 |
| 9.1 | CGI Theran port: 'Atlantis: The Evidence' (2010). BBC Northern Ireland. | 194 |
| 9.2 | Inside a Minoan house: 'Atlantis: The Evidence' (2010). BBC Northern Ireland. | 197 |
| 10.1 | At the theatre in Rhamnous in *Ancient Greece: The Greatest Show on Earth*, episode 1 'Democrats' (2013). Tern Television. | 212 |
| 10.2 | Top shot of Delphi from *Delphi: The Bellybutton of the Ancient World* (2010). Tern Television. | 215 |
| 10.3 | The 'wobble' effect in *Delphi: The Bellybutton of the Ancient World* (2010). Tern Television. | 219 |

## TABLES

| | | |
|---|---|---|
| 6.1 | Evaluative comments on Taylor's television productions of Greek tragedy in the press. | 136 |
| 7.1 | *Ulysses 31* (1985): a comparison of English and French episode titles. | 156 |
| 7.2 | Episodes of *Odysseus: The Greatest Hero of Them All* (1986). | 160 |

# Series Editors' Preface

Screening Antiquity is a new series of cutting-edge academic monographs and edited volumes that present exciting and original research on the reception of the ancient world in film and television. It provides an important synergy of the latest international scholarly ideas about the onscreen conception of antiquity in popular culture and is the only book series to focus exclusively on screened representations of the ancient world.

The interactions between cinema, television, and historical representation is a growing field of scholarship and student engagement; many Classics and Ancient History departments in universities worldwide teach cinematic representations of the past as part of their programmes in Reception Studies. Scholars are now questioning how historical films and television series reflect the societies in which they were made, and speculate on how attitudes towards the past have been moulded in the popular imagination by their depiction in the movies. Screening Antiquity explores how these constructions came about and offers scope to analyse how and why the ancient past is filtered through onscreen representations in specific ways. The series highlights exciting and original publications that explore the representation of antiquity onscreen, and that employ modern theoretical and cultural perspectives to examine screened antiquity, including stars and star text, directors and *auteurs*, cinematography, design and art direction, marketing, fans, and the online presence of the ancient world.

The series aims to present original research focused exclusively on the reception of the ancient world in film and television. In itself this is an exciting and original approach. There is no other book series that engages head-on with both big screen and small screen recreations of the past, yet their integral interactivity is clear to see: film popularity has a major impact on television productions and, for its part, television regularly influences cinema (including film spin-offs of popular television series). This is the first academic series to identify and encourage the holistic interactivity of these two major media institutions, and the first to promote interdisciplinary research in all the fields of Cinema Studies, Media Studies, Classics, and Ancient History.

Screening Antiquity explores the various facets of onscreen creations of the past, exploring the theme from multiple angles. Some volumes will foreground a Classics 'reading' of the subject, analysing the nuances of film and television productions against a background of ancient literature, art, history, or culture; others will focus more on Media 'readings,' by privileging the onscreen creation of the past or positioning the film or television representation within the context of modern popular culture. A third 'reading' will allow for a more fluid interaction between both the Classics and Media approaches. All three methods are valuable, since Reception Studies demands a flexible approach whereby individual scholars, or groups of researchers, foster a reading of an onscreen 'text' particular to their angle of viewing.

Screening Antiquity represents a major turning point in that it signals a better appreciation and understanding of the rich and complex interaction between the past and contemporary culture, and also of the lasting significance of antiquity in today's world.

Monica S. Cyrino and Lloyd Llewellyn-Jones
Series Editors

# Acknowledgements

The idea for this book arose in the general context of an increasingly broad body of critical work on British television and the widening academic engagement with classical antiquity in popular culture, and more specifically through conversations at 'Classics on TV: Greek Tragedy on the Small Screen' (22 June 2012), a symposium accompanying a season of screenings at the British Film Institute in London, curated by Amanda Wrigley as part of the AHRC-funded project 'Screen Plays: Theatre Plays on British Television' (led by Principal Investigator John Wyver at the University of Westminster, 2011–15). It was clear at the symposium, which included talks by Lynn Fotheringham, Lorna Hardwick, Tony Keen, Oliver Taplin and Amanda Wrigley, that there was sufficient interest and energy to collaborate further. Later that same month, we began to scope out what a book-length treatment of a range of British televisual engagements with ancient Greece might look like, soliciting contributions to extend the range of material for discussion and to increase the diversity of critical approaches. Two workshops followed: one at the University of Nottingham, under the auspices of the Classical Association's Annual Conference (15 April 2014), and the second at the University of Liverpool (23 July 2015), funded by Liverpool's Postgate Trust. Here, methodologies were explored, sources shared, and approaches discussed. Due to personal circumstances, some of the original members of our group – Lorna Hardwick, Antony Makrinos and Jackie Whalen – were unable to contribute to the resulting book; we remain grateful for their insights and enthusiasm. Peter Goddard also offered valuable criticism and encouragement at the Liverpool meeting.

Bringing this book to fruition would not have been possible without the dedication and patience of all our authors. Particular thanks are due to Michael Scott and David Wilson, who attended the University of Liverpool's 'Documenting Antiquity' workshop (15 July 2013) and two years later took time to discuss their experiences of making factual television programmes about ancient Greece in an interview, thus providing the basis for our final chapter, which by contrast to the earlier academic studies offers practitioners' perspectives. The Screening Antiquity series editors, Monica S. Cyrino and Lloyd Llewellyn-Jones, have been steadfast in their commitment to the book, as has Carol Macdonald at Edinburgh University Press, and we thank them warmly for their enthusiasm and support.

# *Contributors*

**Anna Foka** is Associate Professor in Information Technology and the Humanities at Humlab, Umeå University. A classicist by training, she researches and publishes on the reception of antiquity in popular culture, cultural history in new media, technology for cultural heritage, and digital humanities.

**Lynn Fotheringham** is Lecturer in Classics at the University of Nottingham. In addition to her work on discourse analysis in Latin, she is interested in the reception of the ancient world in popular culture, including film, television, comics and fiction. She has published on storyboarding in relation to Virgil, the representation of Sparta in novels and comics, and attitudes to Cicero in a variety of media.

**Peter Golphin** completed his doctorate in 2012 with the Open University. His thesis traces the evolution of Louis MacNeice's political and philosophical thought through parallel readings of his poetry, and radio features and dramas against contemporary events from the 1930s to the aftermath of World War II.

**Fiona Hobden** is Senior Lecturer in Greek Culture at the University of Liverpool, where her teaching crosses from the history, society, politics and culture of ancient Greece to the reception of antiquity in contemporary culture. Her current research focuses especially on approaches to the ancient world in television documentaries.

**Tony Keen** is an independent scholar. He writes on the reception of Greece and Rome in science fiction, has co-edited a collection on *Doctor Who* and blogs about academic matters at Memorabilia Antonina (<http://tonykeen.blogspot.co.uk>). He was a Research Consultant for the Open University's project 'Classical Receptions in Drama and Poetry in English from c. 1970 to the Present' and has taught classical studies, history and literature courses at a number of universities, including The Open University and the University of Notre Dame London Global Gateway.

**Sarah Miles** teaches and lectures in the Department of Classics and Ancient History at the University of Durham while researching and publishing on ancient receptions of Greek drama and modern receptions of Greek literature in popular culture, particularly children's media, animation and television.

**Amanda Potter** is a Visiting Research Fellow at the Open University, where she was awarded her PhD in 2014 for her thesis on viewer reception of Greek myth on television. She has published on *Xena: Warrior Princess*, *Charmed*, *Torchwood*, *Doctor Who*, HBO *Rome* and STARZ *Spartacus*. She is interested in how audiences engage with the ancient world through film and television.

**Amanda Wrigley** is a Postdoctoral Researcher in the Department of Film, Theatre and Television at the University of Reading. She is a cultural historian of twentieth-century Britain, interested in the difference that is made when literary and dramatic forms reach new publics via radio and television.

**John Wyver** is a writer and producer with Illuminations and Principle Research Fellow in the School of Media, Arts and Design, University of Westminster. He is Director of Screen Productions at the Royal Shakespeare Company and producer of the *RSC Live from Stratford-upon-Avon*.

# *Abbreviations*

ATV         Associated Television
BBC         British Broadcasting Corporation
BBC WAC     BBC Written Archives Centre
BFI         British Film Institute
BLSA        British Library Sound Archive
CGI         computer-generated imagery
ITV         Independent Television
OU          Open University

# Broadcasting Greece: An Introduction to Greek Antiquity on the Small Screen

Fiona Hobden and Amanda Wrigley

At 10.25pm on Sunday 14 November 1965, the British television viewer had three options. Coming to the end of that year's *Royal Variety Performance* they may have been gearing up to watch the US sitcom *Beverly Hillbillies* on ITV, the Independent Television network, or to enjoy the wit and repartee of Frank Muir and his guests in the word-based game show *Call My Bluff* on BBC2, the British Broadcasting Corporation's second television channel, which had been instituted the previous year. Then again, they may have stayed with BBC1 following the end of a 40-minute excerpt from the Magic Circle's Annual Show, broadcast from London's La Scala Theatre, for *The Drinking Party*.[1] This 'Sunday Night' feature by Leo Aylen and Jonathan Miller was billed as 'a modern recreation' of an ancient Greek philosophical text, Plato's *Symposium*.[2] Within the wider schedule of light entertainment this evening, *The Drinking Party* stands out as a serious-minded, if not entirely sober affair.[3] Although antiquity came late to the television screen by comparison with its sister medium radio, which had since the 1920s drawn on ancient Greece and Rome for programme material,[4] from the late 1950s ancient Greece has offered a creative source of inspiration and content for the medium. Today it may be difficult to imagine a dramatisation of a Platonic dialogue being afforded prime position in the schedule of the principal public service channel, but ancient Greek culture, politics, archaeology, literature, mythology and thought have regularly appeared in British television schedules in various forms to the present day.

It is the purpose of this book to examine television's engagements with ancient Greece across these decades. As the first book-length study of this topic, it cannot be exhaustive. Yet, as a collaborative and cross-disciplinary endeavour that capitalises upon the expertise of researchers with backgrounds in Classics, Ancient History, Classical Reception Studies, English, Media Studies, Cultural History and Digital Humanities, as well as television practitioners, it captures something of the scope, diversity and texture of ancient Greece on television. Rather than attempt a catalogue of Greek-themed programming, which would be of limited critical value, each of the chapters drills down into specific examples of different genres, combining close analysis of individual television programmes, production contexts and (where possible) audience engagement. Together they engage with questions of form, style and aesthetics; adaptation processes; technological development; visual markers of antiquity; tastes and interests of directors; the Britishness (or more frequently Englishness) of ancient Greeks on television; the relationship between Classics and elite education versus the broadening of access through a democratic medium committed, to varying degrees, to education and entertainment; and the mixed response of audiences and critics. As well as demonstrating the complex and creative dynamics of ancient Greece on television and proposing a method of study, the book offers pathways for future interdisciplinary work in the burgeoning fields of historical material on television and television in Classical Reception Studies.

An analysis of *The Drinking Party* suggests something of the rich potential of this work. In a *Radio Times* article published in advance of the programme, its producer and director Jonathan Miller identifies his concern to set Plato's *Symposium* 'into a modern context' – yet without 'bringing it up to date'.[5] The result is a very English tableau, with not a toga in sight. Shot on location at Stowe School in Buckinghamshire, *The Drinking Party* opens with a bucolic scene marked by a silhouetted church in the distance, nestling among the trees, and a field of long grass to the fore. This rural idyll is resonant of the 'green and pleasant Land' of England familiar from William Blake's *Jerusalem* (albeit accompanied by the early Baroque *Banchetto musicale* by Johann Hermann Schein).[6] Through the grass wade young men dressed in black tie, carrying umbrellas. The narrator explains that they are on their way to a 'picnic dinner' with their former 'Classics master', who joins them on the porch of a grand neoclassical building (Stowe's Queen's Temple, a folly built in 1742–8). There, amidst fluted columns, they drink wine, waited upon by a servant; and while they drink they deliver excerpts from

Figure I.1 *The Drinking Party* (1965): former pupils cross the fields to join their old schoolmaster for dinner; 'Phaedrus' (John Fortune) is the first to speak on the topic of love. BBC.

Plato's dialogue in upper-class accents, with the occasional elaboration or aside (see Figure I.1). The young men are the epitome of elite education and privilege of the sort that have come to be associated with representations of the nineteenth-century Oscar Wilde in popular culture and Evelyn Waugh's novel *Brideshead Revisited* (1945; it would later be serialised by Granada Television for ITV, 1981).[7]

Like stage plays produced for television at this time, *The Drinking Party* communicates via theatrical and televisual languages.[8] On the one hand, the porch of the Queen's Temple operates like a fixed stage on which characters enter and depart via a grand staircase. On the other, cameras move around the table, capturing in long takes of medium shot and close-up not only individual speakers in soliloquy but also the expressions and reactions of the guests. The viewer almost becomes one of the party, watching and listening like Aristodemus, the silent guest who is represented here by a local photographer (the only one not in black tie) and who, having been hired to document the evening, says little. Written as a prose dialogue, the *Symposium* offers a combination of verbal exchanges and set-piece monologues delivered by characters whose identity is established by the content of their speech.[9] In this respect, Plato's work possesses inherently dramatic qualities, and indeed, since reading was primarily a spoken activity in antiquity, it was already a performance piece, long before staging Socratic dialogues became popular in the eighteenth century.[10] However, the articulation of that dramatic potential through televisual filming techniques results in an intimate and immersive performance of the ancient text.

The fifth-century BC Athenian philosopher Socrates and his companions have been transposed into a very English (albeit classically resonant) setting and transformed into characters who had received an English public school education. The idyll here may have borne some resemblance to Miller's own social and educational experiences, as well as that of some of the cast. Miller had himself been a public school boy, educated at St Paul's in London and at the University of Cambridge where he had served time in the Footlights. Alan Bennett, who plays Eryximachus, and John Fortune, Phaedrus, were also of this generation of Oxbridge comics.[11] For all it is fundamentally English, almost nostalgically so, the depiction nonetheless would have had little connection to the everyday lives of the majority of the British viewing public who would have been educated by the state and were probably living and working in urban contexts in industrial post-war Britain (and for those in Northern Ireland, Scotland and Wales, the discomfiture must have been stronger). The distance between the world represented here and the everyday reality of most viewers may be understood as part of Miller's strategy to modernise Plato without bringing the *Symposium* completely 'up to date'.

Despite this distancing strategy, one of Miller's aims was nevertheless the 'demystification' of the 'marmoreal' Greeks.[12] As noted already, *The Drinking Party* was broadcast in the BBC's 'Sunday Night' strand of single-topic programmes which had recently replaced *Monitor* (1958–65), the BBC's arts magazine programme which Miller had edited for the last year before its demise. Miller's editorship had been criticised for its eclecticism, its intellectual content and an inability to communicate with ordinary viewers. Miller's view was that 'people thought posh people were the only people licensed to talk. I think the BBC thought they could brush aside crumbs from the rather grand dining table, which could then be picked up by people humbly sweeping it up on their knees.'[13] In dramatising Plato for television, Miller may appear both to conform to the paternalistic, or patronising, approach he derides and to live up to his over-intellectual reputation. Analysis of *The Drinking Party* and its reception does, however, demonstrate his sensitivity to the potential inscrutability of his source material and his desire to make it both practically accessible via television and imaginatively accessible by setting it in a recognizable twentieth-century English context.

*The Sunday Times* considered that *The Drinking Party* was 'likely to start a philosophy boom' and *Queen* magazine applauded it for 'making philosophy accessible to a mass audience'.[14] The BBC's Audience Research Report reveals that only an estimated 1.4 per cent of the British population had tuned in (compared with the 25 per cent estimated to be watching light entertainment on ITV) although amongst the forty-two members of the viewing panel who responded to the questionnaire on which the report was based it achieved an average Reaction Index of 69.[15] Many of these 'thought it extremely well carried out' and 'perfect in every way'. However, even some of those who regarded the programme positively found it 'a bit over their heads' and confusing; a few reported being 'decidedly bored'. The variety of reactions extended from those who 'had doubted if they would enjoy it, or be able to understand it', finding it 'unexpectedly interesting and enjoyable', to others who offered evaluations of the fidelity of the adaptation 'to the spirit and the text of the original' (whether the Greek was meant here or an English translation). On the nature of the adaptation, the modern setting was described by viewers variously as 'anachronistic and rather pointless', 'unusual enough to hold attention' and a 'vivid recreat[ion]', with the Stowe School setting 'ideally chosen, creating just the right atmosphere'.[16] These mixed perspectives point towards the possibility offered by television of attracting and engaging a broad audience with differing expectations and prior knowledge (and the impossibility of pleasing all). As a mass medium, television has long been regarded as a democratising force. From the early days of the BBC, thanks particularly to the influence of its first director-general, John Reith, and his commitment to 'inform, educate and entertain',[17] this has involved broadcasting a wide range of what was perceived to constitute the nation's cultural life and history (from Bach to jazz and music hall, from Billy Smart's Circus to Pinter and Euripides, from cricket to the Coronation and *Coronation Street*) to all households with access to a television.[18] This democratisation is evident not only in the effort to bring ancient Greek philosophy to the small screen, but in the confidence and eloquence of viewers within the context of the BBC survey in expressing opinions about this adaptation of Plato's *Symposium*.

In *The Drinking Party*, the perceived distance between the ordinary viewer and the particularities of the setting is underscored in the closing sequence when Socrates takes his leave. As he walks down the stairs and out of shot, the camera pulls back to observe the young men sitting at table, amidst the neoclassical columns that speak not only of the ancient Greece that inspired them, but the power and prestige that these eighteenth-century architectural features evoked as facades of the homes and public buildings of Britain's wealthy and political elite. Here the young men remain seated: drunk, silent and inert, their heavy eyelids indicate imminent sleep. The camera's physical movement up and away from this static scene draws an end to the tableau and establishes a critical distance and an opportunity for reflection. This 'modern recreation' of Plato's *Symposium*, which replays the perceived association between Classics and Britain's white, male, highly educated elite,[19] and offers the viewer (rather ironically, given the scenario and dinner-time setting) 'crumbs from the rather grand dining table', therefore opens possibilities for critical thinking on the chasms of difference in social class and education. Furthermore, in setting forth ancient philosophical ideas, *The Drinking Party* unavoidably highlights differences between Greek antiquity and contemporary society and reflects on present-day social tensions. This is especially evident in the subtle defence by the Classics master, dropping out of character as Socrates, of Plato's presentation of affection between men as superior to the coldness that marks relationships today, at a time when homosexuality was still illegal and the Sexual Offences Act, which legalised same-sex intercourse in England, still two years away.[20]

With its rich and resonant recreation of Plato's *Symposium*, *The Drinking Party* provides a useful way in to the kind of interconnected issues open to analysis in discussions of television engagements with ancient Greece and serves to demonstrate the value of such study, especially at a time when all eras of history are experiencing a resurgence not just in television, but also in novels, films and video games (for example). This resurgence has been accompanied by increased academic interest in the production of popular historical forms and their impacts on knowledge, memory and national identity.[21] Within this work, however, ancient Greece has received limited attention.[22] Additionally, in scholarship within Classical Reception Studies, aside from volumes devoted to single series,[23] television programmes with ancient world subjects and themes are customarily bracketed together with cinema.[24] While television and cinema are both platforms for audiovisual depictions of the past, and there has been an increasing trend across recent decades towards shared features of technology, production, content and style,[25] television and cinema both possess their own production systems, exhibition methods and audiences that inform their specific engagements with classical antiquity.[26] As our analysis of *The Drinking Party* shows, a sense of the place of a television programme within the specific technologies and practices of its form and medium as well as broader cultural contexts in Britain, well beyond anything to do with ancient Greece, is essential for a meaningful interpretation of the rich evidence for the diversity of the responses from viewers preserved in the archives.

For all that the television has long been an international business and watching it a global occupation, each country has its own broadcasting history.[27] While programmes frequently cross national boundaries, in terms of their making and financing, limiting attention to just one national context allows interpretations to be grounded in a specific socio-political and cultural environment.[28] Britain itself is a notion more than a nation: geographically Great Britain describes the islands that make up the countries of England, Scotland, Wales and the Isle of Man, the first three of which have been bound in political union since 1707 and with Northern Ireland since 1920, when the southern half of Ireland seceded from British control to form the Republic. There is cultural, linguistic, economic and political diversity not only between the constituent countries, but within them. However, as the United Kingdom, Britain has a national history and, through shared socio-political practices, a discernible way of life that permits mutual identification alongside awareness of difference.[29] Indeed, by speaking from and to the 'regions' and contributing to the cultural life of the nation, television has played a role in shaping that.[30] Furthermore, for all that 'Western' and 'European' societies broadly claim a lineal association with ancient Greece (see Hobden, Chapter 1), individually each one has its own particular history of engagement.[31] By focusing these case studies on programmes commissioned, made and/or shown in Britain, this book lays the groundwork for a diachronic and cumulative understanding of how, why and to what effects television producers and audiences engaged with Greek antiquity. It thereby opens up to scrutiny a hitherto largely unexplored strand in the historiography of British television, in addition to exploring further the meanings and significance that ancient Greece appears to have held in twentieth-century British cultural life.

## POPULAR ANTIQUITY

Britain in the 1960s, when *The Drinking Party* was broadcast, was still a broadly conservative society, one in which the benefits of the 1944 Education Act (which had raised the school leaving age to 15) were being felt, but more liberal attitudes were taking hold, especially amongst the younger generations, many of whom now had the chance of greater personal, social and cultural freedoms. This was the decade of 'Swinging London', revolutions in popular music, and swift technological change. An increasing number of households had access to television sets and in this decade television as a cultural form – made by the BBC and, from 1955, commercial contractors for ITV – is said to have come of age. For all the first signal was transmitted in 1929, and the first exciting experimental service in 1936–9 reached homes up to 40 miles around London's Alexandra Palace, it was in the years following World War II (after a hiatus during the conflict), and more specifically from 1953 with the live broadcast of the Coronation of Elizabeth II, which drew in 20 million viewers, that television started to become the dominant form of mass media entertainment in the domestic sphere, ahead of radio.[32] A new wave of drama written especially for the medium – characterised by landmark social realist works such as *Cathy Come Home* (BBC, 1966) and popular serials such as *Coronation Street* (ITV, from 1960) – captured the imagination of viewers, whilst comedic forms such as *That Was the Week That Was* (BBC, 1962–3) and *Steptoe and Son* (BBC, 1962–5; rev. 1970s) made them laugh and magazine programmes on the arts, sciences and philosophy (such as *Horizon*, BBC, 1964–present, *Omnibus*, BBC, 1967–2003, and *Tempo*, Associated Television [ATV] for ITV, 1961–7) made them think.

It was in this period, from 1958, that substantial television engagements with ancient Greece began. Earlier, there had been some Greek-inspired drama, such as Maurice Valency's comedy *The Thracian Horses* (BBC Television, 16 July 1946; transposed to radio in 1948), Terence Rattigan's *Adventure Story*, which was set in fourth-century BC Greece (BBC Television, 30 July 1950; originally a 1949 stage play), and *The Fate of the City*, a play set in ancient Greece that was written for television by Winifred Holmes ('For the Children' strand of *Children's Newsreel*, 4 October 1951). There is also a seam of programmes from the late 1940s and into the 1950s on the post-war condition and reconstruction of modern-day Greece, including *Out of the Ruins* (10 February 1947), which *Radio Times* describes as also depicting 'the modern world's debt to Greece in the fields of culture, science, law, and government'.[33] Looking back from the recent destruction to antiquity, the title has a pleasing duality. In such programmes, human devastation was particularly underlined: for example, *Return from the Valley* (27 February 1952) was a 'short film showing Villagers returning to their mountain homes in Greece to start life again after a long absence enforced by war'. This is precisely what *Women of Troy*, the first production of Greek tragedy on British television, did in 1958. The harrowing tragedy by Euripides that follows the fates of the women after Troy has been sacked and their husbands killed was produced by Casper Wrede and Michael Elliott for the BBC's *Television World Theatre* series.[34] Its close-ups of intimate scenes of natural groupings of chorus women, talking as they cook around campfires, amidst rubble, emphasised the human cost of war. One or two other programmes before 1958 highlight Greece as a holiday destination – a place one might, once again, visit, as indeed viewers did thanks to Mortimer Wheeler's *Armchair Voyage* in 1958.[35]

By this time there was also already a rich, fascinating and by some considerable degree larger tradition of BBC Radio engagements with ancient Greek literature, history and thought which extended back to the early days of broadcasting in the early 1920s. The 1950s and 1960s, in particular, saw a phenomenal number of programmes on BBC Radio's Third Programme and Home Service, which drew in many creative ways on ancient Greek and (rather less often) Roman source material. These included performances of Greek tragedy, comedy and their modern adaptations (whether originally written for the stage or radio broadcast); creative reworkings of other ancient texts such as Homer's epic poems and the Socratic dialogues, often for dramatised performance; individual talks or series on a wide range of archaeological, historical or literary topics broadcast as part of school or adult education curricula; and a significant number of creative re-imaginings of (usually historical) ancient Greek texts and topics in the form of feature programmes, many of which were written and broadcast as propaganda in World War II (an important precursor for television documentary – see Golphin, Chapter 2).[36] Television soon caught up with radio's diversity in engagement, with documentary investigations (see Wyver, Chapter 3),[37] adaptations of Athenian drama for schools and adults (see Wrigley, Chapter 4), and reworkings of Greek myth within the new science fiction-fantasy serial *Doctor Who* (see Potter, Chapter 8) developed from the 1950s and into the 1960s. As the landscape of British television has continued to develop over the decades, with a general movement towards diversity in production and a proliferation of broadcasting channels within an increasingly global environment (or marketplace),[38] ancient Greece has maintained a steady presence in the schedules: from drama productions (see Keen, Chapter 5; and Fotheringham, Chapter 6) to children's programmes (see Miles, Chapter 7), through to documentaries (see Hobden, Chapter 1; Foka, Chapter 9; and Hobden with Scott and Wilson, Chapter 10), for example.

The archival evidence demonstrates that this kind of broadcasting was, in the main, experienced by listeners as both entertaining and educational in a rather straightforward way, even if the BBC's idea of ancient Greece (and other aspects of what was considered to be 'high culture') has subsequently been critiqued as both paternalistic and patronising. The significance of this is, however, that the early television viewer's experience of engaging with radiogenic forms of ancient Greek material may well have contributed to the perceived approachability, and therefore the popularity, of corresponding television programmes. A similar, and indeed related, point can be made about newly accessible print forms of ancient Greek texts. Radio broadcasts had for some time operated alongside and often in tandem with the publication of relatively cheap Penguin paperback translations from 1946, for example, giving works from ancient Greece a new and strong public identity away from the school and university classroom where, over the course of the twentieth century, the study of ancient Greek had become increasingly marginalised. Penguin Classics, and other paperback series operating from the same ideological ground, have had, archival evidence shows, a culturally and personally liberating effect on their readers, just as radio has had on so many millions of its listeners. Indeed, television in turn might send readers towards books. Companion volumes, such as Oliver Taplin's *Greek Fire*, written by the presenter of the 1989 documentary of the same name and published by Channel 4 (as 'A Channel Four Book'), offered readers further insights into topics and themes, long beyond the date of broadcast. Then again, television programmes could inspire a rush among viewers for original ancient texts. So the popular historian Michael Wood observes that after his BBC2 series *In Search of the Trojan War* in 1985, Penguin had to increase their print run of the *Iliad*.[39] The intermedial relationships between print, radio and television, as well as cinema and other cultural forms and activities (including digital output for recent years), are a dimension of British cultural history that has only partially been explored,[40] but work thus far has established that it has significance for what is known about audience expectations and experience just as it has for working practices, form, style and aesthetics. This much becomes clear through the content and thematic approaches in radio features during the early 1940s, as discussed by Golphin (Chapter 2), and many of the programmes subsequently studied, be they documentary or drama.

In its presentation of ancient Greek texts and themes, television also follows on from a wider and long-standing engagement with the written and material remains of Greek antiquity in other, earlier educational and cultural contexts. As studies have shown, by the nineteenth century this was a cross-cultural engagement that cut across classes, although the precise ways people encountered the ancient world would have differed according to their situation and their interests. Greek language and literature formed part of a classical education in private and selective schools at the same time as translated texts and story books became affordable and available in public libraries; Greek myth and history provided topics for theatre and burlesque (and in the early twentieth century for film and radio); classical sculptures and paintings with ancient Greek themes were displayed in private homes and public galleries; and archaeological sites and discoveries were illustrated in the press and at public talks (for the latter see Wyver, Chapter 3).[41] From here on, the cultural heritage of ancient Greece – its plays, its histories, its artworks, and so on – became a constituent component and reference point in British cultural life. At the same time, architects recreated Greek styles for private homes and public buildings; and historians and political thinkers drew lessons and ideas from the Greek past to find models for and to critique contemporary events and practices.[42]

## ENCOUNTERS WITH HELLENIC PASTS

In consequence, when ancient Greece began to be televised, it plugged into a long-running engagement that balanced veneration with invention and familiarity with novelty.[43] Indeed, it is from a position of veneration that factual treatments of ancient Greece tend to commence. As Hobden (Chapter 1) shows, discussions of Hellenic history, politics, society and culture almost invariably reference the 'legacy' of ancient Greece to 'us' or 'our' Greek 'inheritance'. This can be linked both to early engagements with Greek texts following their Renaissance rediscovery and the subsequent elevation of Greek culture and ideas by educated elites who viewed themselves through this prism, and to a more general sense of connectivity resulting from the pervasive retelling of Greek myth and history across contemporary culture, as sketched above. However, at the same time, there remained a sense of distance and difference, evidenced by the ruins that increasingly featured on tourist itineraries and by the very fabric and action of the world represented in literature and art, on the stage and screen, and over the radio waves. In television documentaries, this duality in thinking is conveyed audiovisually through presenter performances, on-location filming, and montage sequences in combination with narrative exposition and expert interviews. Thus, assertions of 'legacy' and 'inheritance' are variously sustained, nuanced and complicated. The blending of past and present through analogy, for example, can confirm the universality of human experience encoded in Athenian drama; or undermine the supposed 'rationality' of the Greeks and as a result our and their democratic systems; or emphasise noticeable differences in daily life. Then again, the 'legacy' can be shown to be adaptable and contingent, a perception rather than a fundamental reality, or an idea that might be activated in ways that are morally unacceptable today. However, the notion that the Greeks provide a legacy for Britain, as part of 'European' or 'Western' civilisation, is never rejected. The cumulative result is a multifaceted understanding of ancient Greece set in relation to a modern society which is simultaneously, and by and large singly, defined by that relationship. The diversity of contemporary Britain (or the so-called West) is suppressed through the ideological assertion of connectivity.

The alignment of past and present found in television documentaries has a precursor in the radio features written and produced by the poet Louis MacNeice during World War II, and analysed by Golphin (Chapter 2). However, here the Hellenic past is matched specifically to present-day Greece, as well as to contemporary Britain. Across a range of dramatisations created to serve the propaganda needs of a government leading a country engaged in live military alliances and offences, MacNeice rewrote Xenophon's *Anabasis* from a soldier's perspective; repeatedly evoked comparisons between the Graeco-Persian Wars of 490 and 480–479 BC, in which the freedom-loving, heroic Greeks stood up against and were victorious over the forces of tyranny, and the invasion and occupation of Greece by the Italians and Germans from 1941 to 1944; utilised Pericles' funeral oration, as reported by the Athenian historian Thucydides, to outline the democratic ideal for which the Greeks and the allies generally were fighting; and presented the Theban Sacred Band and the patriotic self-sacrifice of ancient Greeks more generally as models of inspiration. This partisan employment of the history (and historians) of ancient Greece relied upon a sense of continuity between past and present, at the same time as it aimed to evoke a sense of community between the British radio audience and the Greeks, whose suffering and travails in the current conflict were vividly dramatised.

The juxtaposition between ancient and modern Greece crafted in the mind's eye by MacNeice's radio features acquired a visual dimension in television's earliest documentary treatments: *Armchair Voyage: Hellenic Cruise* (1958) and *The Glory that was Greece* (1959), both of which were filmed on location in the Aegean region.

It was a move that was ground-breaking and trend-setting, but also, Wyver argues (Chapter 3), a logical transfer of habits in tourism and education from the nineteenth and earlier twentieth centuries into the new medium. Sitting in their living rooms, viewers were taken on a journey, guided by charismatic presenters – the archaeologist Sir Mortimer Wheeler and author Sir Compton Mackenzie – who lent their knowledge to the virtual tour. Furthermore, with its moving sound-images, television offered a more sophisticated version of the slide-show lectures that promised entertainment and elucidation about foreign cultures and societies – including ancient Greece – earlier in the century. In this way, television acted as a democratising medium, offering to wider audiences experiences and knowledge that were otherwise restricted to those with time and money, albeit mediated through the small screen.

The Greek plays broadcast during the 1960s as part of a developing provision for schools fulfilled a similar function. Marshalling a wide array of material including programme listings, supporting leaflets for teachers, reports produced by the School Broadcasting Council, internal memoranda from and letters to the BBC and camera scripts, Wrigley (Chapter 4) investigates the place of Athenian tragedy on television within British classrooms. Produced to fulfil an explicitly educational remit on the public service broadcaster BBC and the new commercial channel ITV, special adaptations of works by Aeschylus, Sophocles and Euripides were watched by pupils across the full spectrum of schools, but mainly in non-examination streams of secondary moderns. Such school drama programmes not only introduced pupils (and many others watching television at home) to canonical plays in televised performance. They also, through both introductory programmes and specially published leaflets offering background and interpretation, encouraged and facilitated discussion of their moral and political themes, framed, for example, through character analysis or contemplation of the plays' relevance today.

The staging of Greek plays for schools reflects a longer-standing habit of producing theatre plays for the small screen. This resulted in a number of Greek play productions over the decades. Most notably, in addition to the 1958 version of Euripides' *Women of Troy* mentioned above, these include the 1962 Associated-Rediffusion production for ITV of Sophocles' *Electra*, given in modern Greek with no subtitles;[44] the BBC's pared-down production of the same play in 1974 (a still from which is reproduced on the front cover of this book); the BBC's *Oresteia* of 1979, broadcast as *The Serpent Son*; and *The Theban Plays* and *Iphigenia at Aulis*, written and directed by Don Taylor in 1986 and 1990, respectively. More recently, with Steven Berkoff's *Oedipus*, broadcast on the subscription channel Sky Arts 2 in 2013, and *Antigone at the Barbican* on BBC4 in 2015, filmed recordings have brought original theatrical performances (at the Nottingham Playhouse, and the Barbican in London) to the television screen.[45] As both Keen (Chapter 5) and Fotheringham (Chapter 6) show, the transposition of ancient Greek tragedy from theatre to television can challenge the dominant aesthetics for performing the Greeks. *The Serpent Son*, for example, possesses a striking science fiction aesthetic. The style of shooting, costumes and sets, Keen observes, make it visually 'just like *Doctor Who*', the long-running BBC sci-fi drama (whose own engagements with Greek myth are explored by Potter, Chapter 8). This similarity in part reflects general production practices and the involvement of specific personnel; and, whether the science fiction effect was intentional or not, it contributes towards a depiction of pre-classical Greek antiquity that eschews realism and mobilises stylistic devices for representing the future to distance the audience from the ancient past. Realism was an issue too for Don Taylor, whose productions of Sophocles' *Oedipus* plays and Euripides' *Iphigenia at Aulis* also possessed their own distinctive visual aesthetic. Here, however, the conscious attempt at eschewing realism was part of a wider strategy to popularise and make accessible 'classic drama' by a committed socialist and former 'working-class boy made good'. The discrepancies evident between this aim, its execution and the response of viewers and critics to Taylor's television plays are skilfully traced by Fotheringham. In her attempt to understand what was to become the last ancient tragedy on British television for over twenty years, putting a temporary end to an occasional habit of Greek play production, she illuminates underpinning tensions around their 'theatricality', often framed by the question of what television should or should not do.

In crossing genre as well as media, *Ulysses 31* and *Odysseus: The Greatest Hero of Them All* met with greater success and, indeed, acclaim. Broadcast in 1985 and 1986, close in time therefore to Taylor's *Theban Plays* but in the daytime Children's BBC slot, each adapted the story of Odysseus' return to Ithaca from Troy as found in the epic poem the *Odyssey* for young audiences. The two series stand distinct. *Ulysses 31* was an animation, and a Japanese–French collaboration that was distributed internationally. The adventures of its titular hero unfolded in space, resonating in character and plot with the Homeric poem; indeed at one point they intersect directly with the ancient action, with the futuristic Ulysses (whose name follows the Roman tradition) helping to realise Odysseus' return to Ithaca. Furthermore, the aesthetics were those of contemporary science fiction film. By contrast *Odysseus: The Greatest Hero of Them All* was a very British creation. Developed out of the *Jackanory* story-to-camera format, *Odysseus* was written by Richard Curtis and Tony Robinson, the latter of whom also presented it, and filmed on location in English urban and seaside settings (reminiscent, in fact, of documentary storytelling). While following the narrative of Odysseus' homecoming in ancient time, the story was infused with contemporary perspectives and British humour. Setting the two side by side, as Miles does (in Chapter 7), highlights the potential for diversity in engagement with a single Greek myth and a single Greek poem within the landscape of children's television in Britain during the mid-1980s, as one series looks outwards and to the future and the other inwards and to the present.

Moving from single to multiple myths, Potter (Chapter 8) takes us back first to the 1960s and on into recent history in her analysis of Greek myth in *Doctor Who* (BBC1, 1963–89, 2005–present; a family drama) and the spin-off series *Torchwood* (BBC1, 2006–11; for adults) and *The Sarah Jane Adventures* (BBC1, 2007–11; for children). This long-running science fiction series, which in its recent incarnation has been a major international export for the BBC,[46] is at heart the story of an alien called the Doctor who travels with companions through space and time and solves problems. As might be expected, this premise has afforded several opportunities for the Doctor to visit the ancient world. However, Greek myth offers more than a 'historical' setting, as it does in 'The Myth Makers' serial from 1965, which finds the Doctor in the Greek camp during the Trojan War. Not infrequently, it provides a frame for action that unfolds on alien worlds and in the future. Sometimes the protagonists straightforwardly encounter monsters; at others names and eventualities map in more sophisticated ways onto myths. While early programmes were explicitly intended to be 'educational', more generally, for those with some pre-existing knowledge of the stories, there is an additional payoff in recognising the myth; but ultimately it is subsumed into a *Doctor Who* world, known to fans as the 'Whoniverse'. The style and frequency of engagement have varied over the decades, and viewer reports and audience surveys undertaken by Potter demonstrate a range of responses to 'Greek myth' elements and episodes. Importantly, with Greek myth remaining a go-to resource for the production team in the development of fresh storylines, the series continues through re-imagination to engage new generations of children with ideas and themes originating in the ancient Greek imagination, whether or not it is immediately apparent.

Engaging with ancient Greece on television fundamentally involves telling stories: whether examining the history, politics, society or culture in documentaries; restaging tragedy as televised drama; animating or re-enacting epic poetry; or reworking myths for new story worlds (*Doctor Who* comprising its own distinctive mythology). Narratives about and from the ancient world are realised through the medium's audiovisual technologies, forms and modes of communication. The specifics and the style of each new take are informed by pre-existing habits of engagement or trends in representation, and they innovate in distinctive social, political or cultural moments. That moment, furthermore, can be distinctively technological. In recent years, computer-generated imagery (CGI) has become a standard tool in the production process, providing fantastical landscapes and terrifying monsters in *Doctor Who*, for example. However, such digital technologies have also impacted on documentaries. 'Atlantis: The Evidence' (BBC2, 2010) is one such example. As Foka details (Chapter 9), this episode of the long-running history series *Timewatch* (1982–present) is rich in digital imagery, which is marshalled to support the underpinning contention that the city of Atlantis, whose destruction opens the philosophical discussion of two Platonic dialogues, was the Bronze Age town of Thera on modern-day Santorini. In a basic way, spliced CGI footage of exploding volcanoes actualises audiovisually the spoken narration. However, the programme also contains CGI reconstructions of Theran streets and houses, as settings for dramatised action; and those settings contain images and objects that map onto artefacts from the excavated town. The digital *ekphrasis* is immersive and, again, persuasive, acting affectively as evidence for the real world. Finally, the reality of life in Thera is supplemented by computer reconstructions of domestic architecture, following the physical record and Plato's description, and utilising software for cyber-archaeology. The result is a posthuman environment, an imagined 'Atlantis' that is digitally composed, a reality that cannot be inhabited *in reality*. In 'Atlantis: The Evidence' different digital techniques come together to sketch the historical world of Bronze Age Thera in ways that are convincing and rhetorically effective. The documentary claim on the 'real' is supported via artificial fabrication.

The potential for digital technologies to redefine television engagements with ancient Greece was also observed by the historian and presenter Michael Scott, when interviewed along with the producer and director David Wilson by Fiona Hobden, one of this book's editors (Chapter 10). Since 2010 the pair have worked on three documentary series for BBC4: *Delphi: The Bellybutton of the Ancient World* (2010), *Guilty Pleasures: Luxury in Ancient Greece* (2011) and *Ancient Greece: The Greatest Show on Earth* (2013), the latter made in conjunction with the Open University (OU). These programmes cross the terrain of religion and politics, economics and society, and drama, politics and society. In this interview, the title of which plays with Robin Osborne's seminal work on Greek history, *Greece in the Making, 1200–479 BC*,[47] Scott and Wilson discuss the practicalities of producing a programme on ancient Greece in a contemporary environment. Drawing upon individual and shared experiences, they outline the processes of moving from conceptualisation to realisation. At every stage the shape and content are refined, reflecting commissioning priorities, team discussion, budgets, and eventualities on the ground when filming. In comments that resonate with earlier chapters in the book, Scott and Wilson provide practitioners' perspectives on the interaction between past and present, the relationship between education and entertainment, and the limits and potential for telling stories about ancient Greece in an audiovisual medium including – and we might here think back again on *The Drinking Party* – how or, indeed, whether you might successfully do ancient philosophy on television.

Like the presenter of a television documentary today, who follows in the footsteps of Sirs Mortimer Wheeler and Compton Mackenzie on their Hellenic journeys, this book travels a rich terrain that has not been previously explored at length or in detail. From a 'modern recreation' of a Platonic dialogue, via radio's propagandistic features (an important precursor to future television formats), it progresses onwards through factual and fictional treatments of Greek society, politics, culture, history, literature and art. Moreover, moving forward across time, each chapter facilitates a sense of what was happening on screen at different points in television history: during the late 1950s and 1960s, when television was coming into its own as a medium for entertainment and education; or in the 1980s, when one popular format – the screen play – was coming to an end, but new forms of engagement were emerging through animation and shot-to-camera storytelling; or in the 2010s, a time of comparatively prolific interest in ancient Greece, when documentary-makers deployed long-standing methodologies and benefited from new technologies to craft historical narratives. However, several diachronic studies en route point to longer-term patterns and trends. Of particular note, to accompany the persistence of Greek engagements across almost seventy years of British television history, is a continuing desire to situate ourselves in a relationship with ancient Greece and its legacy, a move that is complicated by reappraisals of the relationship between ancient Greek and contemporary society, but that is further evidenced by that continuing return to antiquity for television content. And in addition, there is the openness of the remains of ancient Greece to reinterpretation: like the makers of *Doctor Who*, television more widely adopts and adapts the 'myths' of ancient Greece – defined broadly as the stories available through surviving literature and art – to meet the interests of producers and audiences today. Ancient Greece is always 'in the making', as the present volume shows.

## PROGRAMME DISCUSSED

*The Drinking Party*, billed in *Radio Times* as 'by Plato. A modern recreation by Leo Aylen and Jonathan Miller'. Prod. and dir. Jonathan Miller. BBC1. 'Sunday Night' series. Sunday 14 November 1965, 10.25–11.10pm.

## NOTES

1 This was the case if they were watching the ITV London schedule; Southern and Anglia viewers, for example, had the option of watching chat-show host Eamonn Andrews in action instead.
2 *Radio Times*, 11 November 1965, p. 19.
3 It was not the only serious programme of the evening: a 1954 cartoon film version of George Orwell's political allegory *Animal Farm* (1945), directed by John Halas and Joy Batchelor, was featured on BBC2, 8.00–9.10pm. Despite conforming in style to contemporary American animations for children, the content possessed an adult edge and political overtones. For those who know Orwell's book these are not the leftist overtones expected: see Leab (2007) on the influence of US government and intelligence agencies during the production process.
4 Detailed in Wrigley (2015a).
5 For that, in his view, would be 'an abuse of a great artist' (Miller (1965)), a phrase reminiscent of the (dominant) fidelity discourse in adaptation studies. On 'fidelity', adaptation studies and the need for a more fluid and inclusive theory of intertextualities, see the introductory chapters especially of Geraghty (2008) and Albrecht-Crane and Cutchins (2010).
6 On the romanticism of such rural imagery in nationalistic discourses about England and Englishness, formed in counter to the industrial imperialism associated with Britain and Britishness, see Wellings (2002: 99–102).

7  The world of Wilde was of course impregnated with Classics, and specifically Hellenism. See Blanshard (2010: 93–6), with Dowling (1994: 67–103) and Wrigley (2011g: 23–52), on the place of Hellenism – and especially Platonic theories on love – in nineteenth-century homosexual culture at the University of Oxford, where Wilde studied and excelled at Greats (i.e. Classics).
8  See, for example, discussion of filming techniques in television adaptations of previously staged performances of Shakespeare by Wyver (2014a).
9  Aspects explored by Corrigan and Glazov-Corrigan (2004).
10  See Puchner (2010: 37–72).
11  *The Drinking Party* might also be seen in relationship with contemporary work satirising academia such as the 'Oxford Philosophy' sketches from the comedy stage revue *Beyond the Fringe*, featuring Alan Bennett and Jonathan Miller.
12  See Romain (1992: 30), quoting Miller in interview.
13  Observed by Irwin (2011), with quotation at 335. On Miller and *Monitor*, see Wyver (2007: 30–1).
14  These positive quotations from reviews were printed with the *Radio Times* listing (7 July 1966, p. 27) for the repeat broadcast of *The Drinking Party* in 1966; the repeat accompanied the first airing of Miller's related 'Sunday Night' feature *The Death of Socrates*.
15  For an introduction to the Listener Research Department and Audience Research Reports to 1950, see Nicholas (2006).
16  BBC Written Archives Centre (BBC WAC) VR/65/646.
17  The triumvirate that still underpins the BBC mission statement: <http://www.bbc.co.uk/aboutthebbc/insidethebbc/whoweare/mission_and_values> (accessed 10 February 2017).
18  See Crisell (2002), whose study of developments over the decades demonstrates the limitations of this interpretation of what 'democratisation' might mean in principle and practice.
19  The association of course belied a more complex set of cultural dynamics: see, for example, Stray (1998), who explores the educational context, and the 'Classics and Class' project (<http://www.classicsandclass.info/>, last accessed 10 February 2017), which documents the extensive popular engagements with Classics during the long nineteenth century.
20  In light of its topicality, it is striking that the homosexual content of Plato's dialogue and thus *The Drinking Party* receives no comment in surviving reports and reviews. Asked about it during an interview at the 10th Annual Fantastic Film Festival (National Media Museum, Bradford, June 2011), Miller commented upon the homosexuality underpinning the educational experience at Oxford during his time there (and so implicitly in the world of this work), but was not otherwise drawn: see Penny Goodman's comments at: <https://weavingsandunpickings.

wordpress.com/2011/06/17/jonathan-miller-and-the-drinking-party> (accessed 10 February 2017).

21 On the diverse ways history is encountered in popular culture, see de Groot (2009) and Aurell (2015), together with other contributions to *Rethinking History* 19.2 (2015). Dillon (2010) focuses on history on British television since 1946 and the role of programmes in the creation of national identity and collective memory. Cannadine (2004) draws upon the expertise of producers, presenters and historians in discussions of the two-way relationship between history and British media. Studies in Bell and Gray (2010) critique a range of non-fiction history programmes produced in Europe since World War II, while Gray and Bell (2013) narrow the focus to British history on television in the period 1995–2010, examining the commissioning and production contexts as well as the character of factual history. None pay particular attention to ancient world representations, although the documentary *Cleopatra: Portrait of a Serial Killer* (BBC1, 2009) raises issues around international productions while *Rome Wasn't Built in a Day* (Channel 4, 2011) merits analysis in the context of historical re-enactment in Gray and Bell (2013: 178, 154–6); and de Groot (2009: 199–201) sets *Rome* (BBC1, 2005–7) alongside the Western *Deadwood* (HBO, 2004–6) as an exemplar for the grittiness of today's 'authentic' historical dramas. Recent analyses of historical documentaries often prefer other subjects: for example, Hanna (2009) on World War I.

22 Although interest is gathering pace. For structural and thematic analyses of ancient Greece documentaries, see Makrinos (2013) and Hobden (2013b, with 2013a and 2017). Hughes (2009) specifically provides insights into the commissioning and making of *The Spartans* (Channel 4, 2002), which the author co-wrote and presented. Examples of Greek drama on television are analysed by Wrigley: see (2014a) on the 1964 BBC *Lysistrata*, (2015b) on the 1962 Sophocles' *Electra* on ITV. Wrigley (2017b) covers various productions of Aeschylus' *Oresteia*; Wrigley (forthcoming) is a book-length study of all Greek plays on British television. The American mythological fantasy series *Xena: Warrior Princess* (1995–2001), a spin-off from *Hercules: Legendary Journeys* (1995–9) and broadcast similarly in the UK on Channel 5, has especially aroused interest: most relevantly from a 'classical' perspective, Early and Kennedy (2003) contains three *Xena* essays, with a focus on gender and fan fiction and a contextualization of the series' Amazon hero within wider representational trends for women warriors; and Potter (2009) explores reviewer responses to the series alongside 'mythical' episodes of the American witches series *Charmed* (1998–2006).

23 Specifically on the HBO–BBC co-production *Rome* (2005–7): see Cyrino (2008, 2015); and STARZ' *Spartacus*, 2010–13: see Cornelius (2015) and Augoustakis and Cyrino (2016).

24 Film and television are successfully blended to explore representa-

tional themes in Pomeroy (2008); in Renger and Solomon (2013) and Cyrino (2013) television is a sideline to more extended discussion of films. Joshel, Malamud and Wyke (2001), Nisbet (2008) and Lowe and Shahabudin (2009) situate television case studies more broadly within popular culture. Note that in the more recent volumes, the television interest is primarily provided by *Rome* and *Spartacus* (see previous note): see also Elliott (2013a, 2013b), who approaches the former from within the contexts of technological developments in television and transnational viewing, respectively. Pomeroy (2017), which provides an array of investigations into 'ancient Greece and Rome on screen', appeared just as the present book went to press; while we have been unable to read all items in that book, we have tried where possible to reference relevant chapters in individual studies below.

25  See Ellis (1982): the formal and stylistic division between film and television that emerges through his separate analysis of both media, in addition to video, has been moderated in recent years by some generic convergence in terms of production, broadcasting and aesthetics. See Andrews (2014) for the increasingly complex interplay between cinema and television in the British context. Treacey (2016) offers a useful survey of the literature on 'screened history', crossing and distinguishing between film and television.

26  Although see Blanshard and Shahabudin (2011: 218–19), who credit the familiarity and popularity of Roman epic cinematic film to the way they were later 'continuous[ly] disseminat[ed]' on television between *The Fall of the Roman Empire* (dir. A. Mann, 1964) and *Gladiator* (dir. R. Scott, 2000).

27  For a survey of international trends and of national/regional television traditions, see Smith (1998). Wheatley (2007) and Mee and Walker (2014) are good examples of the development of a historiography of British television, the latter prioritising Britishness over medium in its evaluation of cinema and television side by side.

28  Perhaps the best example of this relating to the ancient world on television is Joshel (2001) on the resonances of the celebrated costume drama *I, Claudius* (BBC, 1976) in the United States, where it was broadcast by PBS at a time of political and social anxiety in 1977–8. See also Monoson (2011: 69–71), who analyses the depiction of Socrates in 'The Death of Socrates', an early episode of the US historical news programme *You Are There* (CBS, 1953–71), in terms of McCarthy-era anti-communist politics, alongside other American engagements with the philosopher.

29  Not in a neutral or straightforward way, however: see Langlands (1999), who asks 'how do the other [non-English] populations within the state relate to Britishness' and whether there is 'a distinctive Englishness distinguishable from Britishness'. The present volume does not address such thorny issues of identity head on; but the perceptible lack of

regional specificity in all but one case study (see Miles, Chapter 7) may suggest ways in which these particular programmes promote a national rather than local engagement that may in turn support the hegemonic conflation of Englishness and Britishness that Langlands dissects.

30 Hajkowski (2010) examines the BBC's role in the national identity to 1953, with chapters on Scotland, Wales, Northern Ireland and the empire; Dillon (2010: 3) considers that 'Television organises and motivates how national character has been valued, presented as fact, reality, reconstruction and myth.'

31 For responses within Europe, albeit restricted to the nineteenth century, see Klaniczay, Werner and Gecser (2011). The depth of engagement within and beyond the so-called 'West' is evident in Stephens and Vasunia (2010). Chapters in Part 2 of Kallendorf (2007) provide more schematic studies focused on particular places; of particular note, British interactions with Hellenic culture over the centuries are summarised by Jenkyns (2007: 274–8), drawn in distinction to engagements with Rome. Cf. Jenkyns (1980) for a more in-depth study of nineteenth-century trends.

32 From the perspective of viewers of the Coronation, television was 'in some ways something extraordinary, and in other respects well on its way to becoming an element of the everyday life of the audience', observes Örnebring (2007: 174). See also Briggs (1995: 420–35), Wyver (2016). For the very early history of British television, see Aldridge (2012).

33 *Radio Times*, 7 February 1947, p. 35. Also, *News Map*, on the 'present position in Greece', 16 January 1948.

34 For a critical overview of this production, see Wrigley (forthcoming).

35 For example, *Family Affairs* on 15 June 1955 included a 'Holiday in Greece' segment.

36 Wrigley (2015a) offers a first account of this rich terrain, with selective production chronology.

37 Indeed, see Wyver and Stevens (2018) on how from the late 1950s onwards a number of the creators of the emerging 'poetic' television documentaries, such as Denis Mitchell and Philip Donnellan, transformed distinctive techniques of radio features into highly effective visual forms.

38 Parts 2 and 3 of Crisell (2002) bring the survey of developments in British television up to date until the time of publication, while the 'global marketplace' is examined from a British perspective by Steemers (2004).

39 Wood reflects on this boost in sales in a companion documentary to the DVD edition of *In Search of the Trojan War*, released in 2004 (a VHS video had previously been released in 1985). The presenter also authored a companion book of the same title, published in 1985 to accompany the series as a BBC book. It was then revised and published

by Penguin in 1996; this edition has been reissued several times since. There was also a 1989 Oasis audio book. *Greek Fire* (Channel 4, 1989) is discussed by Hobden (Chapter 1). Jenkins (2015) suggests possible directions for exploring the interactions and impacts of different cultural products with classical themes from an American perspective.

40 Müller (2010) thinks through some issues regarding television specifically; see other contributions to Ellestrӧm (2010) for a wider examination of the issues and implications around intermediality. For one step in this general direction relating to the ancient world, see Hobden (2016) on the intermedial and intergeneric characteristics of contemporary documentaries about the ancient Roman town of Pompeii.

41 In addition to works already mentioned, Hall and Macintosh (2005) covers Greek tragedy on the British stage to 1914; for more on Victorian burlesque see Monrós-Gaspar (2015); Coltman (2009) considers classical collecting by individuals and institutions, while Nichols (2015) explores Greek and Roman sculpture in a public setting at the Crystal Palace to 1936; for Greece on film, see Shahabudin (2006) and Berti and García Morcillo (2008), with MacKinnon (1986) and Michelakis (2013) on tragedy in film specifically; relevant material is also addressed alongside silent and epic films with Roman and other ancient world content: see Michelakis and Wyke (2013) and Paul (2013a) respectively.

42 See note 31, above, for relevant studies.

43 A dynamic witnessed frequently in the case studies presented by Silk, Gildenhard and Barrow (2014).

44 On the modern Greek *Electra* (1962), see Wrigley (2015b).

45 The Sky Arts 2 transmission of Steven Berkoff's *Oedipus*, which he directed for Nottingham Playhouse, is mentioned by Safran (2017: 196–7) in relation to other screen versions of Sophocles' play. A short clip is available at the website of the production company, Team Media: http://www.team-media.tv/production/theatre-stage-performance (accessed 10 February 2017). *Antigone at the Barbican*, directed by Ivo van Hove, given in Anne Carson's new translation and with Juliette Binoche in the title role, was transmitted on BBC4 (available to digital television viewers) at 8.00–9.30pm on Sunday 26 April 2015 as part of its season 'The Age of Heroes: Ancient Greece Uncovered'.

46 In 2011 *Doctor Who* was the BBC's most successful export, or leading 'power brand', as reported by Sweeney (2011). The impacts of this international distribution, especially to the United States of America, on the supposedly quintessential British show are explored by Porter (2012).

47 Osborne (2009).

# 1 Are We the Greeks? Understanding Antiquity and Ourselves in Television Documentaries

Fiona Hobden

Sir John Wolfenden: 'I think it's true to say, don't you, that what the Greeks did in the questions they raised, in their thinking, the books they wrote, the poetry they wrote, the experiments in living, in political democracy, all those things, they all start there ... Wherever you look in the fields of art or history or political living, it all starts in Greece ... Well, I would go so far as to say, myself, if I were really pushed, that Western civilization as we talk about it, including American civilization, the whole of western Europe really, when you get down to it, what it doesn't get from the Bible it gets from the ancient Greeks.'

Sir Mortimer Wheeler: 'Well, that I will argue with you after dinner.'

'Venice to Mycenae', *Armchair Voyage: Hellenic Cruise*

Standing on the deck of a cruise ship destined for Greece, Sir John Wolfenden, a prominent educationalist and guest speaker on the tour, is asked by the well-known archaeologist and presenter of *Armchair Voyage: Hellenic Cruise* (BBC, 1958; henceforth *Hellenic Cruise*), Sir Mortimer Wheeler, to explain the 'extraordinary pull' of Greece today. After considering the natural landscape and the buildings and statues the ancient Greeks left behind, Wolfenden turns to the political and cultural inheritance. These, he asserts, are the basis of modern civilisation in the West. Wheeler appears unconvinced, and yet, as the ship travels on to Olympia and footage of the ruined sanctuary appears on screen, he observes, 'the newcomer most readily finds contact with that sense of beauty and humanity that are the basic contributions of Greece to the modern world'. Wolfenden's proposition is sustained. *Hellenic Cruise*, the first British television documentary to engage with ancient Greece at the time of broadcast,[1] establishes the relationship between the Hellenic past and Western present as one of inheritance. In this, the programme was far from unique. For example, in 1821 the English romantic poet Percy Bysshe Shelley wrote passionately that 'We are all Greeks – our laws, our literature, our religion and our art have their root in Greece', when attempting to encourage his British compatriots to support the Greek struggle for independence from Turkish rule.[2] Exactly a century later, in the introduction to *The Legacy of Greece* (1921), a multi-authored collection of essays for general readers, Gilbert Murray, Oxford University's Regius Professor of Greek and a committed public Classicist, similarly argued that 'the beginnings of nearly all the great things that progressive minds now care for were then being laid in Greece'.[3] The sentiments foregrounded by *Hellenic Cruise* in its very first episode reiterate a longstanding and widely held view, represented by but extending well beyond these brief examples.[4]

In the years since, this perceived relationship has continued to inform documentary approaches. Its centrality to *The Greeks: A Journey in Space and Time* (henceforth *Journey*), a four-part series broadcast on BBC1 in autumn 1980, is emphasised by the invitation posed to viewers taking part in the BBC Audience Research panel to assess how far episodes succeeded 'in making clear the great debt all subsequent civilizations owe the Greeks'.[5] As described by the director and presenter Christopher Burstall at the beginning of episode one, the motivation for this series was his growing realisation that 'ancient Greek ideas and drama and poetry and history and art are the bedrock of our world today, what we call western civilization'. This appreciation of an inheritance from the Greeks led Burstall to the question 'who were they?'[6] Noteworthily, the more recent BBC2 series *Who were the Greeks?* (2013) also asserts the Hellenic legacy before embarking upon its investigation. Understanding the ancient Greeks continues to require reference to the assumed inheritance, situating viewers within a modern Western context that is defined by the society whose history, politics and culture are under scrutiny.

And yet, as Wheeler intimated in *Hellenic Cruise*, this premise is debatable. Indeed, in episode one of *Who were the Greeks?* the notion of indebtedness is established in the prologue by reference to hearsay, as something presenter Michael Scott remarks is 'often said', rather than as a straightforward fact. Furthermore, although episode two ends by confirming a legacy, the strangeness of the Greeks in their daily life is repeatedly brought to the fore (as will be discussed below). By taking an interest in the minutiae of Greek society, the notion of inheritance becomes complicated. Again, this is neither entirely new nor unique to television. Indeed, the existence of such a conversation around the turn of the twentieth century is indicated by the efforts Gilbert Murray makes in *The Legacy of Greece* to accommodate potential critics. To the charge that in their lifestyles the people who supposedly achieved such high cultural and intellectual attainments 'resemble savages', Murray can only admit that, located 'somewhere between a Viking and a Polynesian', Greeks of the fifth century BC 'were separated by a thin and precarious interval from the savage'.[7] By this sleight of hand Murray keep the Greeks on their pedestal, whilst admitting the challenge posed by recent anthropological approaches.[8] Underpinning the opposing argument is a perception of difference founded upon an opposition between the primitive and the civilised: the Greeks 'were sunk in the most degrading superstitions: many practised unnatural vices'.[9] This paradigm and its terminology may be out of fashion, but the conversation exemplified by Murray's hypothesis and the arguments attributed to his imaginary detractors continue through televisual treatments of ancient Greece.

By constructing perspectives on the supposedly special relationship between ancient Greece and modern society that uphold and challenge notions of comparability and inheritance,[10] documentaries take up and advance a long-running debate. It is the purpose of this chapter to evaluate the shape and tenor of this debate on British television.[11] The investigation begins by examining the basis and endpoint of the legacy argument: the assumption of similarity. Three programmes broadcast on the BBC's factual channels (BBC2 and BBC4) since 2010 illustrate the ways in which similarity is established and contested when Greek culture is approached through an explicit prism of inheritance. Attention then switches to an earlier series that tackled the legacy head on. Developed by an international consortium and shown on Channel 4 in 1990, *Greek Fire* articulates a more provocative and partisan perspective on the notion of a Greek inheritance, in conformity with the new channel's edgier remit. The final section returns to the present to investigate instances in topic-based programmes where the alleged debt to Greece is problematised by demonstration of its undesirability or its undesirable consequences. By tracing the documentary depiction of ancient Greece through analysis of audiovisual and narrative strategies, this chapter illuminates the terms in which television responds to and carries on the wider debate, which might be summarised by the question 'Are we the Greeks?' Moving forward and backward in time facilitates reflection on the changing socio-political contexts in which the programmes under study develop as well as the particular ideology underpinning contemporary engagements. Underlying problems also emerge with the assumed association between the Hellenic past and Western present at a time when the definition of 'us' is far from stable.

## FROM SIMILARITY TO DIFFERENCE

In evaluating how television documentaries navigate the assumption of similarity embedded in the legacy concept, *Ancient Greece: The Greatest Show on Earth* (BBC4, 2013; henceforth *Greatest Show*) offers a useful place to start. The three-part series presents an investigation into Greek drama that traces its origins and development from fifth-century BC Athens to Imperial Rome to the modern theatre stage. At one level, the narrative is one of progression. However, from the very first there is an assumption of continuity in psychology and experience. This is intimated in the opening sequence of episode one, during which the presenter, Dr Michael Scott, is shown seated in a small cinema, intently watching the screen. On it appear scenes from *Trojan Women* (1971), an adaptation by the Greek film director Michael Cacoyannis of Euripides' tragedy of the same name, conventionally dated to 416 BC.[12] As emotions flicker across his face, Scott recalls in voiceover how the first time he encountered the film he cried. This scene establishes an emotional connection that arises from the original play's treatment of 'the most charged aspects of human life – love, war, sacrifice, fear and death ... it is still utterly gripping today'. Furthermore, the emotional content prefaces a legacy statement. As he turns to the audience, Scott remarks, 'That civilisation [i.e. ancient Greece] has influenced almost every aspect of our lives. Not just drama, but politics, language, philosophy, art and architecture. To understand ourselves, it turns out, we need to understand the ancient Greeks.' The programme thus sets 'ourselves' alongside the Greeks in a pool of shared humanity, to the extent that by learning about them we learn about ourselves.

The underpinning notions of shared psychology and experience extend across the series, for example in a series of conversations staged between Scott, a Greek historian at Warwick University,[13] and Dr Rosie Wyles, an expert in ancient theatre at the University of Kent. As the two exchange ideas, the performance of Greek plays today is explained by reference to a shared humanity. So Aeschylus' *Persians*, a dramatisation of the defeat of the Persians at the battle of Salamis in 479 BC that was staged for the victorious Athenians seven years later, has 'echoed ever since' because of its treatment of war, 'one of these eternal themes'. Similarly Sophocles' *Antigone*, produced during 442 BC, is 'timeless' and 'enjoys universal appeal' in depicting the eponymous heroine's challenge to civic authority, represented by her uncle, the king Creon (both episode one). The sex-strike by which the women of Greece attempt to bring about peace in Aristophanes' *Lysistrata* (411 BC) 'strikes a chord in our continually conflict-ridden world' (episode two). More broadly, Menander's family-oriented sitcoms, produced in the early third century BC, 'always work no matter where you are' (episode three). By this consistent analysis, Athenian drama transcends the moment of its inception to address fundamental human experiences.

The implication of continuity and comparability is further developed by the sequence dedicated to Theophrastus' *Characters* (episode two). By Scott's argument, espoused as the presenter sits reading in an Athenian café, the portraits penned by the philosopher in the late fourth century BC offer 'a fantastic window on the people of ancient Athens' that 'can be applied to any city, anywhere in the world'. As each character's special qualities are recited in voiceover, Scott looks up from his book and glances to the side; the camera then shifts to members of the public sitting nearby. This cutaway gives the impression that the person on screen is under the presenter's gaze. By this trick the man on the street becomes 'The Mean Man' (sitting quietly on his own), 'The Garrulous Man' (talking and waving his arms around) or 'The Exquisite Man' (smoking a continental cigarette). At the same time Scott takes on the role of the 'people-watching' Theophrastus. Coinciding with the series' broader argument, the Athenians on screen represent all humanity, past and present.

In this latter scene, the potential for such effective comparisons arises from the propensity in documentary for on-location shooting and the filming of presenters in situ, that is to say in the modern places where historical events happened.[14] However, this very strategy can complicate notions of similarity. 'The Greek Thing', the third episode in *Ancient Worlds* (BBC2, 2010), illustrates this well. Presented by the University of Sydney archaeologist Dr Richard Miles, this six-part series constructs a historical narrative of ancient civilisations from Mesopotamia through to Rome. In addition to its chronological sweep, coherence is instilled by Miles' description in the prologue to episode one ('Come Together'): 'It's not the story of ancient worlds long past. It's the story of us, then.' Each episode proceeds to examine how humans have lived together at different places, in different times. Within this set-up, 'The Greek Thing' might have fallen back on easy associations. Certainly, the episode begins by acknowledging that 'Today "the Greek thing" has become a sort of shorthand for the values that we like to think are at the root of who we are: rational, cultured, humane, civilised.' Immediately, however, this assumption is unsettled. 'But beneath the civilised skin was a fierce, volatile pulse that gave the Greek thing its energy, passion, life, and its capacity for sudden shocking violence.' At the same time, scenes of political unrest in the streets of modern-day Athens – advancing protesters and armed police clashing against a soundscape of chanting and blaring sirens – jostle with images of marching hoplites on marble sculpture and single combat on black-figure pottery. The sequence ends with a grimacing Gorgon's face. By reconstructing the ancient scenario through the present, drawing the imagery of twenty-first-century political protest into alignment with the ancient iconography of war, similarity is proposed. Here is the violence claimed for antiquity in the present day. The footage confirms Miles' implication that the terms of a Hellenic legacy merit reconsideration.

The proposition is sustained when the passions and sectarianism of the classical Greek city, or *polis*, are addressed head on. Alternating between direct address from inside a football stadium and voiceover, Miles describes the importance of the *polis* in building Greek identities and the intense emotions involved in political membership, namely a fierce, passionate attachment to the community balanced with hatred of others. In the background and then to the fore, individual AEK Athens F.C. supporters light flares, wave flags, jump arm in arm, chant, jeer, whistle and burn a rival team's scarf; but filling the screen en masse, dressed in the tribal yellow and black, they act as one (Figure 1.1). Together the supporters channel a dangerous energy. The dynamics and the perspectives of the football crowd, a community of supporters united in their allegiance and their antagonism to the opposing team, map onto the ancient Athenian *polis*, with its 'rancorous edge' and ever-present potential to 'blow up', as it is described by Miles. This portrayal again speaks against the typical view of the ancient Greeks cited earlier, and for the alternative perspective. As this is 'the story of us, then', the footage of aggression on the streets and at the football stadium asks what it means if 'our' roots do lie in ancient Greece. This represents a challenging perspective on the Hellenic legacy and civilisation.

In both *Greatest Show* and *Ancient Worlds*, the presenter plays an important role in mediating present-as-past by providing on-the-ground perspectives, facilitated by the modern-day Greeks around him. In *Who were the Greeks?*, by contrast, the integration of the presenter into contemporary situations effects an impression of

Figure 1.1 Football crowd scenes in *Ancient Worlds*, episode 3 'The Greek Thing' (2010). BBC Productions.

difference. Originally shown on BBC2 in June 2013, the first of two episodes features re-enactment scenes in which the presenter, again Michael Scott, repeatedly demonstrates his inability to act like an ancient Greek. On one occasion, Scott is thrown to the floor during the training session of an Athenian *pankration* team. While in voice-over he observes the efficacy of the martial art, which combined elements of boxing and wrestling, on screen, pinned flat on the ground, he taps his hand in submission. In another scene, the presenter's face creases in revulsion, as he identifies the underlying flavours of vinegar and blood in the Spartan black broth, described by one costumed re-enactor as 'tough food for tough men'. And finally, spilling wine down his chin whilst attempting to drink from the distinctive Athenian *kylix*, a stemmed vessel with a broad cup, whilst lying in the reclining position typical of Greek drinking parties, Scott declares his own 'epic fail' at the *symposium*. If drinking in the right way 'proved who was in and who was out', as the presenter asserts, his ineptitude places him firmly on the outside. In part this reflects the general effect of historical re-enactment. Donning the dress of people from the past and behaving like them means doing things otherwise. Hence, re-enactment always articulates the 'essential otherness of history'.[15] However, the repeated 'fails' take this to an extreme. Through his physical performances, Scott embodies the difference between ancient and modern.

This display of ineptitude chimes with the broader depiction of ancient Greece in *Who were the Greeks?* As observed in the introduction above, the same episode begins by asserting the legacy of the Greeks. Standing outside the Parthenon, the temple on the Athenian Acropolis that continues to stand for the high cultural, political and artistic attainments of ancient Greece,[16] the presenter recites the usual list of debts, describing 'language, literature, art, philosophy, politics, architecture, sport, [and] culture' as 'the very bones, sinews, muscles and lifeblood of our modern world' – a doubly striking metaphor given Scott's body-based demonstrations of difference. But, as in *Ancient Worlds*, this is immediately qualified. Below the surface lies 'what can seem to us a seething tornado of alien, unsettling and downright outrageous customs and belief'. As the episode progresses, difference is found in the character of the ancient city ('these weren't like our modern cities today'), child exposure ('it seems shocking that a culture we so admire practised ... infanticide and eugenics'), religious belief (combining 'what are to us rational and irrational'), sexual practices ('very strange indeed'), drinking parties ('not what you might think'), slavery ('offensive as it is to our modern concepts of liberty') and public displays of excellence ('very different to us today'). In tandem with the re-enactments, these descriptions build a social environment for the ancient Greeks – the lifestyles, values and experiences of individuals and communities – marked by alterity. However, episode two continues the investigation into 'who were the Greeks?' by addressing a more standard narrative of cultural transmission. Hence, perhaps, Scott's qualifying remark as episode two draws to a close: 'The legacy is so strong that *in a way* I believe we are all Greeks' (my emphasis). Ancient Greece remains both 'icon and enigma'. The series thus makes a virtue of the discomfit. Following the logic of *Ancient Worlds*, Scott concludes, 'Asking who were the Greeks means asking who we are, and it stops us becoming too comfortable with the answer.' Difference is not set aside or elided, but rather it is a critical tool for a deeper reflection on and more nuanced understanding of the relationship between ancient and modern.

## REFRAMING THE LEGACY

Each of the above analyses of documentaries dedicated to ancient Greek theatre, politics and society is framed by direct reference to the Greek inheritance, albeit variously conceived as a matter of shared humanity (*Greatest Show*), interpersonal and community dynamics (*Ancient Worlds*) and cultural continuity (*Who were the Greeks?*). While the latter two do challenge the terms in which the legacy can be read, the notion of a debt owed is never fully or explicitly critiqued. In this, these contemporary programmes step away from the more complex interrogation of *Greek Fire* (Channel 4, 1990).[17] This was a ten-part series made by the London-based Transatlantic Films in co-production with broadcasters in England, Sweden, the United States of America, Holland and Greece. The channel, date and international dimension will be important for interpreting the series' engagement with the question 'are we the Greeks?', as it reframes the Greek inheritance.

From the beginning the tone is exploratory. As explained early in episode one, 'Source: Know Thyself', the title comprises an analogy. Like Greek fire, the chemical compound that burns in water, 'The Greek legacy is a flame that time cannot douse. The legacy is vast. Its richness is the magic of its endurance.' Across the series, ancient Greece is a permanent and pervasive feature of the physical, cultural and mental landscape of the modern world. However, it is also polymorphous. As Dr Oliver Taplin of Oxford University, the series' Classics consultant and the episode's first talking head,[18] explains:

> What we have, then, is not one huge monument that always looks the same, wherever you look at and whatever time you look at it from, but something shifting, something with so many angles, so many facets, that each age will perceive it differently, each age will make different things from it.

Certainly, future episodes will go on to examine regular 'legacy' topics such as politics, drama, architecture, art, science and philosophy. However, by Taplin's reading, the legacy is not fixed and direct, but contingent and invented. With this interpretation, Taplin anticipates the turn in scholarly approaches to classical antiquity in post-antique contexts epitomised three years later by Martindale: '*Meaning ... is always realized at the point of reception*' (original emphasis).[19] The Hellenic legacy can be whatever anyone wants it to be.

In the remainder of 'Source' (and the series), the implications of this radical reappraisal are made clear. For new Americans establishing frontier communities in the Midwest, for example, the importance of ancient Greece lay in its symbolic potential. As Police Lieutenant Francis Harr explains in relation to the Wisconsin town of Sparta where he works, 'The *idea* of Sparta was brought about by one of the early settlers who believed that the quality, the necessary traits of the settlers, was *indicative* of the Spartan people of ancient times' (my emphases). A reminder from the narrator, actress Juliet Stevenson,[20] that historical Sparta was a 'strange, militaristic city', with compulsory military training for boys, child exposure and state surveillance, disconnects the actuality of Sparta from the present, which is seen through the open window of a moving car. As part of an American townscape of trunk roads, shopping malls and Main Street, the Spartan Motel, the Spartan Lodge and a giant cartoon statue of a Spartan humorously reinforce the point that if residents consider themselves Spartan, it is in spirit, not in everyday living (Figure 1.2). Indeed, criticism of the notion that ancient Sparta might be considered more than a useful reference point is effected by juxtaposing an advert from the Greek National Touristic Organization with footage of ruined stones, isolated and overgrown. While the former invites Americans of all ethnic origins to 'come home to Greece', the latter is overlaid by a question from the narrator: 'This is ancient Sparta. Can we go home to this?' Drawing upon the familiar equation of ruins with decay,[21] the broken remains stand as visual evidence that

Figure 1.2 'Greek fire burns even here in a valley in the American Midwest': views from a car window, driving through Sparta, Wisconsin, in *Greek Fire*, episode 1 'Source' (1990). Transatlantic Films.

once-powerful Sparta is now 'fragmented and cryptic'. The narrator's question and the archaeological view dissociate ancient Greece from the modern world, and thereby undermine the tourist-board rhetoric of cultural descent. Ancient Sparta is inscrutable; it is the notion of Sparta that constitutes the Greek legacy.

The Greek legacy thus arises within the imagination, serving the needs of the community. In the United States it is 'a touchstone of confidence for a culture without its own deep historical roots'. Ancient Greece is a 'source' in so far as we return to it, like ancient pilgrims to the temple of Apollo in Delphi. This analogy is sustained visually by a camera-led progression up the sacred way and onto the temple floor. But the influence is 'recurrent' rather than 'permanent', because each interpretation is 'revolutionary', insists Bernard Knox, former Director for the Center for Hellenic Studies in Washington, DC. It does something new. Again the Greek legacy is fundamentally utilitarian. For Marx, Nietzsche and Freud, whose photos are superimposed onto the Delphic temple, their ideas of ancient Greece stimulate their famous theories of society, the self and the mind. However, 'Source' also argues for a deeper connection, grounded in the Delphic sanctuary's famous maxim: 'Know thyself.' For the literary critic George Steiner, 'interpretations of ancient Greece have moulded our cultural unconscious. Our return is an attempt to excavate those interpretations, to understand the forces that have made us what we are.' There is an inheritance: 'bequeathed' desires and ambitions – for a balanced life, to advance and progress – that 'the Greeks seem to have established inside us'. The functionality of the idea of ancient Greece in the imagination is balanced by the absorption of Greek ideas into our shared cultural psyche.

This presentation raises questions, however, about who 'we' are. This first episode focuses heavily on the resonance of ancient Greece in US contexts, not simply through the example of Sparta, Wisconsin, but also through the frequent return to America's urban landscape. Visuals include extended sequences at the Tennessee Parthenon, replayed footage of runners passing the Lincoln Memorial in Washington, DC, and shots of American buildings – a strip club, a police station – during a longer montage of neoclassical architecture. When the English-accented narrator asks, 'We have inherited that Greek desire, but how consciously, how critically? Are we aware of the hidden Greek presence all about us in our world? Do we see the latent influence, or simply the blatant one?', the people and places on screen are largely American. The British viewer (or their counterparts in Sweden, the Netherlands and Greece) is subsumed into a cultural continuum coded through American culture. Any potential dissonance is diffused by the discussion of engagements with ancient Greece by Byron, Marx, Nietzsche and Freud, which, together with Steiner's presentation of ancient Greece speaking to 'the Western world', broadens the scope beyond the US experience and environment. Later episodes draw attention to political, cultural and intellectual developments from a range of countries: for example Britain, Switzerland and France as well as the USA, in the 'Politics' episode discussed below. Imagining ourselves in relation to the ancient Greeks – accepting the Greeks are lodged inside – involves imagining ourselves within a continuum from Europe to North America. National or cultural distinctions are suppressed in preference for a broadly drawn Western identity.

Whilst asserting a pan-Western process of imaginative engagement (amongst the 'we' posited by Wolfenden in *Hellenic Cruise*), *Greek Fire* also asks how far Greek practice and ideas are really embedded in modern societies. In episode two, 'Politics', the political character of contemporary countries is weighed against that of democratic Athens. Only Switzerland, with its participatory ethos, bears comparison. In Greece, the United States and Great Britain, vertical hierarchies prohibit effective deliberation or involvement by ordinary citizens. These are more than tokens of difference, however. A strong polemic runs throughout the episode. Talking head Benjamin Barber, an American political scientist whose published commitment to stronger citizen participation is evident in his criticism of one-way communication and the lack of opportunities to pose questions to power, boldly asserts that 'what has to happen' is for citizens to demand their constitutional rights.[22] And Martin Jacques, the editor of *Marxism Today*, voices anxieties over recent attempts by the UK government to control information, describing modern-day Britain as an *ancien régime* in which parliamentary sovereignty is uncontested, the government and head of state are unelected, and citizens have no rights. These negative remarks are echoed during a radio phone-in conversation and compounded by the testimony of mechanic Jesus Ledo, who articulately conveys the average person's frustrated ennui. At the heart of these criticisms are the impotence, lack of interest, and disengagement that characterise supposed democracies. The extent to which Greek ideas have been interiorised is thus questioned and – with a disregard for balance possible in Britain only on Channel 4, established in 1981 with a brief to provide 'opinionated and experimental' content – the Athenian alternative is promoted over the political status quo.[23]

With this agenda, *Greek Fire* begins to fulfil the critical imperative claimed for the Greeks: the quest to 'Know Thyself'. In 'Source', as a goldfish swims in front of a model temple inside a bowl placed on a fluted column, set in front of a television – an evocative if somewhat ineffable scheme – the narrator insists 'The past presents alternatives, frees us to question prejudice and preconception, or at least to trace their origins.' Later, following saccharine scenes of American life shown on multiple television sets (excerpts from Ronald Regan's presidential campaign video), it is suggested that in the current media environment we are dangerously shut off from 'a past which shaped us, a past which can guide us into our future, out of the parochial present'. In the stimulus to 'know ourselves', *Greek Fire* adopts a characteristic claimed for ancient Greece, also defined in the 'Source' episode as 'a world of questions rather than answers'. To progress, we do not need to become the Greeks, but we do need to ask questions as they once did.

In its evaluation of the Greek legacy, *Greek Fire* establishes a new relationship between modern cultures (us) and the ancient Greeks (them). The notion of an inheritance is supported, but it does not involve a neutral transfer from ancient Greece to the West. Instead, elements of ancient Greek culture continue to be extracted and deployed within contemporary contexts, in the service of individuals and communities. In this way, the Greeks are internalised. Furthermore, the view of legacy promoted by the series is itself contingent, arising within a distinctive historical context. In 1989, the year the series was made, the Berlin Wall fell and Czechoslovakia's Velvet Revolution followed, bringing an end to Soviet occupation in the region. Beyond Europe, under intensified pressure, the South African government was beginning to dismantle apartheid legislation, while pro-democracy campaigners in Tiananmen Square were massacred by the Chinese army (a news report of this event can be heard during the radio-station sequence mentioned above). Back in Britain, in a context of economic recession, there were worker strikes and in Scotland, if not yet elsewhere, popular revolt against the new poll tax. Around the world and at home politics was being played out through dissent. As new horizons looked to be opening, opportunities appeared for modern societies in the West to activate the Greek legacy – to ask questions, to insist upon more democratic politics – as it is framed in *Greek Fire*.

## PROBLEMATISING THE LEGACY

In its radical reappraisal of the Greek legacy and its impetus towards action (or indeed enaction), *Greek Fire* steps beyond the earlier and later BBC documentaries discussed so far. However, awareness of its contingent and shifting character is reflected in *Treasures of Ancient Greece*, broadcast in April 2015 as part of a BBC4 season on 'The Age of Heroes: Ancient Greece Uncovered'. By offering a historical survey of the development of Greek art that regularly lauds the Greek achievement and its direct impacts on Western art, the first two episodes follow a traditional narrative of inheritance. By contrast, the final episode, entitled 'The Long Shadow', delves into some discrete moments when these impacts were accomplished. Of particular note are the contexts and motivations of artists and patrons as described by the presenter and writer, Alastair Sooke. For example, the commissioning of copies of statues to purchase 'Greek sophistication' by the Roman emperor Hadrian; the incorporation of the Laocoön statue group into an atmosphere of artistic experimentation following its excavation under Michelangelo's supervision; the appropriation of Greek models into a fashionable domestic aesthetic by the British collector William Hamilton and pottery manufacturer Josiah Wedgwood; and the acquisition and display of four bronze horses in Paris by Napoleon as a statement of power. In each instance, the ancient artwork gains significance through its modern appropriation.

The final example – Adolf Hitler's promotion of the fifth-century Discus Thrower by Myron as the incarnation of Nazi ideology – illustrates the same trend. The fascists saw in the statue 'the perfect Aryan body, the athletic *habitus*, the beautiful ideal white male and ... the Herrenrasse [Master Race]', observes Professor Rolf Michael Schneider from the Ludwig-Maximillians University in an interview with Sooke. Incorporated into propagandistic film, photographed in proximity to Hitler and his associates, and presented to the people of Germany in the Munich Glyptotech as a source of inspiration, as documented by the archive material presented on screen, the ancient statue became an expression of a malign cultural and political ideal. In Sooke's words, Myron's Discus Thrower 'became the ultimate symbol of Hitler's evil race politics'. Indeed, the measured tones and sombre expression of the presenter throughout the segment convey his lack of enthusiasm for what is described as Greek art's 'darkest turn'. Acknowledging the contingency of the Greek legacy requires admitting that it can serve any master. Thus, in the presenter's closing evaluation, ancient Greece provides 'an ideal, against which the western world has understood itself, revealing who we are and where we come from'. And yet, perhaps because it would unsettle its prior narrative of ancient Greek art as a great achievement at the root of modern art, *Treasures of Ancient Greece* backs off from the full implication, which might be inferred from its own examples, that the ideal is selected and created by the receivers of classical culture, the people who use its artefacts. Instead, the ideal exists in a dissociated and abstract way, so that Nazi manipulations become a corruption. Hence, it is proposed, the Discus Thrower would have resisted its fascistic transformation into an embodiment of the Nazi collective. Alas, as Schneider remarks when thinking about its integration into Hitler's 'perverse ideologies', 'the statue cannot say no'.

Imagining the statue's will to resist retains the purity of the Greek legacy, whilst demonstrating its potential for debasement, according to an evaluatory scheme that few would contest today. In this way, the legacy is problematised as something that in the wrong contexts might become undesirable. A similar position is adopted by presenter and historian Bettany Hughes during a brief segment of the second episode of *Divine Women* (BBC2, 18 April 2012). The series is dedicated to ancient Greek (and Roman) religious practice, an aspect of daily life that is never integrated into the narrative of inheritance. However, when 'Handmaids of the Gods' addresses the underrepresentation of women's importance in ancient Greek society today, Hughes directly addresses the Greek legacy. Standing with the Parthenon in the background, she observes:

> You could argue that what happened in Greece gave us the building blocks for Western civilization. A belief in democracy, a belief in freedom of speech, and a fixed and firm notion that women were definitely second-class citizens.

Describing next the limitations placed on ancient Greek women's movements, dress and education, and their encouragement towards silence, Hughes then attacks the narrow interests of historians in war and monuments at the expense of a 'truer, richer picture'.[24] This works as a programmatic statement for the series, which helps supply the missing elements. But it also offers a pointed feminist critique of the celebration of the Greek legacy. As *Greek Fire* argues, if 'we' are like the Greeks, it is because we have interiorised aspects of the 'heritage'. By associating that heritage with unreconstructed patterns of male misogyny, the notion of an inheritance is preserved, but it seems less desirable as a result. It is striking that it takes a female presenter in a programme about women's history to raise a direct challenge; but, interested in other topics, Hughes moves swiftly on.

## CONCLUSION: ARE WE THE GREEKS?

As the above survey shows, television's answer to the question 'are we the Greeks?' is far from stable or consistent. While the notion of a legacy or inheritance sets the ancient Greeks in an ancestral relation to contemporary societies in the West, the character of this relationship is variously defined. An assumption of continuity in cultural practice may be strengthened by arguments for shared human experience and psychology or unsettled by illustrations of differences in social life and patterns of behaviour. Then again, the Greek inheritance might be an invention of the modern imagination: an idea that services a societal need but that societies do not necessarily live up to. In this guise, the inheritance might also have undesirable consequences, or the implications of the legacy might be unpalatable. There is a pervasive sense, to appropriate an observation by the director of *Greatest Show*, David Wilson (in interview: see Chapter 10, below), that 'the Greeks are something to do with us'.

If television documentaries are regarded as forms of public address,[25] the message offered by these programmes is varied rather than homogeneous. Nonetheless, constant attention to the Hellenic legacy keeps the relationship between ancient and modern to the fore. At no point is that relationship denied. Instead, viewers are hailed as members of a Western civilisation for which the Hellenic legacy is claimed as a hallmark. This act of interpellation, to use Althusser's terminology for the process by which individuals are addressed and come to identify within an ideology, suppresses the great diversity of the audience.[26] This applies especially to the post-2010 programmes, although the political changes in 1989–90 mentioned above make it pertinent to *Greek Fire* too. The West is an idea, rather than a historical entity, applied to Europe and areas of the world where local culture was displaced, suppressed or blended with that of European settlers. Even Europe can be said not to exist.[27] At any rate, it has never been stable. The diversity of engagement with the 'legacy' of classical antiquity in areas that have become the modern nation states is in fact one way of observing that.[28] Even the present European Union, which developed out of a growing economic community, has been in constant flux since it was founded in 1993. New members continue to join, increasing its geographical reach and cultural complexity; weaker economic nations (including Greece, for whom 2010–15 were crisis years) and those who contravene community values (at the time of writing, Hungary, for building a wall to deter immigrants) are threatened with expulsion; and states can withdraw (again at the time of writing, Britain's exit is pending). At the same time populations within member countries are ethnically diverse. For example, in the 2011 UK census, only 81 per cent of residents in England and Wales described themselves as 'white British', reflecting patterns of immigration, especially from Commonwealth nations in Africa, the Caribbean and the Indian subcontinent, since the 1950s.[29] By sustaining the notion of a Hellenic legacy in some shape or form, television documentaries cut across this diversity in population, which of course means diversity in personal heritage and experience. Hailed as individuals for whom the Greek inheritance matters, 'we' are subsumed into a version of Britishness, Europeanness and a Western identity that eliminates multiplicity and divergence.

In this respect, the touted legacy acts as a fetish, as conceived by Slavoj Žižek. Building on Lacanian psychoanalysis, according to which reality is a fantasy that hides its own lack, the cultural theorist postulates 'social *fantasy* as the elementary ideological mode to mask antagonism' (original emphasis). Indeed, 'the fetishist logic' can be witnessed in the filming of presenters on location standing amongst archaeological ruins and walking down streets filled with buildings and people distinctive of modern-day Greece. '*Je sais, mais quand même*' ('I know, but all the same') represents the cognitive dissonance required to balance the otherness of the visual world – compounded by simply appearing on television – with the claim that in some way it is fundamental to who 'we' are.[30] From the proposition of legacy, it is of course possible to dissent.[31] But sustained across programmes and across the years, the notion of a Greek legacy papers over the cracks that undermine the notion of a unified 'Western civilization'. For as Crépon argues, with regard to Europe, discourse requires two levels of identity: one that reflects the 'totality' of its constituent units, and one that accommodates their differences.[32] By upholding the legacy, television documentaries facilitate the former, but their presentation of the relationship between ancient and modern does little to illuminate the cultural richness of contemporary society.

## PROGRAMMES DISCUSSED

*Armchair Voyage: Hellenic Cruise.* 3-part series. Prod. Stephen Hearst. BBC Television.
Episode 1: 'Venice to Mycenae'. Monday 21 July 1958, 9.15–9.45pm.

*The Greeks: A Journey in Space and Time.* 4-part series. Dir. Christopher Burstall. BBC1.
Episode 1: 'The Greek Beginning'. Thursday 11 September 1980, 10.20–11.10pm.

*Greek Fire.* 10-part series. Prod. Revel Guest. Transatlantic Films. Channel 4.

Episode 1: 'Source: Know Thyself'. Dir. Revel Guest and Jonathan Stamp. Thursday 22 March 1990, 8.00–8.30pm.
Episode 2: 'Politics'. Dir. Chris Goddard. Thursday 29 March 1990, 8.00–8.30pm.

*Ancient Worlds*. 6-part series. Dir. Tim Kirby. BBC Productions. BBC2.
Episode 1: 'Come Together'. Wednesday 10 November 2010, 9.00–10-00pm.
Episode 3: 'The Greek Thing'. Wednesday 24 November 2010, 9.00–10-00pm.

*Divine Women*. 3-part series. Dir. Emily Davis. BBC Productions. BBC2.
Episode 2: 'Handmaids of the Gods'. Wednesday 18 April 2012, 9.00–10.00pm.

*Who were the Greeks?* 2-part series. Dir. Ishbel Hall. Tern Television. BBC2.
Episode 1. Thursday 27 June 2013, 9.00–10.00pm.
Episode 2. Thursday 4 July 2013, 9.00–10.00pm.

*Ancient Greece: The Greatest Show on Earth*. 3-part series. Prod. and dir. David Wilson. Tern Television. BBC4.
Episode 1: 'Democrats'. Tuesday 27 August 2013, 9.00–10.00pm.
Episode 2: 'Kings'. Tuesday 3 September 2013, 9.00–10.00pm.
Episode 3: 'Romans'. Tuesday 10 September 2013, 9.00–10.00pm.

*Treasures of Ancient Greece*. 3-part series. Dir. David Vincent. BBC Arts Production. BBC4.
Episode 3: 'The Long Shadow'. Wednesday 22 April 2015, 9.00–10.00pm.

## NOTES

1 See Wyver, Chapter 3, below, for the context, premise and influence of *Hellenic Cruise*. The series is currently available at: <http://www.bbc.co.uk/programmes/p017bby3> (accessed 12 September 2016).

2 The exhortation was written in the Preface to Shelley's *Hellas*, a polemical reworking of the *Persians*, written by the Athenian playwright Aeschylus in 472 BC. In *Hellas*, the Turkish sultan Mahmud is cast in the role of Xerxes, the king of Persia whose defeat by sea in the battle of Salamis is the subject of Aeschylus' play: see Mulhallen (2010: 176–207).

3 Murray (1921: 12, 21). For Murray's classical activities beyond the

academy, see Griffith (2007), with Wrigley (2015a) on his prolific radio contributions.
4. See further Jenkyns (1980) on the nineteenth-century perspective, into which Shelly and Murray both fit.
5. BBC WAC VR/80/370, VR/80/39 and VR/80/399. In all three surviving reports, covering episodes one, three and four, over 70 per cent of respondents deemed the programme 'quite' or 'very' successful.
6. BBC WAC 11.9.80.
7. Murray (1921: 14).
8. For the anthropological background, see Hartog (2005: 26–54).
9. Murray (1921: 14).
10. To extend the 'special relationship' between individuals and classical poets or genre as described by Silk, Gildenhard and Barrow (2014: 98–101) to a societal level.
11. With the exception of *Greek Fire*, the programmes discussed below are available via Box of Broadcasts (bob), a subscription-based on-demand service supported by the British Universities and Colleges Film and Video Council: <https://learningonscreen.ac.uk/ondemand> (accessed 12 September 2016). Quotations, with minor corrections, follow the accompanying transcripts.
12. On the film, compare Bakogianni (2009b), who argues for a very contemporary flavour.
13. And a contributor to this book: Scott discusses his experiences presenting this and other programmes in interview in Chapter 10, below.
14. See Hobden (2013b, 2017) for this strategy's broader application in ancient world documentaries.
15. De Groot (2009: 105).
16. See Etlin (2005).
17. A video set of *Greek Fire* is available to buy in American format, published by Mystic Fire Video, Inc. Note, the episodes are arranged in a different order from that in which they were broadcast on UK television.
18. And author of the series' accompanying book: Taplin (1989).
19. Martindale (1993: 3).
20. Stevenson's appeal as a narrator may have derived from her performance as Antigone in Don Taylor's *Theban Plays* four years before, on which see Wrigley (2012c).
21. See Hobden (2013a).
22. See, for example, Barber (1984).
23. See Ellis (2008: 333, 340–1). For the channel's propensity towards more challenging takes on Greek antiquity, see Wrigley (2012e) for discussion of Peter Hall's *Oresteia* (Channel 4, 1983).
24. This somewhat underplays the presence of women's and gender studies in mainstream scholarship. However, it is an entirely fair representation of the overall focus of historical documentaries, including the series discussed here: see Gray and Bell (2013: 214–18).

25 See Corner (1995).
26 Althusser (1971: 162–4).
27 See Robson (2008), reviewing Stiegler (2005) and Crépon (2006).
28 Exemplified by Kallendorf (2007: section 2).
29 See 'KS201 UK Ethnic Group, local authorities in the United Kingdom', available at: <https://www.ons.gov.uk/peoplepopulationandcommunity/populationandmigration/populationestimates/datasets/2011censuskeystatisticsandquickstatisticsforlocalauthoritiesintheunitedkingdompart1> (accessed 9 April 2018).
30 See Žižek (1989: 3–55); quotations are from Žižek (2005: 314–15), a more digestible read. On television's default representation of other worlds, see Ellis (1982: 112).
31 See Fiske (1987) on resistance to the ideologies encoded in television programmes.
32 Crépon (2006), summarised by Robson (2008: 378).

## 2  Louis MacNeice and 'The Paragons of Hellas': Ancient Greece as Radio Propaganda

Peter Golphin

This chapter examines the ways in which Louis MacNeice employed and, at times, manipulated historical narratives of ancient Greece in radio feature programmes to provide encouraging parallels for the resilience, courage and determination required to survive fascist occupation in World War II and ultimately to overcome it. The primary aim of these programmes was to maintain awareness of and sympathy for an important ally on the Home Front through radio. MacNeice uses the artifice of viewing the present predicament of Greece through the prism of its ancient past. We may term his programmes propaganda in that their effects are intentionally rhetorical, though these broadcast features were not such as would require embarrassed explanations after the war.

At the time of the outbreak of war in 1939, BBC Radio was more established, more developed and much more widely available than its nascent television service, which had been available within a short radius of London's Alexandra Palace since 1936. With the latter shut down for the duration, radio was in any case the primary medium for the broadcasting of information and entertainment. Radio could reach the majority of the population: 'by 1939, 73 per cent of households nationwide owned a radio licence, suggesting a potential audience of perhaps 35 million out of a total population of 48 million'.[1] Transmissions reached a corner of most living rooms and, as Connelly has written, the war forced a change in domestic listening habits, with radio becoming more convenient than the newspapers: 'With people working longer hours in complex shift patterns, the ability to read a newspaper from cover to cover diminished, thus making the radio the crucial source of information.'[2] Given this ubiquity, radio was also an effective means of propagandising the allied war effort, particularly through the evolving features genre.

It was the adaptable format of features programmes that was in the main used for BBC Radio wartime propaganda. Wrigley writes, 'Strictly speaking, features may be described as radio documentaries or information programmes which utilise innovative combinations of dramatization, poetry, music and sound for their effect.'[3] In practice, as Coulton has said, a feature 'could be almost anything'.[4] Therefore, the flexibility of features could involve variations of dramatic dialogue and more directly informational content, in whatever proportions was deemed necessary for a particular propaganda dimension. However, although other radio features written by MacNeice in the war years sometimes included a documentary component, those that drew on ancient Greek history and myth were largely, and sometimes entirely, dramatic dialogue.

The BBC on a wartime footing saw its chief roles as supplying both 'a contribution to the preservation of civilised culture in time of war' and 'implicit or explicit propagandistic contributions to national wartime activity'.[5] Importantly, the latter required careful handling in order to remain effective. The Corporation was aware of the public's suspicion of improbable news and of seemingly misleading or unbalanced information. An internal memo dated early in 1940 and headed 'Wartime Propaganda' read 'no deliberate perversion of truth, as in depreciation of the military qualities of the enemy, avoidance of cheapness and personal ridicule'.[6] Instead, as Stallworthy has written, 'memorably reinforcing aspects of the truth' was all the spin needed.[7]

MacNeice was recruited by the BBC in 1941, having prevaricated over what his contribution to the war effort might be. He had had scripts produced previously, but like several members of the intelligentsia he claimed to find something distasteful about working for a large institution and, for another matter, scripting propagandistic material.[8] On 17 March of the previous year he had received a persuasive letter from T. Rowland Hughes of the BBC Features and Drama section, which suggests why MacNeice was sought by them: it included: 'We in this country have not yet been able to secure a first class poet for such radio programmes and I feel convinced that your lines would speak well.'[9] His reputation had preceded him through publications of his poetry: *Poems* (1935), *The Earth Compels* (1938) and perhaps most of all, his long occasional poem *Autumn Journal* (1939). In the event, he was interviewed on 9 January 1941 by Archie

Harding, chief instructor of the BBC's Staff Training School, 'who seems to have persuaded MacNeice to reconsider his views on patriotism and propaganda'.[10] Indeed, MacNeice's relationship with the corporation was to last for twenty-two years, ending with his death in September 1963. During the war, he was one of several distinguished poets and writers to lend the Corporation their talents; but remaining on the staff after the war he was to take radio features and drama as seriously as he did his poetry, seeing it as equally ripe for experimentation and development. In the meantime, he remained a member of literary London and his radio pieces are the products of a poet's imagination, at times sharing the same preoccupations as his poetry.[11]

For the classically educated MacNeice, using ancient Greek history as a propaganda resource to illuminate the wartime plight of Greece seemed appropriate. With a double first in Greats from Oxford (1926–30), he had taught Latin and Greek at Birmingham (1930–6) and Greek at Bedford College, London (1936–8); and in 1936 he had published his own translation of *The Agamemnon of Aeschylus*. Antiquity is only one of a range of resources used by him in his radio work, 'but it is a dominant one'.[12] However, the poet's view of this material was qualified, which in some senses distances him from more conventional views of ancient Greece. McDonald writes that MacNeice may have meant to 'set himself apart from the kind of academic humanist' engaged with late Victorian attitudes to the classics, which stressed the influence of Thucydides and the golden mean.[13] This places MacNeice in contrast to the orthodox and sometimes reverential future representations of Greece by Sir Mortimer Wheeler and Sir Compton Mackenzie on BBC television in the 1950s, discussed by John Wyver (Chapter 3, below): for example, the former called the battlefield at Marathon 'sacred ground' and the latter offered paeans of praise for the glories of Athens. MacNeice's scepticism about such seemingly uncritical idealisations also differentiates him from the likes of Gilbert Murray, who speaks in his own wartime radio programmes of Greece's supposed exemplary attributes – freedom, free speech, equality before the law, democracy.[14] The empirically minded MacNeice is as sceptical of the meta-narrative of the ancient world as he is of any other. To be sure, he had made this clear in section 9 of *Autumn Journal*:

> And when I should think of the paragons of Hellas
>     I think instead
> Of the crooks, the adventurers, the opportunists,
>     The careless athletes and the fancy boys,
> The hair-splitters, the pedants, the hard-boiled sceptics

>             And the Agora and the noise
> Of the demagogues and the quacks; and the women pouring
>             Libations over graves
> And the trimmers at Delphi and the dummies at Sparta and lastly
>             I think of the slaves.

The poet's ironic 'paragons of Hellas' is borne out by his montage of metropolitan types, who might also be found in any modern city. 'The hair-splitters, the pedants,' might equally be those modern individuals who seek to interpret these far-off things as exemplars of morality, justice, modes of thought; but MacNeice is more a 'hard-boiled sceptic'. The section concludes with:

> And how one can imagine oneself among them
>             I do not know;
> It was all so unimaginably different
>             And all so long ago.
>
>                                   (MacNeice 2007 [1939]: 121-2)

In the wartime radio programmes under discussion here, MacNeice was not concerned with the military strategies of the present war or with its great victories and defeats, but sought to reflect individual experiences, albeit representative ones intended to typify how people were affected by events. His Greek pieces are imaginatively cast as short dramas, which highlight personal danger and sacrifice, great courage, and painful partings wrought by Nazi occupation. This concern for individuality in the midst of an all-pervading war is also a preoccupation in his poetry at this time: namely, the subject under the stress of war. But when re-imagined on the radio it proves an effective means of raising awareness of the plight of Greeks under occupation.

Contemporary events making occupied Greece not only a pertinent subject for propaganda but also a site of wartime barbarity began with an attempted invasion by the Italians on 28 October 1940. But the Italians were rebuffed and the Greeks achieved a significant victory; fighting in the snowbound, rugged terrain of the Pindus Mountains near Epirus through the winter of 1940-1, they forced the invaders back into Albania. On 6 April 1941, the Germans arrived in Greece on a front further east, citing the presence of British and Commonwealth troops as a pretext for their intervention. The latter were forced south to Crete and beyond. But, like the Italians, and despite imposing a far more brutal, uncompromising regime, the Germans also failed to subdue the Greeks or eradicate the guerrilla activities, which constantly disrupted the invaders' attempts to impose fascist rule.[15] The Greeks were to suffer appallingly for this state of affairs: this, needing no exaggeration, provided material for MacNeice's radio work. However, the first of these Greek features underlines determination and resilience of a different type.

## INVOKING ANCIENT HISTORY

A fifteen-minute feature called *The March of the 10,000* was transmitted on the Eastern, Pacific and North American Services on 16, 17 and 18 April 1941 respectively, just a few days after the German invasion. Like many of MacNeice's 1941 scripts – Greek and otherwise – it is primarily intended to encourage America to enter the war as a military participant in the allied war effort, while, as Wrigley and Harrison note, it represents a powerful piece of 'relationship building' with Greece itself.[16] It is an adaptation of Xenophon's *Anabasis* and the only one of these scripts to rely entirely on a narrative from ancient Greece. *The March of the 10,000* tells the story of Greek mercenaries in Mesopotamia, deep inside the Persian Empire, compelled to make their slow way home across the harsh terrain of desert, wide rivers and snow-covered mountains, while sometimes harassed by hostile tribes. Indeed it may provide an echo of the British retreat to the sea at Dunkirk in the previous summer. The Greeks' goal is also the sea, which provokes their famous cry on first laying eyes on it, '*Thalatta! Thalatta!*' ('The sea! The sea!').[17] However, this is not the whole story: 'on crossing the Bosphorus they found political uncertainty and isolation'.[18] MacNeice chooses to sound an optimistic note at the end, rather than the more downbeat actuality recorded by Xenophon.[19]

Other interventions in Xenophon's narrative by MacNeice are intended to heighten its resonance with listeners by including dialogue among 'Common Soldiers' (C.S.), whose troubles are meant to align them closely with modern Greeks:

C.S. 2: I'm not fighting for any lousy dictator.
[...]
C.S. 3: What freedom is there in Greece?
C.S. 2: I'll tell you what freedom there is – freedom to say what you like and live the way you want to – that's what there is in Greece, and that's what I want.
C.S. 1: You're right, mate. And no bullying Great King is going to talk me out of going back to Greece. (pp. 38–9)

As well as freedom, dialogue also foregrounds another recurrent theme in these pieces, namely democracy, through the election of Cheirisophus and Xenophon himself as generals by the men they will lead and to replace the dead Clearchus. This atmosphere of liberty and democracy was anathema to the fascists and certainly a reminder to listeners of the fundamental issues at stake in the then current war. However, MacNeice highlights a form of direct election which was unknown in Britain too, and it prefigures his further implicit and politically motivated criticism of British democracy in scripts of 1943.

*The March of the 10,000* is entirely dramatic dialogue, as was the case with MacNeice's next Greek work, *The Glory that is Greece*, transmitted on 28 October 1941, the first anniversary of the thwarted Italian invasion.[20] The title brings into the present tense Poe's frequently quoted words, 'the glory that was Greece, the grandeur that was Rome', which MacNeice had also alluded to in *Autumn Journal* with a hint of scepticism:

> The Glory that was Greece: put it in a syllabus, grade it
>   Page by page
> To train the mind or even to point a moral
>   For the present age.
>                             (MacNeice 2007 [1939]: 121)

The tonal difference between the two references is significant. The latter is ironic, even cynical; but the propagandistic version on the radio seeks to align past glories with the current war. Wrigley describes MacNeice searching Herodotus and Aeschylus for 'vivid details' to work up an engaging story: specifically, Herodotus' lead-up to the battle of Marathon (6.94–117) and battles of Thermopylae and Salamis (7.201 to 8.100), and Aeschylus' *Persians* for scenes involving Xerxes.[21] First, we hear an Italian family discussing the invasion of Greece and generationally divided over its wisdom and fairness. Grandfather prefers his Aeschylus to modern military adventures enthused over by his children. More directly, we hear the ancient Greek battle cry in defence of the homeland, a fundamental justification for war, *'nun huper panton agon'* ('Now the struggle is for all'), from Aeschylus' *Persians* (402–5), the battle cry of the Greeks whilst fatally attacking the Persian fleet at Salamis. At this time of great danger, it is still evocative and inspiring: the cry's force 'lies in protecting family and cult and in keeping the country, the land of the fathers, free by taking up arms in defence'.[22]

We hear the Greek prime minister, Metaxas, call upon his people to prepare to fight for their country and prove themselves worthy of their ancestors, invoking the exemplary deeds of those seemingly perfect role models. Furthermore, the analogous binary between totalitarian Persia and Nazi Germany on the one hand and democratic Greece both then and now on the other makes for potent propaganda.

This leads to the central argument of the piece, which is simply to draw a straight line between ancient military victories and the recent one in the Pindus Mountains. The most explicit allusion comes at the end with a 'Woman Announcer' moving forward chronologically: 'Marathon / Thermopylae / Salamis / Plataea; Tripolitsa, Missalonghi, the Pindus gorges' (p. 73).[23] The time shift suggested by the title is reflected in the structure of the piece as scenes cross-fade between present – where frequent 'radio announcements' help to contextualise the action – and distant past, between fascist-occupied Greece and the fifth century BC, where the Persian emperor Xerxes is topically a megalomaniac dictator who scoffs at the Greek devotion to freedom and democracy. He will invade Greece with an army vastly larger than anything the Greeks can muster, as similarly envisaged by Mussolini and Hitler. The device of cross-fading, juxtaposing ancient and modern to suggest a strong similarity, is one which prefigures a theme adopted on television in the 1950s by presenters such as Wheeler and Mackenzie who stressed the continuity between past and present (see Wyver, Chapter 3, below; cf. Hobden, Chapter 1, above).

It is the erudite Stavros and his fellow soldiers Janni and Kosta whom listeners follow through the snow, high into the mountains close to the border with Albania, and who carry the present-day strand of the narrative through dialogue which conveys passing events to listeners. And Stavros repeatedly links these events with fifth-century BC Greece: 'All this has happened before' (pp. 57 and 70); 'This recalls the classic age' (p. 66), a line which furnishes a neat link back to Xerxes; 'The set-up's much the same. The bloated tyrant who thinks he can walk in and take us' (p. 57), equating Hitler with Xerxes again. As Kosta dies of his wounds, Stavros recites from Pericles' funeral oration as re-imagined by Thucydides, rendering the analogy yet stronger: '"The whole earth is the sepulchre of famous men; and their story is graven not only on stone over their native earth, but lives on far away, without visible symbol, woven into the stuff of other men's lives"' (p. 75).[24] And soon we have a second extract from Thucydides when Stavros paraphrases lines that elevate the deeds of modern Greeks: '"If a noble death is the highest part of virtue, this is what has fallen to us above all men. For, anxious to clothe Greece with freedom, we lie enjoying an honour that grows not old"' (p. 75). Through his character's 'noble death', MacNeice reminds his listeners of the glory of the sacrifices of thousands of people like Kostas.

As in *The March of the 10,000*, there is an optimistic uplift at the end of the piece. The heroic defeat in the pass at Thermopylae was at the hands of Xerxes, but in part facilitated the Athenian naval victory at Salamis in the same year; and this is held out by Stavros' wife, Maria, and her friend:

> Maria: We are still at the stage of Thermopylae –
> Angelice: But some day we shall have a Salamis. (p. 77)

*The Glory that is Greece* derives its thrust as propaganda essentially from the notion that history is repeating itself and will do so again. Fascist invasion and occupation, which are equated with Thermopylae, must be followed by a Salamis. The drama also makes clear the Greeks' refusal to concede defeat and be subjugated as well as the occupiers' inability to halt the sabotages, the blowing up of fuel dumps and railway lines, the cutting of telephone wires – no matter how many hostages they shoot. And MacNeice revisited this resistance in 1942, when he responded promptly to and provided imaginative versions of actual situations in his dramas.

## RESISTING NAZI BARBARITIES

The Greeks' refusal to submit to the Nazis was double-edged. Revenge atrocities resulted, which included persecution and enforced starvation. *The Times* seized on guerrilla activities and consequent efforts by the occupiers to quell the unrest as illustrative of the heroism of the former and the brutality of the latter. On Tuesday 19 January 1943, it reported in a leader under the banner 'In the Greek Mountains':

> Recent news from Greece has shown that Germans and Italians alike have been adopting violent methods of repression in the vain attempt to deter a courageous and patriotic people from assisting the increasing bodies of *guerilleros* [sic] in the mountains. They have been shooting hostages, deporting 'suspects', sending retired officers of high rank to concentration camps in Italy, with the added indignity of fetters, and generally behaving with a barbarity which, in the case of the Italians, denotes something approaching panic.[25]

The article gives a sense of the atmosphere into which MacNeice's propagandistic features were transmitted and the situations to which he was responding. Such are the actualities fuelling his imagination and which must be creatively recycled. Another article, reporting a statement by the National Organisation of Greek Women, published in *The Times* on 6 February 1943, describes further the inhumanity of Nazi repression, but also the resolution of the Greeks:

> We may starve, we may have become human shadows, nevertheless we bear our hunger with pride. We may see our children gradually pining away. Our

hearts are torn, but we will not give in. Every day our kinsmen fall fighting in the towns and the mountains. Our hearts ache, and we mourn for them, but we fully realise how indispensable is their sacrifice for the great thing called liberty.[26]

In 1942, sixteen MacNeice scripts were produced, only two of which were influenced by events in Greece. These were two dramatic miniatures, which responded to the tenor of newspaper reports and needed no exaggeration to achieve their propaganda impact. *Salutation to Greece* was transmitted on 22 March and *Salute to Greece* 25 October, both on the Home Service. Both are fifteen-minute dramatic features which open with the Greek national anthem, signalling their intended effect on listeners: namely, to maintain awareness of an occupied ally being mistreated by the enemy.

The dialogue of both is set in the present day, dwelling on the 'repressive measures' and the starvation, such as reported in *The Times*. *Salutation to Greece*, broadcast three days before the Greek Independence Day to which it refers, derives its propagandistic thrust from the detention on the street by a bersagliere of an old man who is pushing a pram. The incompetent Italian, who has just failed to stop an uproar by the hungry locals, is chastised by a German major, who reminds him of Italian failure in the Pindus Mountains. The major assumes that the pram contains illicit goods, 'stolen food' and forbidden literature, all of which should be confiscated. He orders his sergeant to remove the pram cover. The shocked man is initially unable to report his finding:

> German Major: Well, answer me. What is in that pram?
> Sergeant: A Dead child, sir.
> German Major: A child?
> Sergeant: A <u>dead</u> child, sir. Looks as if he died of hunger.
> Old Man: He did die of hunger. I watched him. It was all because you Germans took away all the food.
> German Major: Hold your tongue.
> Old Man: You took away all the bread and the oil and the olives and the fish and the figs and the tomatoes.[27] (p. 9, original emphasis)

Cross-fading with this emotional kernel of the piece – which is sustained suspensively over almost four pages – is the parallel narrative of Yannis. Yannis is known to the local Gestapo for his resistance activities: cutting telephone wires, stealing a lorry-load of petrol, printing a secret newspaper and helping the British to escape during the Nazi invasion. When he is inevitably arrested, a woman speaker reads from the funeral oration as in the previous year's *The Glory that is Greece*, beginning, 'If a noble death . . .' (*Salutation to Greece* typescript, p. 11). Then she delivers without embellishment an emblematic reminder of past glories: 'Remember Marathon, Thermopylae, Salamis and Plataea.'

*Salute to Greece* is similar in thrust and sentiment, with a similar scenario involving the risks taken by young Greeks, who continually plot to disrupt the occupation.[28] Nikos speaks of the starvation of babies; Penelope tells a Nazi officer, 'You will never sleep easy in Greece'; Linas' sweetheart, Kostas, has been killed fighting with UN forces in the Libyan desert, which Penelope likens to the dead of 'Missalonghi and Marathon. Of Salamis and Thermopylae' (*Salute to Greece* typescript, pp. 2–6). Again a character named Yannis is arrested for resistance activities at the end, facing certain death. And this time it is Penelope who repeats the same lines from the funeral oration.

## PERICLES AND BRITISH DEMOCRACY

From these imagined but typical situations in present-day Greece, MacNeice turned once again to ancient sources in 1943. Coulton describes how MacNeice had proposed a project called *The Four Freedoms* to his boss, Lawrence Gilliam, in a memo dated 28 December 1942 which, accompanied by annotation and marginalia, suggests his enthusiasm for it.[29] *The Four Freedoms* are those enshrined in the Atlantic Charter, an agreement between Churchill and Roosevelt in 1941. The series of six fifteen-minute pieces was intended to underline the notions of freedom and democracy for which the allies were fighting. The first episode was 'Pericles', transmitted on 21 February, and the last was 'What Now?' on 28 March, and both are concerned with ancient Greece. The others were 'The Early Christians', 'The Renaissance', 'The French Revolution' and 'John Milton'. All were carried on the Home Service on Sunday evenings.

The central purpose of 'Pericles' is to foreground democracy as a corollary of freedom and equality, reminding listeners of an important reason for their wartime sacrifices; but in a new approach, MacNeice's treatment of the subject is politicised. As in *The Glory that is Greece*, he returns to the apt binary from the Peloponnesian War of totalitarian Sparta and free and democratic Athens as analogous to the Axis powers and the Western allies respectively; but now his strategy is quite different. Whilst a large component of the piece consists of speeches allegedly spoken by the Athenian statesman Pericles, as reported by Thucydides in his *History of the Peloponnesian War*, MacNeice is anxious to cast a particular light on Athenian democracy. The piece opens with an announcer, who tells listeners, 'If you went back there you'd find it all very strange ... <u>Would you</u>?' (p. 87; ellipsis and emphasis in the original). *Autumn Journal* had declared that it was difficult to 'imagine' what it was like back then in Athens, but here he suggests that perhaps it would not be so difficult. Thus again, he was anxious to align present-day London with fifth-century BC Athens. In 'Pericles', however, MacNeice implicitly suggests that their modes of government are quite different.

Ostensibly, 'Pericles' represents Athenian democracy as effective and direct. Its claims to egalitarianism are articulated by a citizen of the city to a stranger in town, Xenos, who is implicitly a refugee. 'I am by nature a democrat', he says, 'Where I come from I couldn't lead my own life. I couldn't even raise my voice. There was no such thing as free speech' (p. 87). So, as a foil for the Citizen, Xenos invites an outline of the political arrangements in Athens.

As they converse in the street, a hurrying fish porter, called Rough, collides with them:

> Rough: Out of the way there! Out of the way, you fatheads! What are you two mugs doing blocking the traffic? D'ye think you own this street?
> Citizen: Certainly I own this street.
> Rough: Then so do I!
> Citizen: Certainly you do, my dear fellow – but need you be in quite such a hurry? Where are you off to? The fish-market?
> Rough: Fish-market! Pah! Urgent affairs of state.
> [...]
> Xenos: What did he mean by 'affairs of state'?
> Citizen: He means 'affairs of state'.
> Xenos: But the fellow's just a fish-porter.
> Citizen: Well, what of it? <u>He</u> has his share in the State, he has his say in whether we go to war. (p. 88; original emphasis)

Participation in affairs of state by the Athenians was brought about through male suffrage, which in granting them such a role also made them politically active. As Wrigley writes, MacNeice 'was not, however, blind to the fact that in some important respects ancient Athens could not possibly be considered a haven of freedom in all senses', but he does pass over these in 'Pericles'.[30] Lane Fox has elaborated on the actual nature of Athenian democracy:

> The Athenian version counted on a very strong willingness of all citizens to participate ... To modern eyes, there were still conspicuous exclusions: 'all citizens' did not mean 'all residents'. Non-Athenian residents (the *metoikoi*,

or metics, meaning those living away from their home), inhuman objects of property (the many slaves) and the unreasoning second sex (women) were excluded without hesitation.[31]

Not only, therefore, is MacNeice selective in his choice of material for 'Pericles', but also he appears as politically motivated as his fish-porter. The direct form of this Athenian democracy, involving men voting on specific issues – such as the election of the generals in *The March of the 10,000* – was not a right the British, man or woman, would recognise. Certainly, MacNeice offers the participative political involvement of the Athenians as an ideal; but for his listeners, comparison with the British infrastructure is inescapable. They had not been able to vote in a parliamentary election for eight years and certainly did not vote on whether or not they should go to war against the Axis powers.

In 'Pericles', MacNeice provides an ironic critique of the society and political structure to which its listeners were themselves subject and thereby differentiates it from his other, more conventional, more 'realistic' Greek features. To be clear, he was politically motivated elsewhere in these years. *Autumn Journal* included this eloquently expressed hope for a more egalitarian society:

> Where skill will no longer languish nor energy be trammelled
>     To competition and graft,
> Exploited in subservience but not allegiance
>     To an utterly lost and daft
> System that gives a few at fancy prices
>     Their fancy lives
> While ninety-nine in the hundred who never attend the banquet
>     Must wash the grease of ages off the knives.
>                       (MacNeice 2007 [1939]: 105)

Furthermore, some of his non-Greek features around this time – for example, *The House of Commons* (7 July 1941, Overseas Service) and *The Debate Continues* (10 May 1942, Home Service), which contain a similarly suggestive ambiguity to 'Pericles' – also testify to MacNeice's willingness to include his personal convictions in his radio work.

Our awareness of its probable fictiveness does not detract from the rhetorical force of Pericles' funeral oration in honour of the Athenian dead of the Peloponnesian War. Extended extracts are included in 'Pericles', which contribute further to the underlying sense that MacNeice intended his listeners to hear his propaganda as double-edged. For example, here is Pericles eulogising Athenian democracy and the principle of equality on which it is founded:

> Our form of government stands outside and above competition with others. We do not copy our neighbours; we are an example to them. Athens is a democracy. The business of government lies with the many and not with the few. The law secures equal justice to all; at the same time the claims of excellence are recognized; individuals are preferred to the public service, not as a matter of principle, but as the reward of merit. Nor is poverty a bar. No man, however poor – or however obscure, is forbidden to do good to his country. In our public life there is no exclusiveness.[32] (pp. 92–3)

The values that MacNeice holds out to his listeners are the exemplary values for which they are fighting or making sacrifices on the home front – a participative democracy, 'equal justice' before the law, and an inclusive meritocracy. Simultaneously, he treats Athens as the paragon, knowing that British arrangements are quite otherwise. These were not the actual conditions of British life, and this listeners at home would surely register. Furthermore, 'Pericles' was transmitted three days after the Commons debated the contents of the Beveridge Report. This Report recommended social and economic reforms reflecting the aspirations and popular hopes for a fairer, more equal society, including provisions for old age and for unemployment, greater security of employment, better housing and a national health service. However, there was widespread scepticism that it would survive pressure from 'vested interests', like the major insurance companies or, for that matter, from Churchill's government.[33] Broadcast in this atmosphere, 'Pericles' can be perceived to be striking a contentious chord, one that attentive listeners would surely hear.

The suggestion of political intent here is further increased in the final feature of *The Four Freedoms*, called 'What Now?' (broadcast on 28 March 1943). However, three days before its transmission, on 25 March, MacNeice's more orthodox *Long Live Greece*, a thirty-minute dramatic feature on the Home Service to commemorate Greek Independence Day, reverts to reflections of newspaper reports and thereby highlights the political peculiarity of both 'Pericles' and 'What Now?' *Long Live Greece* demonises Nazi vindictiveness to Greek civilians, such as revenge atrocities for non-cooperation with occupying forces. Once again, MacNeice focuses on human predicaments. Greek brothers serving with the allied armies in North Africa do not know whether their father or the wife and baby of one of them have been killed or taken prisoner in a reprisal attack on their village. It is a more conventional piece of propaganda and in the same vein as those of the previous year. However, it serves to differentiate, or throw into relief, the strategies of 'Pericles' and of 'What Now?' This provided another change of tone.

'What Now?' is unusually self-referential, querying preconceptions about Athenian democracy and alluding to 'Pericles'. MacNeice is aware that his listeners are suspicious of propaganda, have become aware of when they are hearing it and have evolved strategies for listening to it. The scenario here is that an elderly brother and sister are waiting for 'What Now?' to start and discuss what a radio programme about freedom might be like:

> Robert: I can tell you exactly what it would be like. A series of clarion calls. Freedom from fear: fanfare. Freedom from Want: fanfare. Freedom of worship: organ. Freedom from –
> Evelyn: Don't be so cynical, Robert. It's a serious subject, isn't it?[34] (p. 3)

They do not question the idea of freedom, but the predictable manner in which it is being promoted on the radio. 'What Now?' is essentially concerned with what its characters already accept as valid and important. Its listeners know they are not being offered a balanced view; this propaganda includes a debunking of itself without actually spoiling its own propagandistic message. 'Pericles', transmitted five weeks earlier, is then discussed:

> Robert: But they didn't point out the snags in Athenian democracy – slave labour at home and imperialism abroad. The B.B.C. just left that out of the picture.
> Evelyn: I know, dear, but perhaps they hadn't got time.
> Robert: I don't think it's that. I think that they're afraid that, if they put in the shadows, their public will get all confused. Why take our democracy ... (p. 4)

Robert acknowledges neither the double-edged nature of the version of democracy in 'Pericles', nor MacNeice's subversive employment of it – MacNeice interrupts him before he can express any doubts on the British version. Robert's superficial point is that effective propaganda is simple and direct, without complications, but MacNeice is still dissembling. He foregrounds that in her youth Evelyn was politically active as a suffragette before World War I and that women's suffrage was a hard-won victory, but without stating that Athenian women in fifth-century Athens were not allowed to vote. For contemporary listeners with no script to read and re-read, however, these ironies were surely harder to detect. For example, the radio critic of *The Manchester Guardian* declared 'What Now?' to be 'prosaic', 'almost rambling' and 'oblique' in its approach.[35] Thus, for one reviewer, at least, its subtleties were ineffective.

## THE SACRED BAND

Following the apparent machinations of 'Pericles' and 'What Now?' MacNeice returned to a more standard mode of keeping up awareness of the Nazi occupation of Greece and Greek heroism with *The Sacred Band* (7 January 1944, Home Service), the last of MacNeice's wartime propaganda features to utilise a notion from ancient Greece as its touchstone. At forty-five minutes, it is also the longest, carrying a more sustained storyline, which nevertheless bears comparison with the earlier, shorter ones in terms of tone and content.[36] The inspirations of the piece are two historical fighting forces which have been known as the Sacred Band: the fourth-century BC Theban unit, characterised by '300 infantrymen... bound together by homoerotic pairing', and a Hellenic battalion formed during the Greek War of Independence (1821–9), which claimed the same ethos. An opening announcement describes their relevance to the present day: a new sacred band of Greeks is fighting in the Middle East alongside the Western allies. Like its ancient predecessor, this is a do-or-die unit of elite, highly trained men.[37] The association is made even more explicit in a *Radio Times* notice for *The Sacred Band*, where this line of descent is visually reinforced by the use of a photograph of modern Greek soldiers in desert trenches (see Figure 2.1).

We hear dialogue between cheerful soldiers waiting to hear their leader's address before the battle of Chaeronea (338 BC) where they will face the might of Philip of Macedon, followed by a mother trying unsuccessfully to dissuade her son from borrowing the farm's horse and the family's old musket and making his way to fight the Turkish janissaries at Missolonghi. These two short sequences provide the cornerstone of the remainder of the drama and are all the historical background information the listener gets. The ensuing storyline traces the contour of Greek fortunes in the then current war through the adventures and hardships of three young men and, through a parallel narrative, the young wife of one of them who has helped British soldiers escaping from the invading Nazis.

Separately, Yannis, Kostas and Petros join the army fighting in the Pindus Mountains through the winter of 1941–2. Initially, we hear their sad farewells with loved ones. Typically, MacNeice lingers over this emotive aspect of the intrusion of the war on individual lives, before introducing the technique of allowing his characters to read each other's thoughts. Despite being several miles apart in the mountains, the three men are able to communicate with each other through a form of telepathy – an effective device first developed by MacNeice

## Louis MacNeice and 'The Paragons of Hellas'

Figure 2.1 Notice for Louis MacNeice's *The Sacred Band* (1944) in the *Radio Times*, 31 December 1943, p. 16.

in *The Commandos*, a feature concerned with the commando raid on Dieppe on 18–19 August 1942 (broadcast on the North American Service, 11 October 1942, and Home Service, 17 October 1942):

Yannis: ... Now then. Who's got an olive?
Kostas: I have if you want to know –
Yannis: Who the –
Kostas: Kostas the name is but I'm several mountains away from you. So I think I'll eat it myself. (*The Sacred Band*, pp. 13–14)

They learn that they have each slept with a single blanket:

> Kostas: Nothing like action at dawn after you've slept in one blanket –
> Yannis: You needn't tell me. I slept in one blanket too.
> Petros: So did we all, gentlemen – you needn't look around, you can't see me. I'm five miles southwest of you. (p. 14)

Thus a lasting comradeship begins. And Petros soon finds he can similarly communicate with his wife, Lina. Through Lina we are again reminded of starvation as a weapon, when a merchant tells her that 'The Germans are depleting the country; they want us to starve' (p. 21).

The narrative continues with the now familiar story of Italian retreat and German invasion. The British are compelled to retreat south, as are the escaping Greeks, including our three young men, who end up in the same boat bound for Egypt. Lina is now helping to hide British soldiers, placing herself in great danger. But one evening finds her reading some lines by the Greek romantic poet Andreas Kalvos:

> Here, when we have given
> Greece her ancient sceptre,
> Every mother will bring her children
> And say: 'Let the Sacred Band
> Be your model, children – a band
> Of heroes, the pride of youth.' (p. 25)

In Egypt, against the backdrop of El Alamein – in November 1942, the first British victory of the war – the three men join their own Sacred Band and undergo advanced training to equip them for more dangerous missions. They affirm, in the tradition of the first Band, that they will return with their 'shield or on it' (p. 26).

In the closing pages of the script, Kostas is killed in action and Lina is arrested for the possession of a wireless set with which she listens to 'enemy broadcasts'. She assures the Nazi who has come to collect her that she does indeed listen to enemy broadcasts: 'I listened exactly an hour ago to the news of the battle of El Alamein' (p. 29). She is incarcerated and, although *The Sacred Band* ends with the uplift of the 'Winged Victory', Nike, it is not before she 'talks' to her husband, Petros, for the last time, through her thoughts:

> Petros: I'm sorry, Yannis ... I was thinking about something else. I was thinking about ...
> Lina: Me? You may think about me, darling, but I'm glad that you can't see me – and you don't know where I am. I'm somewhere quite inconceivable. And I shan't last very long here; nobody does. I shall

be dead before you return to Greece. But when you return, Petros, you must avenge me and when I say 'me' I mean all of us. (p. 30)

MacNeice provides a poignant close to remind listeners of Nazi cruelty and the terrible human cost of the war. Our pity for doomed Lina turns to anger with her plea for vengeance.

This is the last of MacNeice's Greek propaganda programmes, and it is founded on the idea of the ancient tradition of fighting to the death for the freedom of the homeland, and *'nun huper panton agon'* ('Now the struggle is for all'). The link back to the ancient Sacred Band of the fourth century BC only provides an expressly stated starting point before fading into the background of the present era. Even so, the link is established and the Band's traditions honoured.

The strategies employed by MacNeice in these features are intended sometimes to persuade listeners to a particular point of view, sometimes merely to remind them of things they already know. Analogies are ennobling; they provide a heightened sense of heroism and of brave deeds; they remind listeners of Greek victories against the odds long ago. Implicitly, we may anticipate similar victories in the present war: all of these programmes mention Marathon, Thermopylae, the Athenian naval victory at Salamis, and Plataea. These names are repeated to cast Greeks caught up in the struggle against fascist oppression in the light of an ancient tradition, which their ancestors lived through and survived before. MacNeice's imagined, modern scenarios are meant to recreate events and situations which seem 'real', in which his characters in their current predicaments refer often to the distant past, which is dramatically brought to supply, as Wyver suggests in Chapter 3, below, 'a sense of continuity between past and present' – a sense which found great potency during World War II. MacNeice relied on the same assumption in the war years in order to create a sense that human experience and human values are essentially unchanged over time.

## PROGRAMMES DISCUSSED

*The March of the 10,000*. Prod. Royston Morley. BBC Radio, Overseas Service. Several transmissions, 16–18 April 1941.

*The Glory that is Greece*. Prod. Laurence Gilliam. BBC Radio, Home Service. Tuesday 28 October 1941, 8.00–8.45pm.

*Salutation to Greece*. Prod. Malcolm Baker-Smith. BBC Radio, Home Service. Sunday 22 March 1942, 8.45–9.00pm.

*Salute to Greece*. Prod. Louis MacNeice. BBC Radio, Home Service. Sunday 25 October 1942, 8.45–9.00pm.

*The Four Freedoms*. 6-part series. Prod. Louis MacNeice. BBC Radio, Home Service.
Episode 1: 'Pericles'. Sunday 21 February 1943, 8.45–9.00pm.
Episode 6: 'What Now?' Sunday 28 March 1943, 8.45–9.00pm.

*Long Live Greece*. Prod. Louis MacNeice. BBC Radio, Home Service. Thursday 25 March 1943, 9.40–10.10pm.

*The Sacred Band*. Prod. Louis MacNeice. BBC Radio, Home Service. Friday 7 January 1944, 8.15–9.00pm.

## NOTES

1. Nicholas (1996: 63).
2. Connelly (2004: 162).
3. Wrigley (2013: 11).
4. Coulton (1980: 130).
5. Briggs (1970: 113).
6. Balfour (1979: 87).
7. Stallworthy (1995: 292).
8. Golphin (2012: 18–20).
9. Stallworthy (1995: 287); Wrigley (2015a: 155).
10. Stallworthy (1995: 290).
11. Coulton (1980: 53).
12. Wrigley (2015a: 151).
13. McDonald (1998: 48).
14. Murray (2013: 80–3).
15. Hastings (2011: 199).
16. Wrigley and Harrison (2013: 32); this volume publishes the script in its entirety, with introduction; and the Appendix at 409ff. notes which of the programmes discussed in this chapter are extant in the British Library Sound Archive (BLSA).
17. See Xenophon, *Anabasis* 4.7.24.
18. Wrigley and Harrison (2013: 32).
19. As noted by Flower (2012: 109–10), in Xenophon's story the troops' sighting of the sea offers a 'false closure', as their struggles, and the *Anabasis*, go on.
20. Published in its entirety, with an introduction, in Wrigley and Harrison (2013: 43–79).
21. Wrigley and Harrison (2013: 46).
22. Wrigley and Harrison (2013: 53 n. 12).
23. Page references following quotations are to Wrigley and Harrison (2013), which published these scripts for the first time.

24 See Thucydides, *History* 2.43.3. Note that Stavros' next 'quotation', cited below, is not matched directly within Thucydides' version of the speech.
25 Anon. (1943c).
26 Anon. (1943b).
27 A typescript for *Salutation to Greece* is held in the BBC WAC Script Library.
28 Typescripts for *Salute to Greece* are held in the BBC WAC Script Library and in the WAC's separate collection of Louis MacNeice's typescripts.
29 Coulton (1980: 62).
30 Wrigley (2015a: 165).
31 Lane Fox (2005: 93–4).
32 Cf. Thucydides, *History* 2.37.1.
33 Rose (2003: 67).
34 Typescripts for 'What Now?' are held in the BBC WAC Script Library and in the WAC's separate collection of MacNeice's typescripts.
35 Anon. (1943a).
36 Typescripts for *The Sacred Band* are held in the BBC WAC Script Library and in the WAC's separate collection of Louis MacNeice's typescripts. These collections also hold a 'short version' of thirty minutes for broadcast on the Home and Overseas Service on 25 March 1944.
37 Lane Fox (2005: 181).

# 3 The Beginnings of Civilisation: Television Travels to Greece with Mortimer Wheeler and Compton Mackenzie

John Wyver

At the end of the 1950s both the eminent archaeologist Sir Mortimer Wheeler (1890–1976) and author and secret service veteran Sir Compton Mackenzie (1883–1972) presented film documentary series about ancient Greece for BBC Television. Although aspects of the classical world had been considered in earlier television programmes, Wheeler's *Armchair Voyage: Hellenic Cruise* (BBC, 1958) and *The Glory that was Greece* (BBC, 1959) with Mackenzie were the small screen's earliest sustained engagements with the subject.[1] The television critic of *The Manchester Guardian* described the first episode in Wheeler's series as 'an instance of television really opening a window upon the world and genuinely giving people a foretaste of something tremendously satisfying that they can go and do for themselves'.[2] For *The Listener*, K. W. Gransden welcomed Mackenzie's initial offering as 'a most impressive and enjoyable film, both for classicists like myself and, I should guess, for those to whom it was all new'.[3] Sequences filmed at significant classical sites in Greece feature in both series, although the documentary languages that each develops and their approaches to representing place and space are distinct. Seen almost sixty years on they also reveal contrasting concerns, as Wheeler addresses archaeological questions within a broadly humanist framework while Mackenzie develops a more explicitly political discourse with an embrace of contemporary parallels.

This chapter outlines the precursors of and influences on Wheeler's and Mackenzie's series, exploring within a broad cultural frame the legacies of early modern travellers and of the Grand Tour, the development of sightseeing and popular tourism from the eighteenth century onwards, representations of Greece in literature, painting and photography, technologies for virtual voyages, illustrated lectures and film travelogues as well as the mediation of travel by radio and early television. I argue that elements of each of these antecedents contributed to the formation of the two series, along with the public service understandings of the BBC's mission, the social and educational aspirations of a post-war, middle-class audience and the personal interests of the two presenters. Yet while both series can be seen as pioneering certain techniques that would quickly become established for presenter-led documentary series, the visual language of neither is entirely successful. Only in Mortimer Wheeler's subsequent series, *The Grandeur that was Rome* (BBC, 1960),[4] do we see the confident deployment of tropes that would become fundamental, including on-location address to the camera. Even so, by building on the strategies of older technologies including panoramas and film travelogues, Wheeler's and Mackenzie's series about ancient Greece exemplify television's development of techniques of virtual travel that have emerged as dominant in factual television.

## 'AN EXCELLENT SUBSTITUTE FOR THE REAL THING'

First shown after 9.00pm on three consecutive Monday evenings from 21 July 1958, *Armchair Voyage: Hellenic Cruise* (hereafter *Hellenic Cruise*) is a trilogy of half-hour television films that journeys with members of 'The Hellenic Travellers' Club' on an Aegean cruise undertaken earlier that year.[5] The first episode travels from London to Venice and on to Mycenae, the second visits Miletus, Istanbul and the islands of the eastern Mediterranean, while the third sails from Delos to Athens. Mortimer Wheeler accompanies an organised tour visiting the key sites of a history and culture that many would have studied at school, and maybe also university. In addition to explorations of archaeological remains there are sequences that celebrate the folkloric aspects of contemporary Greece, such as traditional dancing on Lesbos. There is, however, no mention of the recent civil war, which had ended less than a decade before, or of the continuing political instability of the country. The acute tensions of the struggle by Greek Cypriots for independence from the British similarly have no place in the narrative.

Throughout the series Mortimer Wheeler contributes an informed and informal narration, enlivened by a dry humour. But while his voiceover at times shares personal responses ('St Paul apart,' he reflects, 'I find little to get excited about at Corinth'), Wheeler at no point, whether on land or at sea, addresses the camera directly. He is frequently pictured on the boat and is filmed, invariably in long shot, walking around the historical sites. There is no synchronous sound at the locations, whereas on board ship Wheeler speaks on camera with a number of scholars who are making the trip. These include Professor William Bedell Stanford (1910–84), of Trinity College, Dublin, who produced commentaries on classical texts (such as his two-volume edition of Homer's *Odyssey*, published in 1947–8) and the educationalist Sir John Wolfenden (1906–85), who was presumably taking a break after the publication the previous year of his committee's report recommending that homosexuality should be decriminalised. Wolfenden is also one of those who contribute lectures for the travellers, and by extension the viewers, and the third episode includes a five-minute section of his dense discourse on Plato's ideal state. The camerawork throughout the series is prosaic, although just occasionally there is an attempt at an unconventional visual effect, as on Delos in the third episode. From a close-up of Mortimer Wheeler filling his pipe, the frame tilts down to the shadow of his silhouette (see Figure 3.1). 'In Delos too,' he asserts, 'you were not allowed to look at your own shadow, less death strike you within the year.' Throughout there are reference stills of key artworks and a small number of drawings, as at Olympia, reconstructing what an ancient town or temple might once have looked like.

Broadcast just nine months later, sir compton mackenzie's *The Glory that was Greece* has a greater visual confidence than *Hellenic Cruise*, with more accomplished camerawork, animated graphics, and expressive montages that aspire to bring drama to the narrative. Appropriating the title and employing the popular but scholarly approach of the 1911 illustrated book by J. C. Stobart,[6] *The Glory that was Greece* offers what *Radio Times* described as 'personal reflections' on the history of ancient Greece.[7] First shown at 9.20pm on Wednesday evenings from 1 April 1959, the trilogy begins with a programme shot largely on Crete in which Mackenzie discusses the myths of Zeus, Minos and Theseus. The second episode recounts the battles of Marathon, Salamis and Thermopylae, visiting the sites on which they were fought, while the third considers the struggle between the democratic state of Athens and Sparta's oligarchy in the Peloponnesian War. Mackenzie's scripts are significantly more discursive than Wheeler's, weaving together history, myths, reminiscence and rumination in a manner that is occasionally wildly idiosyncratic.

*The Beginnings of* Civilisation 67

Figure 3.1 Mortimer Wheeler lighting his pipe in silhouette on Delos: *Hellenic Cruise*, episode 3 'Delos to Athens' (1958). BBC.

Speaking of women depicted in the frescoes at Knossos, for example, Mackenzie says,

> they seem to me absolutely marvellous, and the best of the lot, well I'll be quite frank, [are] these breasts which are bare, or covered with a very diaphanous material. And I can't help thinking, when I think of all our young ladies today who lie about on beaches in the Mediterranean in bikinis and brassieres, if they'd only leave off the brassiere how much better it would look.

There are no academics to support Mackenzie, who, in contrast to Wheeler, at times speaks directly if uneasily to the camera. The series also employs what today appears a bizarre technique of combining sequences shot on location without sound with scenes obviously filmed in a studio in front of back projections. In the first episode, for example, images of Mackenzie on a mule climbing to the Dicteon Cave on Crete are followed by him in a studio walking into frame mopping his brow with the landscape projected behind him. The transition is done without comment, with the clear intention that the viewer believes the closer shots with Mackenzie's words were also filmed and recorded on location. This disconcerting technique appears to have been a unique experiment in a presenter-led series, and to have been employed both for reasons of economy and to help the production team achieve greater control over Mackenzie's performance. Executives at the time, however, were worried about the practice, as is witnessed by an internal memo from Assistant Head of Television Talks Grace Wyndham Goldie (1900–86), in which she wrote:

> [producer] Stephen Hearst is using back projection at Ealing, so that there will in a sense be a deception of the audience. Some of the material will in fact be spoken by Compton Mackenzie at Ealing, and he will purport to be in Greece. I am a little concerned about this for obvious reasons, and I have asked to see the programmes ... so that if we have views about keeping trust with the public in an actuality documentary of this kind, [changes] can be implemented.[8]

Either her concerns were allayed or re-editing proved too complex: the programmes went ahead with sequences that to twenty-first-century eyes appear almost laughably 'fake'.

*Hellenic Cruise* with Mortimer Wheeler drew a positive response from viewers, with the episodes achieving Reaction Indices of, respectively, 75, 73 and 76 ('good figure[s]', according to the BBC's confidential Audience Research Report).[9] Regarding the first episode, a survey respondent identified as 'a Professional Cricketer's wife' 'readily admitted (and others agreed with her) that [the episode] was an excellent substitute for the real thing'. Reacting to the third episode, 'a Teacher' commented, 'I am keen on things Greek and never having visited these places the T.V. is the next best thing.' Recording Reaction Indices of 74, 68 and 79 for its three episodes, *The Glory that was Greece* had a less consistent response from viewers, with Compton Mackenzie prompting strong opinions. 'A large majority of the sample audience', the Audience Research Report for the first episode noted, 'were full of praise for his contribution' but he 'was sometimes compared unfavourably' with Wheeler in *Hellenic Cruise*. 'It was said that [Mackenzie] got carried away by his own enthusiasm,' the Audience Research Report detailed, 'and as a result was inclined to talk too much, and not always clearly.'[10]

Both *Hellenic Cruise* and *The Glory that was Greece* embody the ideals of public service broadcasting as they were understood by the BBC radio and television services in the post-war years. In a memorandum submitted in January 1961 to the Committee on Broadcasting chaired by Sir Harry Pilkington, the BBC noted that its Royal Charter refers to the 'great value' of the broadcasting services 'as means of disseminating information, education and entertainment', and it expressed its corporate view that 'material that is informative can also be entertaining and what is entertaining can also be educative'.[11] Wheeler's and Mackenzie's series aim both to educate and to entertain, and this intention can be seen as intersecting with the aspirations of an increasingly knowledgeable middle-class population, especially with the extension of secondary schooling following the 1944 Education Act. By the mid-1950s, continental travel was starting to be a reality for increasingly affluent Britons and it was in these years that, as historian Rosemary Wakeman notes, 'The tourist industry fashioned an imaginary of European distinctiveness and heritage as a prized commodity essential to prosperity.'[12] Popular interest in the classical world and its remains was also evident from the healthy sales of paperbacks including *The Gods of the Greeks* by Carl Kerényi, first published by Thames & Hudson in 1951 (reprinted by Penguin in 1958), and *The World of Odysseus* by M. I. Finley, published in Britain by Chatto & Windus in 1956. *Hellenic Cruise* and *The Glory that was Greece* extended these contemporary engagements with ancient Greece in print into television. At the same time both series also drew on older and more diverse forms as they sought to give viewers who had not travelled to Greece 'an excellent substitute for the real thing'.

## TOURISTS AND TRAVELLERS

While they may have been among the first to be accompanied by television crews, Mortimer Wheeler and Compton Mackenzie were following in the footsteps of soldiers, scholars and many others across the previous three hundred years. The exploration of Greece by foreigners developed from a tradition of classical study and educational travel that in the late seventeenth century coalesced among the upper classes in the Grand Tour. Greece, however, was not usually embraced by the Tour, at least not until after the landmark publication between 1762 and 1816 of Nicholas Revett and James Stuart's *The Antiquities of Athens and Other Monuments of Greece*. These volumes catalysed the Greek revival movement in architecture and were just one aspect of an increasingly pervasive Hellenism among the intelligentsia of northern Europe.

'The sentimental accompaniment', David Constantine writes,

> of this focussing on Greece was nostalgia. Though it was possible to recover, clarify and substantiate the Hellenic Ideal, that ideal remained, as an ideal, unrealisable, lost. Visiting the land itself, recovering the sites and the works of art, enhances the sense of loss, in that one sees more clearly what once was.[13]

And in the modern medium of television the nostalgic note continued to shape both Wheeler's and Mackenzie's attitudes to the classical world. In his first episode, for example, speaking of Phidias' statue of Zeus in the temple at Olympia, Wheeler laments that, 'Alas, it has gone the way of all gold. So too has the temple, its columns thrown down by men or earthquakes.' Both Wheeler and Mackenzie also share an attitude that John Pemble identifies as pervasive among Victorian visitors to Italy and Greece: 'On the threshold of the South [the British traveller] experienced an apotheosis. He passed from the circumference to the centre of things and his thoughts dwelt on roots, origins, essentials, and ultimate affinities.'[14] In the first episode of *Hellenic Cruise*, as he leans against the ship's rail to converse with Wheeler, John Wolfenden expresses this sense of returning to the singular source: 'Plato and Aristotle, Sophocles, Thucydides, wherever you look in the fields of art or history or political living it all starts with Greece.'[15]

Despite the growth of organised tourism across Europe in the middle of the nineteenth century, the pathways to Greece remained tough to negotiate. Only towards the end of the century was there a gradual extension of general tourism in pursuit of Hellenic ideals, as is evidenced by the publication of John Murray's first *Handbook for Travellers to Greece*, which had reached its seventh edition by 1900. Cruises organised by Henry Lunn (1859–1939) and The Hellenic Travellers' Club made the country somewhat more accessible in the interwar years. In the wake of World War II, however, continental tourism was still a complex business, with currency restrictions in place and, in Greece especially, comparatively few tourist hotels. In 1951 the Society for the Promotion of Hellenic Studies asked W. F. and R. K. Swan, who ran Swan's Travel Bureau, to organise a cruise around the Aegean, and this was repeated in subsequent years.[16] Distinguished academics, including Mortimer Wheeler, were invited along to lecture the travellers, and as is recognised in the opening credits of *Hellenic Cruise* one such excursion provides the narrative framework for the series. But what remains hidden from the viewer is that Wheeler had the year before the filming become chairman of the organising company, now known as Swan Hellenic Cruises.[17] Similarly unrecognised in the episodes is the tension between the democratisation, by both the cruise and now television, of the Grand Tour experience, and the sense that the direct and supposedly authentic encounter with the ancient ruins remains the privilege of those who enjoyed the advantages of education and wealth.

Both the Grand Tour and television's later travels aspire to the authenticity of experience that James Buzard suggests is seen in the modern era to be based not on aristocratic privilege but rather on a democratised form of the mentality that the Grand Tour was intended to impart: 'a loosely defined set of inner personal qualities that amounts to a superior emotional-aesthetic sensitivity'.[18] Essential to this authenticity of experience was a visitor's physical presence, and by the nineteenth century it was widely accepted that standing on the very stones of an ancient site would stimulate in some mystical way a revival of its ancient ethos. Richard Jenkyns suggests that this idea of a secular pilgrimage emerged in one of its earliest forms with the antiquarian Robert Wood, who travelled in Greece in the 1750s:

> The conception of a special magic that places can acquire through their connection with great men and events, or through the associations breathed into them by poetry, is something still fresh in European thought. Stuart and Revett rediscovered Greek architecture, but Wood has a claim to be considered the first pilgrim to Greece.[19]

Both Wheeler and Mackenzie are insistently present throughout their pilgrimages two centuries later, although it is Mackenzie who is more strongly associated in the visuals with the sites themselves. By standing on the Acropolis or visiting the plain of Marathon, the guides for the small screen both bear witness to the authenticity of experience being offered by the episodes and at the same time enhance the allure of what are at times comparatively unspectacular images. At the close of the third episode of *The Glory that was Greece*, for example, Mackenzie reinforces his visual presence at Missolonghi with an intense, near-mystical incantation, 'This, this sacred ground, this is Missolonghi.'

The importance, both for the television viewer and for the presenter as their surrogate, of above all seeing the actual places extends the imperatives of travel in what Judith Adler and others have characterised as the age of observation.[20] As Carol Crashaw and John Urry have written, referencing Adler's work:

> By the end of the eighteenth century the focus of travel in Europe shifted from scholastic pursuits to visual pleasure, from the traveller's ear to the traveller's eye. From then on, sight becomes highly significant in the ordering of tourist and travel discourses. In most such discourses there is a particular emphasis upon the seeing and collecting of sights.[21]

The point is reinforced by Jennifer Craik when she writes, 'Knowledge was acquired through seeing, verifying and ordering the world. Observation, witness and hearsay were techniques of the eye and became the new form of travel – sightseeing.'[22] And very soon this new centrality in travel of sight was underpinned by the technologies of photography that allowed sights to be fixed for the viewer, transported, collected and commodified. One of the great attractions of early photography was that it could, like television a century later, act as a stand-in for travel. Writing of photographic publications from the 1850s and 1860s depicting Mediterranean sites, Claire Lyons observes that, 'As a substitute for the personalised experience of travel, they offered at once a window on to the outside world and a powerful device through which to represent and ultimately to possess it.'[23] *Hellenic Cruise* and *The Glory that was Greece* extend into the emerging medium of television the idea of travel for the seeing of sights, the concern with capturing those sights for viewers at home, and the sense of the viewer's possession.

## ARMCHAIR VOYAGES

Both *Hellenic Cruise* and *The Glory that was Greece* extend techniques and technologies of virtual travel that date back to long before the end of the nineteenth century, when film exploited them. Indeed, Grace Wyndham Goldie described the idea of the former series as taking 'the public vicariously on a Hellenic Cruise by means of television'.[24] Among the earlier forms of such vicarious transports were moving panoramas that featured a long roll painting unfurling past a 'window' at which the spectator sat. Such attractions often took the form of a travelogue, as did Clarkson Stanfield's *The Passage of the Rhine* (1828), presented in a conventional theatre with characters supposedly in a cut-out ship placed before the moving canvas.[25] Stationary travel in space and time of this kind was also central to numerous other pre-cinematic technologies including stereoscopes, magic lantern slides, postcards and a variety of spectacles on offer at world's fairs. By 1900 film travelogues, known to the industry and audiences of the day as 'scenics', were the most popular and potent expression of what Anne Friedberg has theorised as the 'mobilized gaze'.[26] 'These short films', Jennifer Peterson considers, 'presented glimpses of foreign landscapes, peoples, regional industries, and tourist icons to an audience that were not yet accustomed to world travel.'[27] Just as television's travels to Greece in the 1950s were to be legitimised by their educational elements within the context of public service broadcasting, so travelogues and indeed lectures were frequently promoted for their improving qualities. 'The educational impulse of the travelogue', Jeffery Ruoff notes, 'is one of its defining characteristics, even when it is the pretext for other, less edifying, pleasures.'[28]

Charles Musser and others have proposed that travelogues were strongly influenced not only by panoramas and stereocards but also by the pre-cinematic practice of live lecturers narrating alongside the projection of sequences of lantern slides. One of the central figures in this tradition was Burton Holmes (1870–1958), who can be recognised as a direct precursor of Mortimer Wheeler and Compton Mackenzie. Burton Holmes shot and presented film travelogues across the world from 1897 to 1949, and indeed his business manager, Louis Francis Brown, is credited with coining the term 'travelogue' for a series of lectures in London in 1902.[29] Musser argues that travel lecturers like Holmes 'were the figures with whom audiences could identify and derive vicarious experience and pleasure'.[30] For such identification to be successful it was important that the lecturer appeared in the slides, and later films, demonstrating his presence in the remote location; that the slides and films were understood as often reproducing his point of view; and that he spoke from the podium alongside the projected images. In both *Hellenic Cruise* and *The Glory that was Greece*, the first two conditions are reproduced precisely within the films, and for the third is substituted the voiceover narration and sequences in which the presenter speaks directly to the camera. The most direct link between Burton Holmes' activities and those of Wheeler and Mackenzie are not in fact travel films but three lantern slide lectures from the late 1890s. 'The Olympian Games in Athens', 'Grecian Journeys' and 'The Wonders of Thessaly' were published in the third book of the lavish ten-volume *The Burton Holmes Lectures with Illustrations from Photographs by the Author* (1901).[31] Holmes travelled to Greece in 1896 for the inaugural Olympics, and the printed version of his lecture recounting this voyage has as its first photograph a shot of the Adriatic Sea taken from his ship – just as is featured in the opening titles of *Hellenic Cruise*. The reader – and the audience member for the original lecture – follows Burton's itinerary via a combination of text and numerous images, most of them photographic but with occasional line drawings also. The journey culminates in a visit to the Acropolis, and in several images Holmes appears before the ruins, just as Wheeler and Mackenzie do in their respective series.

Central to Burton Holmes' practice and to both lantern slide lectures and film travelogues in general is a discursive and digressive structure. As Jeffery Ruoff notes, 'the travelogue is an open form; essayistic, it often brings together scenes without regard for plot or narrative progression'.[32] This too is partly echoed by the television travel series of the late 1950s, for although Wheeler's narration employs the ship's voyage as a structure, digressions are provided by folk dancing on Lesbos and an Easter service of the Greek Orthodox Church in Athens. Mackenzie is distinctly more discursive, reflecting for example on the history of water closets in episode one. In their visual languages both *Hellenic Cruise* and *The Glory that was Greece* also reproduce aspects of the form of early travelogues. As Jennifer Peterson suggests,

> The basic formula of the travelogue of the nickelodeon era is a series of single, discrete exterior shots of landscapes and people ... Most shots have been joined together in a manner that preserves the integrity of each shot rather than, for example, making connections between shots via continuous space or matching on action ... This discontinuous editing principle creates the sense that the shots form a *collection* rather than a unified whole.[33]

In episode one of *Hellenic Cruise* the lengthy sequence devoted to Venice is just such a series of discrete exteriors with no sense of the creation of continuous space across the city, and even when Wheeler, almost always in long shot, walks through the ruins of Mycenae, it is hard for the viewer to understand how each framing relates spatially to the ones before and following.

While illustrated lectures and early film travelogues can be recognised as significant precursors of *Hellenic Cruise* and *The Glory that was Greece*, more recent elements in their formation were television programmes about archaeology and, before these, radio programmes about the classical world. Between the 1920s and the early 1960s, the BBC broadcast a wide range of radio programmes about ancient Greece, and these broadcasts complemented other cultural and educational activities, such as the publication after 1946 of relatively cheap Penguin paperback translations, to give works from ancient Greece a public identity beyond formal education.[34] Such radio broadcasts began as early as 24 October 1924, just under two years after what was then the British Broadcasting Company started transmissions. From the regional station 2EH in Edinburgh, Professor of Greek A. W. Mair (1875–1928) gave the first of a pair of fifteen-minute talks titled 'The Heritage of Greece'. In 1926, and anticipating Mortimer Wheeler's *Hellenic Cruise*, Major W. Cross, a Fellow of the Royal Geographical Society, contributed seven talks recounting *A Cruise in the Mediterranean*. The sophistication of interwar radio travel broadcasts is suggested by *Radio Times*' description of an edition of *Travel Talk* broadcast by the National Programme on 27 March 1936, which anticipates aspects of Wheeler's virtual voyage to Corinth in the first episode of *Hellenic Cruise*:

Today Mr Duckett is to take listeners on a Greek steamer through the Gulf of Corinth ... Mr. Duckett will point out the beautiful scenery, narrow fringing lowlands and steep mountain-sides, hill pastures and olive groves; and so he will bring them to Corinth and take them on to Athens.[35]

Travel documentaries on early television constitute a further context, albeit a rather limited one, for both *Hellenic Cruise* and *The Glory that was Greece*. The BBC's first broadcasts from Alexandra Palace from November 1936 onwards were live programming shot with electronic cathode ray tube cameras, mostly from studios, and then increasingly as 'outside broadcasts' at locations from which signals could be relayed back to the transmitter either by cables or by wireless transmission. Programmes originating on film, such as *Hellenic Cruise* and *The Glory that was Greece*, were rare in the immediate post-war years. This was in part because the new medium was widely understood as being inherently 'live', and so only modest resources were allocated to filming, but also because the movie industry and its powerful Association of Cinematograph Technicians' union opposed television's potential challenge to existing structures of the production and exhibition of films. Nonetheless, a programme form was developed which involved a studio-based presenter introducing film sequences, as in *About Britain* (1953–4) with Richard Dimbleby, on which Stephen Hearst (1919–2010), who was later to produce *Hellenic Cruise* and *The Glory that was Greece*, worked as a scriptwriter. By this point film cameras were becoming lighter and somewhat more flexible, although sound recording on location remained technically demanding.[36] From November 1955 the BBC was facing for the first time competition from the commercial ITV network. Several of the ITV franchise holders, including ATV and Granada, were companies with closer links with the cinema industry, and early on they started to use film for both dramas and factual programmes. Working with film on the BBC series *Half the World Away* (1957), with presenter Christopher Chataway travelling to Delhi, Hong Kong and Singapore, Stephen Hearst would have been well aware of these shifts. *Hellenic Cruise*, shot early the following year, was similarly to be a film series, and one with an established presence before the camera.

## AUTHORITY FIGURES

Sir Mortimer Wheeler by 1958 had been a dynamic keeper of the Museum of London, an energetic field archaeologist, founder of the Institute of Archaeology and Director-General of the archaeological survey of India, and he remained secretary of the British Academy.[37] He was also well known to television's growing audiences. He first appeared on the screen in the fortnightly quiz programme *Animal, Vegetable, Mineral?* (1952–9) on 6 November 1952, and he quickly became a regular guest. Writing only two years later, producer Glyn Daniel identified the importance of the show in introducing viewers to archaeology, and also training archaeologists and other professionals 'to perform with ease, or at least with an air of natural sincerity, in front of the battery of cameras and lights which fill a television studio'.[38] In part thanks to subsequent appearances on the archaeology series *Buried Treasure* (1954–9) but far more significantly because of Wheeler's continuing popularity on *Animal, Vegetable, Mineral?*, by the late 1950s he was regarded by BBC executives as one of their few 'star' presenters of factual programmes. Moreover, it is clear from the BBC's written archives that the decision to produce *Hellenic Cruise* was less the result of a considered and strategic decision to mount a series about the classical world and considerably more to do with a desire to appease Wheeler's concern to secure regular on-screen appearances and, as a consequence, a comfortable retirement income. After an extensive correspondence in the latter half of 1957, on 22 January 1958 Head of Television Talks Leonard Miall (1914–2005) confirmed in an internal memo that not only had the BBC guaranteed Wheeler 'at least the same money as he received from the television service last year in return for an exclusive contract' (that is, no appearances on ITV), but also discussions had begun for 'four major documentaries involving a Greek cruise'.[39] By mid-March the arrangement was confirmed and the dates of the cruise fixed for 1–18 April.

Early in 1958 the BBC Talks department envisaged that it would shoot two 'cruise' series with Swan's Tours during the year (a second, Scandinavian voyage to be filmed two months after the trip to Greece appears not to have come to fruition). Filming around Greece, however, seems to have gone largely to plan, although when the team returned to England it became apparent that there were technical problems with the rushes, with many shots underexposed or filmed with other errors. As a consequence, it was felt that there was no option but to reduce the series from the planned four programmes to just three. Throughout the process the project was coordinated by producer Stephen Hearst, who was central to both the editorial and logistical control of the programmes. The detailed written outlines of each programme were prepared by Hearst, who also compiled the schedule and attempted to control the budget. Hearst had come from Austria to Britain with his family immediately after Hitler's *Anschluss* in 1938, and after war service with the Pioneer Corps he joined the BBC in 1952. For the next three decades he had a central position in the development of BBC cultural programming on both television and radio, and by the summer of 1958 he was already planning to return to Greece with another eminent figure born in the Victorian era.

Compton Mackenzie had been broadcasting for rather longer than Mortimer Wheeler, having first given a fifteen-minute radio talk titled 'Siamese Cats – and Some Islands' for 5XX Daventry on 24 September 1928. He was a frequent contributor to radio discussions, and he wrote, devised and presented numerous radio programmes about the theatre and literature as well as permitting his novels to be adapted for the medium (for example, *The Passionate Elopement*, Home Service, April–May 1953). Mackenzie also made occasional appearances on television, but when *The Glory that was Greece* appeared he had neither a screen identity as fixed nor a manner as practised as Mortimer Wheeler's. He was also well known for having been military control officer in Athens in 1916 and then a spy for the British in the Aegean between the wars. As Gavin Wallace's *Oxford Dictionary of National Biography* entry records, 'His support for the anti-monarchist faction in Greece during the First World War, and afterwards for Greek independence, won him from the population a pseudo-Byronic adulation.'[40] And it was his fervent support for the Greeks in their centuries-long struggle with the Turks that was to cause considerable concern at the BBC during and after the series' production.

The idea for what would become *The Glory that was Greece* was suggested by Mackenzie himself, and during the summer of 1957 there was some discussion about whether he might be integrated in some way into what was quite separately shaping up as *Hellenic Cruise*.[41] Having met with the author, however, Stephen Hearst was keen that Mackenzie be given his own six-part series that would make 'enthusiastic use of Sir Compton Mackenzie as a returning humanist, traveller and teller of personal memories and reflections'.[42] By the time that the films were completed in March the BBC recognised that this series was of a different order from Wheeler's, as is indicated by Grace Wyndham Goldie noting in an internal memo that, 'What comes over in addition to some lively photography, and a great deal of ingenuity, is Sir Compton's own personality.'[43] Her enthusiasm, however, was not shared by Controller of Programmes for BBC Television Kenneth Adam, who after the transmission of the first programme wrote to Leonard Miall:

> It was, in my view, a slightly confusing programme, and I was particularly disappointed at the very obvious back projection ... I am afraid I felt rather cheated by this programme. It did not have the clarity, the pictorial quality or the overall distinction for which I was hoping.[44]

Moreover, the BBC had had to deal with a political row sparked by Mackenzie just after he returned from filming. He was quoted in the *Glasgow Herald* as saying of the recent murder of a British woman on Cyprus, 'That was done by a Turk ... I am satisfied with that myself. I have seen the evidence. Eoka had nothing to do with that.'[45] EOKA was the National Organisation of Cypriot Fighters, a group of Greek Cypriots engaged in armed resistance to the British rule of the island. The Press Attaché to the Turkish Embassy in London objected to Mackenzie's assertion and then wrote to Gerald Beadle, Director of Television Broadcasting, seeking assurances that the forthcoming series would not be anti-Turkish. Beadle and colleagues were unmoved, and while it is certainly the case that the final films are not explicitly anti-Turkish they remain strikingly strong statements of the importance of Greek independence.

## ONE SUBJECT, TWO APPROACHES

The politics of *The Glory that was Greece* is in fact one of its crucial differences from *Hellenic Cruise*. Wheeler's earlier series had itself caused some ripples of diplomatic concern, although Beadle was able to reply with some confidence to a Foreign Office enquiry that, 'The proposed television programmes will be entirely concerned with archaeology.'[46] There are lengthy sequences of *Hellenic Cruise*, such as the scenes from Venice in episode one, dancing on Lesbos in episode two, and the third episode's Athenian street scenes, that have little to do with archaeology and can be characterised as straightforwardly 'touristic', but when the camera visits ancient sites the focus is narrowly archaeological and the dominant documentary mode is of wide shots illustrating Wheeler's narration. Throughout, there is an emphasis on the origins of Greece and on a sense of continuity between past and present. 'Does it take much imagination', Wheeler asks in episode three, 'to think that the interests and passions of the Greeks have remained much the same for two thousand years?' Wheeler implicitly reinforces what Deborah Harlan describes as 'a deep history for the modern state'.[47] That state in the late 1950s was far from uncontested, since only just over a decade before the British had, with direct military aid, helped defeat in a bitter civil war the resistance fighters of ELAS (the National Popular Liberation Army). The result was an 'uncompromisingly anti-Communist, royalist and undemocratic' Greece, 'its allegiance to NATO and to its American colleagues considerably firmer than any commitment to the political institutions or laws of its own state'.[48]

Nor were relations between Greece and Turkey in any way stable in 1958, thanks to profound tensions over disputed control of Cyprus. All of these political problems are entirely absent from Mortimer Wheeler's hymn to the glories of Athens and its neighbours in the fifth century BC. *The Glory that was Greece* strives, as noted, for a more expressive use of the camera and, in Mackenzie's narration, a more partisan position. For the opening of the first episode, Mackenzie quotes Homer's description of Crete before introducing the characters of Minos and Zeus. At which point, to the accompaniment of dramatic music and storm effects, the film frame crashes over onto its side. The series also employs animated graphics and, in episode two, the rapid intercutting of images from vases with shots of the battlefield site filmed at Marathon to conjure up the sense of violent conflict. Subjective shots are used frequently, as in episode two to suggest the point of view of the running Phidippides, who is supposed to have brought the news of the Athenians' victory at Marathon to the city. The overall effect is far more strongly 'cinematic'. This is underpinned by the confident and stylish monochrome images of Charles de Jaeger (1911–2000), the cameraman whom Stephen Hearst had hoped but failed to secure for *Hellenic Cruise*. Within the drama that Hearst, de Jaeger and their team conjure up around him, Mackenzie determinedly puts across contemporary parallels with the myths and legends he recounts. In episode two, he describes the arrival of hoplites from Plataea coming to the aid of Athens at Marathon in 490 BC as 'very like the gesture of Greece when we [that is, the British] stood alone in October 1940 and Greece came in and stood beside us'. He is most insistent in his remarkable peroration to episode three, already noted above, which was filmed at Missolonghi, site of a desperate siege in 1825–6 during the Greek War of Independence, and he references the decisive naval battle of Navarino in 1827:

> This, this sacred ground, this is Missolonghi, where heroic Greeks fought hard and desperately to free their country from the barbarous yoke of Turkey ... This is a sacred memory for us and it was we, after all, who at Navarino were able to complete what Missolonghi began. And as I stand here on this sacred ground I pray that never in the future shall we betray Greece.

Yet in detailed contemporary press reviews of both *Hellenic Cruise* and *The Glory that was Greece* in *The Manchester Guardian*, *The Sunday Times*, *The Observer* and *The Listener* there is no mention of the implicit or explicit politics of either series.

## CONCLUSION

Just over a year after Compton Mackenzie expressed his prayer that Britain might never abandon Greece on the nation's television screens, those same electronic devices lit up with the image of a deserted landscape, foreground rocks and a tree to the right of frame. 'In the beginning . . .' intoned a familiar voiceover, as the camera panned slowly right to reveal Mortimer Wheeler in mid-shot seated by a wall and speaking directly to camera. After a moment or two the camera cut to a closer shot as Wheeler continued to confide about an ancient empire. Here, in the opening of *The Grandeur that was Rome*, for the first time in a television series about the classical world we can recognise the combination of the essential elements of the presenter-led, location-shot series that would reach its apotheosis in *Civilisation* (1969). Most crucially, Wheeler is addressing the viewer directly from a historical site. Less than a decade later Sir Kenneth Clark would take the viewer on a virtual voyage around Europe and across the Atlantic in thirteen films that explored the art and ideas of the West from the end of the Roman Empire to the present day. *Civilisation*'s producers would employ techniques pioneered by the teams led by Stephen Hearst on *Hellenic Cruise* and *The Glory that was Greece*. Viewed with an awareness of the achievements of later series, however, it is apparent that producer Stephen Hearst failed to draw the viewer in by not having his presenters address the audience directly from the ancient sites. In addition, on *The Glory that was Greece* he experimented with back projection and found the technique wanting. *The Grandeur that was Rome*, by contrast, applies lessons from those experiences and brings forth the configuration that, in essentials and with added colour, *Civilisation* embodied. That later series was created under Hearst's guidance as, from 1967, the head of television arts features. From *Hellenic Cruise* onwards, Hearst and his colleagues had developed for the ever-more-confident medium a form that was dependent on a cultivated traveller as the viewer's surrogate on a Grand Tour that is both historical and contemporary, together with the emphasis on sightseeing and the authenticity of the host's experience in the actual places legitimating his particular understanding of the past, and of the present. *Civilisation* and other much-lauded projects such as *Alistair Cooke's America* (BBC, 1972), about the history and culture of the United States, developed directly from Wheeler's and Mackenzie's series, and just as those earlier series did, they drew on understandings and approaches evolved by travellers, artists, writers, photographers, panorama showmen, lecturers, film-makers and others, stretching back at least three hundred years.

## PROGRAMMES DISCUSSED

*Armchair Voyage: Hellenic Cruise*. 3-part series. Prod. Stephen Hearst. BBC Television.
Episode 1: 'Venice to Mycenae'. Monday 21 July 1958, 9.15–9.45pm.
Episode 2: 'Istanbul and the Islands'. Monday 28 July 1958, 9.30–10.00pm.
Episode 3: 'Delos to Athens'. Monday 4 August 1958, 9.45–10.15pm.

*The Glory that was Greece*. 3-part series. Prod. Stephen Hearst. BBC Television.
Episode 1: 'The Age of Minos'. Wednesday 1 April 1959, 9.20–10.00pm.
Episode 2: 'The Age of Victory'. Wednesday 8 April 1959, 9.20–10.00pm.
Episode 3: 'The Age of Civil War'. Wednesday 15 April 1959, 9.20–10.00pm.

*The Grandeur that was Rome*. 3-part series. Prod. Stephen Hearst. BBC Television.
Episode 1: 'The Skeleton of an Empire'. Friday 13 May 1960, 9.30–10.00pm.
Episode 2: 'Gods and Men'. Friday 20 May 1960, 10.15–10.45pm.
Episode 3: 'Roman Art and Architecture'. Friday 27 May 1960, 9.25–9.55pm.

## NOTES

1 *Hellenic Cruise* is available online: <http://www.bbc.co.uk/bbcfour/collections/p018818x/archaeology-at-the-bbc> (accessed 28 December 2016). Arrangements to view *The Glory that was Greece* can be made with the British Film Institute (BFI) Viewing Service.
2 'Television Critic' (1958).
3 Gransden (1959).
4 Also available online: <http://www.bbc.co.uk/programmes/p017b9xg/episodes/player> (accessed 28 December 2016).

5 The title of the series on the films themselves is simply *Hellenic Cruise*. The slightly ungainly *Armchair Voyage* appears to have been added after the films were completed but before the programmes were listed in *Radio Times*. This was perhaps prompted by a concern that the original was somewhat obscure and that 'Hellenic' might be unfamiliar to viewers.
6 Stobart was the BBC's first Director of Education, serving from 1925 to 1932.
7 *Radio Times*, 27 March 1959, p. 17.
8 Goldie, Grace Wyndham, 'The Glory That Was Greece', memo to H. T. Tel, 18 December 1958, BBC WAC T32/816/1.
9 Audience Research Report, *Armchair Voyage*, 6 August 1958, BBC WAC VR/58/393.
10 Audience Research Report, *The Glory That Was Greece*, 17 April 1959, BBC WAC VR/59/178.
11 BBC (1961: 210).
12 Wakeman (2012: 427).
13 Constantine (1984: 4).
14 Pemble (2009: 8).
15 On this episode and theme, see further Hobden, Chapter 1, above.
16 See Barker (2005).
17 See Stone (n.d.).
18 Buzard (1993: 6).
19 Jenkyns (1980: 7).
20 See Adler (1989).
21 Crashaw and Urry (1997: 178).
22 Craik (1991: 28).
23 Lyons (2005: 39).
24 Grace Wyndham Goldie's letter to Michael Maclagan, 17 March 1958, BBC WAC T32/439/1.
25 Huhtamo (2013: 106).
26 Friedberg (1993: 2).
27 Peterson (2005: 640).
28 Ruoff (2006: 3).
29 Anon. (n.d).
30 Musser (1990: 127).
31 Holmes (1901), available at <https://archive.org/details/burtonholmeslecto3holm> (accessed 28 December 2016).
32 Ruoff (2006: 11).
33 Peterson (2013: 18), original emphasis.
34 See Wrigley (2015a: 1–3).
35 *Radio Times*, 20 March 1936, p. 67.
36 Neither *Hellenic Cruise* nor *The Glory that was Greece* includes synchronous sound recording. Both were shot on 35mm film, but for *Hellenic Cruise* sound was recorded only on the ship. *The Glory that*

*was Greece* was shot mute, while the sound sequences were filmed with Mackenzie in England; additional effects and music were added in post-production.
37  See McIntosh (2004).
38  Daniel (1954: 202).
39  Miall, 'Sir Mortimer Wheeler', memo to Television Booking Manager, 22 January 1958, BBC WAC file: Sir Mortimer Wheeler, 1937–1958.
40  Wallace (2004).
41  The BBC film-maker Richard Cawston was also working on an ultimately unrealised project to be shot in Greece with the author Kay Cicellis, and Grace Wyndham Goldie was in contact with Basil Wright, who was preparing his own privately financed short film. Wright's *Greece – The Immortal Land* was released in 1959 and can be viewed here: <https://www.europeana.eu/portal/en/record/09204/EUS_36B6FA46F30B4F1981F0A16AA3F7CB3D.html> (accessed 8 February 2018).
42  Hearst, Stephen, '*The Glory that was Greece*: A Film Series with Sir Compton Mackenzie', 20 June 1957, BBC WAC T32/816/1.
43  Goldie, Grace Wyndham, 'The Glory that was Greece', memo to D. Tel. B, 12 March 1959, BBC WAC file: Talks, Mackenzie, Compton, 1937–1962.
44  Adam, Kenneth, memo to H. T. Tel., 1 April 1959, BBC WAC T32/816/1.
45  Anon. (1958); clipping in BBC WAC T32/816/1.
46  Beadle, Gerald, letter to Ralph Murray, 24 March 1958, BBC WAC T32/439/1.
47  Harlan (2009: 435).
48  Judt (2005: 505–6).

## 4 *Tragedy for Teens*: Ancient Greek Tragedy on BBC and ITV Schools Television in the 1960s

Amanda Wrigley

From the inception of schools television in late 1950s Britain, programmes produced by both the BBC and independent companies such as Associated-Rediffusion and Grampian brought the experience of theatre plays in performance to thousands of teenage school pupils across Britain, as well as a 'great army of eavesdroppers', as the *Radio Times* described individuals tuning in to schools programming within the home.[1] The pedagogic motivation behind these programmes frames the terms of television's engagement with works from the theatre, with both play and performance often contextualised in a number of ways. For example, introductory programmes and talks were variously used as ways of offering background on content, genre, context and conventions (to 'put the class in a better position to receive what they are to see');[2] narrator figures were sometimes used to facilitate engagement; and almost all series were accompanied by the publication of illustrated pamphlets for pupils and leaflets for teachers, both of which provided background information and guides for further teaching and learning activities. Schools television series were intended to supplement, not supplant, the school curriculum and traditional teaching methods, but some series had a close relationship with core elements of the school curriculum (such as mathematics) whilst others (such as drama) were decidedly 'off-syllabus'.[3] Writing in 1966, the BBC's Controller of Educational Broadcasting, Richmond Postgate, stated that the very few 'preconceived ideas' behind the commission of BBC television series for schools included one that they should offer 'something that [pupils] would not otherwise get at all, or not so well'. Indeed, regarding dramatic performance, 'the evidence seemed to be that television had a distinctive role to play in bringing the theatre to the classroom; in giving children an opportunity to see plays of quality performed'.[4] Given general indications in the archival evidence on the demographic diversity of pupils who were watching drama series, and the School Broadcasting Council's finding that 'off-syllabus' programmes were more likely to be shown to schoolchildren in non-examination streams, it is reasonable to consider that for a substantial proportion of the audience these television programmes would have offered a rare opportunity to engage with theatre works on either the page or the stage. This makes the drama output of schools television a matter of social, cultural and educational significance.

The BBC had been transmitting radio programmes for use in schools since 1924, but it was not the first broadcasting organisation to make and transmit schools television. Rather, Associated-Rediffusion, the independent contractor for London and surrounding areas, did this in May 1957 – remarkably, just a little over eighteen months after it first began to make television programmes. ITV thus stole a march on the BBC, which had in 1952 conducted a closed-circuit trial amongst six schools and had, ever since, been very carefully planning a much larger experiment with money-strapped local education authorities and lukewarm government support. The BBC, taken by surprise by Associated-Rediffusion's bold move, hastily speeded up and expanded its plans, starting to transmit television programmes for schools in September 1957.[5] By the mid-1960s, the BBC and ITV were making around fifty schools television series each year, with each series composed of individual programmes stretching across one or more school terms.[6] Series that focused on theatre plays were a core offering from both the BBC and one or more of the commercial companies each year. Within months of the start of their schools television services, both the BBC and ITV were transmitting excerpts from Shakespearean and Jacobean plays, and they both swiftly went on to transmit a remarkable range of plays from British and foreign-language playwrights (in translation) from the full Western theatrical repertoire – including a significant amount of Greek drama – but with a noticeable concentration on drama from the late nineteenth to the mid-twentieth centuries. The BBC's 1960 *Twentieth-Century Drama* series for schools, for example, testifies to a general preference for plays from earlier decades over near-contemporary work in its offer of three Edwardian plays, one interwar play and another from the war years. The leaflet for teachers which was published to support the delivery of these programmes in the classroom acknowledged that 'No one is certain where the masterpieces are. Today Shaw is better known than Arnold Wesker. Tomorrow Wesker may supersede Shaw – or both may have been eclipsed by someone not yet born.'[7] Here, at least at the BBC, confidence in the established theatrical canon is set alongside a degree of uncertainty about its future at a time when theatre was rapidly turning to social realism (as in the plays of Wesker and John Osborne) and absurdist forms (for example, Samuel Beckett and Harold Pinter). For the moment, however, at the start of this new decade – in which the new teenage generation would experience seismic social changes – the established canon of Western theatre offered a safe harbour in which teens might be encouraged 'to explore unchanging human predicaments' and to learn how 'to explain ourselves to ourselves'.[8]

The first ancient Mediterranean play to be included in a schools television series appears to be *The Haunted House*, a two-part English-language production of *Mostellaria*, a Latin comedy by Plautus, which the BBC programmed as the opener for its autumn 1960 drama series on an Italian-Roman theme (featuring also Niccodemi's *The Poet*, Pirandello's *Sicilian Limes*, Shakespeare's *Julius Caesar* and Shaw's *Androcles and the Lion*).[9] In 1961, the first Greek tragedies were featured in schools television series, just three years after the first-ever Greek tragedy on British television – the BBC's 1958 *Women of Troy* (discussed in the Introduction, above). In January 1961, Associated-Rediffusion's *The Angry Gods* (comprising mainly Aeschylus' *Oresteia* trilogy and Shakespeare's *The Winter's Tale*) was transmitted by ITV and, in September, the BBC followed with a studio production of Sophocles' *Philoctetes*, which was repeated in October 1962 in a double bill with a new production of Euripides' *Bacchae*. The BBC also produced Sophocles' *Antigone* for schools in October 1962 and in the same month Associated-Rediffusion produced scenes from the same play in a schools series titled *Patterns of Love*. In November 1962, Associated-Rediffusion scored a spectacular, if unexpected, hit with a modern Greek production of Sophocles' *Electra*, a studio version of the Peiraïkon Theatron's internationally touring stage production, which was transmitted by ITV, without subtitles, across the UK.[10] Doubtless this unusual success, which achieved a degree of notoriety, underscored by the report of the Pilkington Committee in June 1962 which famously criticised commercial television's output for triviality, encouraged the appetite for serious drama in educational strands on independent television. Associated-Rediffusion followed with productions of Euripides' *Medea*, in three parts, as part of the series *Theatres and Temples: The Greeks* (ITV, March 1963); there were also productions of Euripides' *Trojan Women* (Rediffusion for ITV's *Take It from the Top* series, December 1965) and *Medea*, with Sybil Thorndike in the title role (ABC for ITV's *Tempo* programme, April 1968); and Sophocles' *Antigone* and Aristophanes' *Peace* were transmitted as part of a sequence of programmes under the title *Heritage* which explored aspects of ancient Greek culture and mythology (Thames for ITV, January–March 1969). Worth mentioning, too, is a BBC Further Education programme, *In Rehearsal*, which in April 1969 focused on ways of performing scenes from Euripides' *Bacchae*. From 1971, a new higher educational strand of television (and radio) was established with the birth of the OU, which relied heavily upon the BBC for both co-production and dissemination of a substantial amount of course material. OU–BBC co-productions for television broadcast included Aristophanes' *Clouds* in 1971 and Sophocles' *Oedipus the King* in 1977. Nestled in amongst this potted history of educational Greek drama programmes are some high-profile, bigger-budget studio productions: for example, Sophocles' *King Oedipus* (BBC1, 1972), Sophocles' *Electra* (BBC1, 1974) and Aeschylus' *Oresteia* trilogy under the title *The Serpent Son* (BBC2, 1979) and, in the next decade or so, the flourish of Don Taylor's four monumental studio productions of Greek tragedy, which would be the last Greek plays on television for a quarter of a century. The large-scale BBC productions of the 1970s, together with the OU–BBC collaborations and the increasing appetite for drama in the popular social-realist mode, may go some way to account for what appears to be an absence of Greek tragedy in schools television drama series in the decade following its efflorescence in the 1960s.

The remarkable moment of regular televised Greek tragedy for teens in 1960s Britain has not been documented or discussed within scholarship; indeed, the wealth of televised theatre for schools more generally is a topic which has only recently begun to receive attention.[11] This is not for want of evidence. A rich mine of historical sources for these educational television productions of theatre plays – comprising recordings, camera scripts, institutional planning documents, printed pamphlets, reports on audience feedback, etc. – exists in the archival collections of the BBC and the BFI. These tragedies for teens comprise only one strand in the broader history of television as a pedagogical and cultural medium for literature, drama and the arts, not to mention other humanities subjects such as history and geography, the sciences and allied subjects, and numerous programmes on a wide diversity of personal and social topics. A comprehensive evaluation of the contribution and significance of these programmes within the broader education and experience of teenagers, as well as part of the televisual offering to the domestic audience beyond the classroom, is needed. As a first step in that direction, this chapter offers a comparative impression of how the BBC and Associated-Rediffusion produced Greek tragedy for a non-specialised teen audience in the 1960s, exploring the different ways in which each used dramatic performance to draw on ancient archetypes in order to engage with the potency and potential of teenagers and their place in society at the beginning of this tumultuous decade. The sample of productions is limited and the quantity and quality of evidence are varied and incomplete, but sufficient exists to give a strong sense of characteristic differences in pedagogic style and broader motivations. The study's focus on Greek tragedy links with other cultural and educational frames: for example, the increasingly marginalised position of Greek as an academic subject in schools over the course of the twentieth century, the long history of regular performative engagements with Greek dramatic (and other) texts on BBC Radio from the 1920s to the 1960s, and the renaissance of Greek tragedy in professional performance in the 1960s.[12] The evidence for the making, televising and viewing of these Greek tragedies for and by teens (and those 'eavesdroppers' watching at home) in non-specialist, off-syllabus contexts in the 1960s contributes a significant new piece to the cultural historical jigsaw of engagements with ancient Greece beyond the academy in twentieth-century Britain.

## BBC: *PHILOCTETES, BACCHAE* AND *ANTIGONE*

It is a Tuesday afternoon in September 1961. A teacher in a secondary modern school, who has been using broadcast programmes in her classes for pupils aged thirteen and above for a couple of years now, switches on the television and the class settles down to watch the first of two thirty-minute parts of an abridged studio production of Sophocles' *Philoctetes* in an English translation by Kenneth Cavander.[13] The teenagers watching this performance are not reading Greek or Latin and they have little familiarity with the ancient world; indeed, their teacher has little too. Most of them, in fact, will not be doing formal examinations or staying in school for much longer.[14] *Philoctetes* and the other plays in this series are being offered in an off-syllabus context. But the pupils are prepared for this new experience because the teacher has read the leaflet accompanying the series, which contains five pages of teaching notes on the play and its broadcast production, and she has engaged the pupils in preparatory discussion. Also, last week the class watched a thirty-minute introductory television programme on the play, in which the moral philosopher Bernard Williams, who had read Greats (i.e. Greek and Latin) at Balliol College, Oxford, and was a lecturer in Philosophy at University College London, 'set the scene of the Trojan wars and defined the main characters and motivations of the tragedy'.[15] Next week, they will watch the culminating part.

Both the introductory programme and the first of two parts of the performance exist in the BBC archive. The production by Ronald Eyre of *Philoctetes* – the tale of Odysseus' scheme to get Philoctetes and his all-powerful bow and arrows to Troy with the help of Achilles' son Neoptolemus – is claustrophobic in its small-scale studio setting, and plenty of close-ups offer good insights into the emotional and psychological state of the lead characters. For example, we see the young man Neoptolemus (Alan Howard) recoil with disgust on picking up rags Philoctetes has been using to bind his leg-wound; the stichomythic exchange (of alternate lines between two speakers) in which Odysseus (Alan MacNaughton) debates with Neoptolemus the issue of lying to Philoctetes (Richard Pasco) in order to seize his prized bow is effectively captured in a series of rapidly alternating head-shots; and the screenshot at Figure 4.1 captures the powerful moment when Philoctetes entrusts Neoptolemus with the bow. There is very little music in Part 1, at least – just a few simple bars played on a flute twenty-four minutes in (as the First Stasimon comes to a close); however, the near-constant low-level atmospheric noise of, variously, the sea, the whistling wind, gravel underfoot and the drip-drip of moisture within the cave provides audio texture to this drama of dialogue. Odysseus and Neoptolemus are dressed in fine clothing, which is customarily short, beautifully draped and adorned with metal buckles. The sailors are more plainly (and scantily) clad. There is some effective make-up on Philoctetes' putrid leg-sores.

In this naturalistic production the set design by Charles Lawrence – a simple rocky outcrop and cave which look effective in the extant black-and-white film of Part 1 – does not distract from the psychological shifts in the action, and the six-strong Chorus of sailors are integrated into the performance in an informal way, tending the fire as they speak lines from the Parodos (the name for the ode they sing on their first entrance on stage), for example, while chatting with Neoptolemus about the condition of Philoctetes. As on the stage, the long-awaited entry of Philoctetes is a significant moment: he emerges

Figure 4.1 Philoctetes entrusts Neoptolemus with his prized possession, the bow, in *Philoctetes* (1961). BBC.

from a crouching position on high; his wild hair makes a useful contrast with the neat-haired, clean-shaven visitors to the island; and he clutches his glorious bow, which stands taller than him. He is a fine orator, telling of his hardships with a wild look in his eye. The budding relationship and inverted power balance between the older, suffering war-hero Philoctetes and duplicitous Neoptolemus, son of Philoctetes' peer Achilles, is thoughtfully portrayed through facial expression, blocking and camera position. Part 1 of the play (to line 838 of the ancient play by Sophocles) ends just after Philoctetes has fallen into a deep sleep following an agonising spasm of pain. 'Don't disturb. Let him sleep', instructs Neoptolemus, to which the Chorus respond, in individual voices: 'Now, sir, what's it to be?', 'Have you thought what to do next?' and 'Can you go on? Can you persist with your plan now?' Neoptolemus' face contorts and the credits roll, thus ending the first half of this production on a tantalising climax. The sound of the waves accompanies the closing credits. This production exemplifies how, although BBC Schools drama productions were made in small studios and with tiny budgets when compared with drama for the mainstream audience, there was nevertheless the ambition to make the most of limited means to convey the power of dramatic action.[16]

To twenty-first-century eyes and ears, the performance may appear somewhat stilted, but in 1961 it was felt necessary to include in the published notes for the teacher a sentence or two on the British 'upper lip ... stiff almost to the point of paralysis' and how the nation's perceived excellence in matters of emotional restraint differs from Greek heroes, 'who are not afraid to express their pity, pain, and anger in the extreme form in which they feel them'.[17] *Philoctetes* was, indeed, the first play in a drama series which offered theatrical works that had been chosen as a way 'to introduce viewers to modern experimental psychology', in which context having the introduction to *Philoctetes* given by a moral philosopher who engaged with ideas from the Greeks and modern psychology, and not a traditional scholar of classics or the theatre, makes good sense. Other works in this series included Sheridan's 1775 comedy *St Patrick's Day*, Chekhov's 1889 farce *The Wedding*, Marlowe's seventeenth-century play *The Tragical History of Doctor Faustus* and a medieval mystery play from *The Wakefield Cycle*.[18]

The BBC was, for the purposes of the School Broadcasting Council's second report on school television, following closely the reception of its schools television programmes transmitted in the 1961–2 academic year. Statistics gathered reveal that, of the 276 separate programmes broadcast in various series, 78 per cent (214) were intended for secondary moderns, 8 per cent (24) for grammar school sixth forms and 14 per cent (38) for primary schools; in total, there were at least 300,000 separate class viewings of programmes.[19] With regard to the drama series of which *Philoctetes* was the first offering, of the 429 schools that tuned in, 233 schools (54 per cent) were secondary moderns and junior secondary, 91 schools (21 per cent) were grammar and senior secondary, and 13 schools (3 per cent) were technical and further education centres. Across the different kinds of school, most pupils were in the 13–15 age range and 40 per cent of the classes watching were categorised as being of 'Good' intelligence, 16 per cent 'Medium', 9 per cent 'Poor', and 34 per cent 'Mixed'.[20] This audience data reveals that teenagers of a broad range of academic ability, in the full range of school settings, were watching this series of theatrical works designed as an introduction to 'modern experimental psychology'; the audiences for schools series on other topics that term were also impressively broad. In short, television programmes for schools were thoughtfully made and intended to be deeply enriching, a significant number of schools tuned in, and, within them, a broad range of academic streams viewed these programmes.

The School Broadcasting Council report notes that televised drama programmes were, almost across the board, offered in an 'off-syllabus' context. This meant that – unlike in the idealised scenario outlined above – teachers did not usually have enough time to do preparation for them themselves or to devote whole classes to preparing pupils.[21] Teachers were 'appreciative of these full and often quite deeply analytical and interpretative notes' published by the BBC, and there was 'a marked difference in the reactions of classes which have and have not been prepared' by teachers engaging with this printed material. But, despite the fact that 'the ability of the teachers to talk with children about performances affected considerably the way they reacted', teachers' engagement with printed materials remained patchy. The BBC recognised the 'need to build into the programmes something to encourage thought about the drama and about the theatre'.[22] Accordingly, each of the plays in the autumn 1961 drama series was accompanied by some kind of background or introductory programme. The introductory programme for *Philoctetes* presented by Bernard Williams was considered to have been a huge success: 'Children were gripped and excited by this and their interest held and grew throughout the two parts of this complex drama.'[23] The notes for the teacher state that the introductory programme aims 'to envision in modern terms some aspects of the situation in which the characters find themselves'.[24] The programme was successful in assisting pupils to find topicality and modernity within the performance of this ancient play:

> Following such a preliminary broadcast the *Philoctetes* of Sophocles scored a great success and the essentials of the play 'went home'. As one school reported: 'It was valuable that the pupils should realize the topicality of something written thousands of years ago. The figures of myth and legend became embodied for them in flesh and blood reality. Some realised that the drama of outer action overlies a much more subtle interplay of mind and motive – as modern as today's dilemmas.'[25]

The 1961 *Philoctetes* was presented again side by side with a new production of Euripides' *Bacchae* in the following academic year's 'For Sixth Forms' series. This series was not 'designed for an audience of specialists': the goal was to offer 'a meeting ground at which arts students and science students ... can come together to view and discuss material of common interest', but viewers were in the main located in grammar and senior secondary schools (78 per cent) in 1961–2.[26] The pamphlet for pupils concludes with some words on the 'moral' of *Bacchae*, drawn from E. R. Dodds' Preface to his Clarendon edition of the play: 'we ignore at our peril the demand of the human spirit for Dionysiac experience'.[27] Williams also provided the introductory programme for *Bacchae*. The recording of this programme in the BBC archive reveals that he uses a range of techniques to convey context, background and an interpretation of the play. Williams is presented as an authority figure, a lecturer with a dry delivery, looking frequently at his notes and once at his watch. He manipulates a mechanical version of an interactive board to reveal the various branches on the family tree of characters: see Figure 4.2 for a glimpse of this behind the legs of life-size representations of Dionysus and Pentheus descending from on high into this 'lecture space'. Props used include a *thyrsus*, and a picture of a Maenad on an ancient cup leads onto discussion of the followers of Dionysus and their rituals. Short sequences of the play are rehearsed by actors not in costume. Heavy use of film clips showing a range of human and animal behaviour underlines Williams' delineation of the central 'moral' of the play – namely, the necessity of achieving a careful balance between competing natural energies and rhythms of life. Barefoot dancing at festivals, lambs suckling, beer drinking, couples cuddling and rivers rushing are contrasted with a sequence showing dervishes in extreme states of possession, security men with dogs on leashes, people being hit with batons, a protest turning violent, birds of prey picking shreds of flesh from a carcass and dogs eating meat. In alluding to things spoken about, but not enacted, in the play, these clips are powerfully

Figure 4.2 Bernard Williams speaking in front of a family tree, with illustrations of characters from *Bacchae* (1962) descending. BBC.

representative of its themes. Certainly, they are likely to have raised the teenage viewer's appetite for *Bacchae* in a way which Williams' dry lecture-with-props format may not have done.

In the same academic year, the BBC transmitted a two-part schools production of Sophocles' *Antigone*, again with an introductory programme, in a *Drama* strand aimed at pupils aged 14–16. The 'Notes for the Teacher' leaflet opens with a quotation from Brecht and states that the pupils who watch this series 'be asked to test all they see against their own experiences'.[28] Alongside *Antigone*, there was Brecht's *The Caucasian Chalk Circle*, a repeat of the previous year's *The Wakefield Shepherds' Play* and two further programmes designed to encourage pupils to try their hand at writing a play; this selection was designed to encourage discussion on ideas of justice and injustice. As with *Bacchae*, the moral heart of *Antigone* provides the pedagogical frame: the teachers' leaflet identifies this as 'the clash of two strong points of view' – 'the good of the community' versus 'family, religion, affection and loyalty'.[29] In addition to offering background information about the playwright, the ancient performance context, the mythic cycle and a brief summary of the action, this leaflet also offers the teacher ten suggested questions with which they might engage their pupils in discussion. As with the advocacy of balance in the discussion on *Bacchae*, the questions on *Antigone* are designed to encourage pupils to consider the situation from the perspective of both Antigone and her uncle Creon, who are at odds over the burial of her brother and his nephew; to analyse the arguments used by Creon and his son (Antigone's betrothed) respectively, and both Antigone and her sister Ismene, whose initial reaction to the family crisis is different. The last couple of questions are more expansive – 'Can you think of more modern situations in which someone has faced a dilemma similar to Creon's?' and 'Should the title of the play be *Creon* rather than *Antigone*?' – stretching pupils to think beyond binaries and relative moralities, assessing the work as a whole and finding modern resonances within.[30]

## ASSOCIATED-REDIFFUSION FOR ITV: *THE ANGRY GODS (ORESTEIA)* AND *THEATRES AND TEMPLES (MEDEA)*

From January to March 1961 *The Angry Gods*, an eight-part Associated-Rediffusion series for schools, was transmitted by independent television networks. The twenty-five-minute programmes offered performances of Euripides' *Iphigenia at Aulis*, the three plays of Aeschylus' *Oresteia* trilogy, and Shakespeare's *The Winter's Tale* in a broad study of guilt and retribution for pupils aged thirteen and above in around 1,500 schools. This was one of six series networked by ITV in this academic term.[31] Many dramatic productions for schools were by necessity abridged versions of plays, owing to the traditionally short length of educational programme slots, but *The Angry Gods* takes a very flexible approach: the dramatic action of *Iphigenia at Aulis* was given approximately ten minutes of screen time in the first episode ('A Sacred Offering'), the three plays of Aeschylus' *Oresteia* trilogy were abridged to twenty-five minutes each (episode 2, 'The Crimson Path'; 3, 'The Black Furies'; 4, 'The Judgement'), and *The Winter's Tale* was given much more expansively over four episodes (5–8, 'Some Ill Planet Reigns', 'Apollo's Angry', 'The Flowers of Spring' and 'The Oracle is Fulfilled'). The teachers' leaflet records that the primary intention of each programme was to offer 'the most vivid interpretation' of these still-powerful centuries-old plays' (and on the rhetoric of continuity, see Hobden, Chapter 1, above):

> to bring the theatre of these two widely different ages [ancient Greece and Shakespearean England] within the small compass of the television screen ... will obviously necessitate free adaptation of the action and text to give the most vivid interpretation, particularly in the case of the Greek plays, but the aim will be specifically to show how the force and power of these dramas continue to the present day.[32]

The series, directed by Pat Baker, featured Martin Worth's commentary and adaptations, music by Eric Spear, designs by Barbara Bates, and narration by Michael Hawkins. Students from the Central School of Speech and Drama took the parts of the Chorus, and main roles were played by Jill Balcon (Clytemnestra/Hermione), Bernard Brown (Polixenes), Zoe Caldwell (Cassandra), Anne Castaldini (Iphigenia), Avril Elgar (Electra), Christopher Gilmore (Florizel), Nigel Green (Agamemnon/Leontes), Neville Jason (Orestes) and Jane Merrow (Perdita). No recordings for *The Angry Gods* exist in the archives but close reading of the camera script offers insights, and other kinds of documentation are similarly useful: stills printed in the promotional material, for example, indicate that a set with a sweep of steps and large walls was used for the Greek plays and *The Winter's Tale*.

The first episode, 'A Sacred Offering', is indicative of Associated-Rediffusion's approach to using television for pedagogical purposes in its broad and energetic contextualisation of the plays and dramatic conventions which may have been unfamiliar to pupils. The script reveals that this programme opens, perhaps unexpectedly, with shots of the Jodrell Bank observatory, a microscope, and a polling station as illustration of the narrator Michael Hawkins' assertion that for the origin of many modern ideas, achievements and cultural activities, including drama, we must look to ancient Greece.[33] But Greece is not idealised: although Athens is posited as birthplace of democracy, 'cruelty and injustice, poverty, and even slavery' also receive mention (2). A paraphrase of Pericles' funeral oration on the nature of democracy, from Thucydides, is offered (a popular reference point, used also by MacNeice in his 1941 radio feature *The Glory that is Greece*: see Golphin, Chapter 2, above), and conventions of ancient Greek theatre such as masks are introduced and illustrated through a brief dramatised extract from Euripides' *Bacchae*. A photograph in the archive shows four chorus members, with masks, wigs and hooded cloaks with a geometric 'Greek' design, standing with their right arms raised before a plaster cast of Dionysus elevated on a pedestal, palms turned towards him in a gesture of respect. The script records the narrator's assertion that Greek plays are 'as exciting and powerful as anything that's been written since' (3). The narrator engages the imagination of viewers by introducing the dynamics of ancient theatre space with what the camera script suggests was a suggestive interplay of words and image that may well have held attention and stimulated the imagination:

> Well, imagine yourself a citizen of Athens over two thousand years ago. It is spring, the most important time of the year to worship the god Dionysus whom you depend on to make the crops grow. As part of the festival in his honour, you know that various plays to be performed [*Mix to 1: Clytemnestra/Iphigenia/Agamemnon with Servant on top of rostra*] are now being rehearsed ... and so, next morning, to the great theatre of Dionysus you set off at sunrise ... and it will be sunset before you leave for home [*camera pans round the first tier of seats in an ancient theatre*] ... all eyes are on the circular area known as the *orchestra* [where] the chorus will perform. (6–7)

To this point in the programme, Greek theatre is introduced using techniques which are familiar from modern-day television documentary forms on ancient Greece,[34] but 'A Sacred Offering' also included a ten-minute abridged version of Euripides' *Iphigenia at Aulis*. The narrator relates Paris' abduction of Helen and the Greeks' subsequent decision to wage war on the Trojans, leaving the story at the point when Agamemnon has instructed his wife to bring his daughter Iphigenia to Aulis to be married to the hero Achilles – a ruse through which he will sacrifice her in order to appease the gods and secure fair winds for the sea-journey to Troy – and thus excluding the graphic Messenger speech telling of the killing of Iphigenia. The camera script indicates that this was a very condensed version of the main action: for example, in addition to the omission of the report of the killing of Iphigenia, each chorus is compressed to around ten lines and Achilles does not appear as a character. But what remains is to the point, getting across the main thrust of the drama. For example, Iphigenia's plea to her father for her life is as follows, abridged from around forty lines in Euripides:

> I have nothing left to offer you
> But tears, my only eloquence. I hang
> A suppliant. Kill me not in youth's fresh prime.
> Sweet is the light of life, while all beneath
> Is naught. He's mad who seeks to die, for life
> Though ill excels whatever's good in death. (14)

These lines are far from everyday speech, but the poetry is made more easily digestible by its brevity. The shortness of this cut-down *Iphigenia*, too, and its setting within a programme which draws heavily on the techniques of documentary form to offer a strong, relatable context, surely made for an approachable introductory programme which served to encourage pupils to appreciate the 'force and power of these dramas'.

Episodes 2, 3 and 4 each present an abridged version of the three plays of the *Oresteia*. 'The Crimson Path', a version of *Agamemnon*, opens with the following words, spoken by the narrator:

> Remember the agony of Agamemnon at Aulis? ... Why were the gods so vindictive towards him? To the early Greeks the gods seemed very often vindictive, revengeful and immoral. ... That evil might be more due to man than God was one of the things which in the fifth century BC was only just being realised – and it's this question, how far Man or God is responsible for good and evil, that dominates the plays we're going to see from now on.[35]

Here, the narrator opens up questions on good and evil, guilt and retribution, which dominate this drama series. He goes on to explain the background to the plot and 'the vicious circle of crime, revenge which itself must be avenged', whilst carefully avoiding the potentially morally problematic issue of adultery.[36] Rather than introduce Aegisthus as Clytemnestra's lover, he simply says that while Agamemnon was at war his wife plotted 'revenge – with someone else who hated Agamemnon too' (3), drawing on another, internecine, strand of the Greek myth. The play opens as in Aeschylus with the Watchman, but the pace of the drama is broken up with the reappearance of the narrator, who offers an interpretation of the Watchman's words:

> He is depressed by the darkness of night, the darkness of a house whose king and glory are absent. From all such darkness, the darkness in fact of sin and

evil itself, he prays for release, for deliverance, for light. But, as we shall see through all this play, when the light comes it brings new darkness with it. (3)

'The Black Furies' and 'The Judgement' both present their respective plays – *Choephoroi* and *Eumenides* – with minimal introduction from the narrator. However, it is not possible to ascertain how much historical contextualisation and discussion of theatrical conventions and themes existed for *The Winter's Tale*, since the scripts for those four programmes do not appear to have been preserved.[37] We do, however, learn from other sources how the programme-makers intended to establish the link between the Greek and Elizabethan theatre in this series. In the notes for teachers, the dissimilarities are first enumerated, with emphasis on the formality and restraint of the Greeks with regard to the off-stage location of gruesome acts of bloodshed, whereas 'The Elizabethans on the other hand loved to see acts of violence: stabbing, strangling and gouging out the eyes are all part of the spectacle which they enjoyed.' 'Many deep and significant similarities' are then listed: first, 'in both periods the theatre was for everybody and the audience drawn from every walk of life'; and performances took place in the open air, in theatres where 'the seats were arranged in a circular formation with the acting taking place in a central space, the orchestra in the Greek theatre, the apron stage in the Elizabethan'.[38] Figure 4.3 demonstrates how the teachers' leaflet used the remains of the ancient Greek theatre of Epidaurus on the cover (whereas the *TV Times* article announcing the series printed a late nineteenth-century illustration of a highly imaginative reconstruction of the Athenian Theatre of Dionysus).

No record of how pupils and teachers engaged with *The Angry Gods* has yet come to light, so a comparison with those responses we have for the roughly contemporaneous BBC Schools television tragedies discussed above is not possible, but the aspiration of those involved in bringing such programmes to the screen is documented in the *TV Times* article. Enid Love, Associated-Rediffusion's Head of Schools Television, is quoted as saying, 'We try to bring actual experience into the classroom; to involve the viewers emotionally with the subject we are presenting, and leave them with their curiosity aroused.'[39] The leaflet for teachers suggested that the series might be used 'not only in its more obvious context as a comparison of certain specific plays and ages, but also as a basis for further study of great civilisations, of the history of drama, of recurrent themes in the plays and, more specifically, as a background for study of set texts, such

Figure 4.3 The theatre at Epidaurus on the cover of Associated-Rediffusion's teachers' leaflet for *The Angry Gods* (1961).

as *Samson Agonistes*', John Milton's 1671 Old Testament-inspired dramatic poem.[40] So *The Angry Gods* was intended to serve as an introduction to canonical works of dramatic literature (ancient and more modern) and to the societies which produced them, but also as a way of stimulating thought and engaging both imagination and emotion – in other words, exploring ethics, teaching empathy and deepening the sense of what it is to be human.

This approach is developed further a couple of years later, when the first four, Greek-themed, episodes in *The Angry Gods* series ('A Sacred Offering', 'The Crimson Path', 'The Black Furies' and 'The Judgement', covering the action of *Iphigenia at Aulis* and *Oresteia*) were recycled in the context of a new, longer series titled *Theatres and Temples*. These four were followed by other programmes that sought to explore further Greek drama both as a cultural form from a long-distant society and also as a vital commentary on the human condition. Three programmes ('The City State', 'The Inquiring Mind' and 'Legend and Belief') worked to convey a sense of the politics, philosophy, myth and art of fifth-century Athens, and the final three ('Theatres and Temples', 'The Path of Vengeance' and 'The Poisoned Robe') offered an unabridged performance of Euripides' *Medea* in Philip Vellacott's translation. The image on the cover of this document (reproduced at Figure 4.4) suggests the high production values in the design of *Medea*, with both costume and set envisaged on a bold scale which underscored monumentality (the walls, columns and altar) and otherness (the headdresses of the chorus). The diagonal angles in this composition are (probably intentionally) reminiscent of the productions shots used to advertise the Associated-Rediffusion modern Greek production of Sophocles' *Electra*, transmitted a few months earlier in November 1962.

The brochure published alongside this series, which was transmitted in 1963, notes the broad aspirations behind it:

> this series may be useful to schools in several ways: as a preliminary study of a civilisation of which most children know very little, as a basis of discussion of the many moral problems raised, and perhaps most of all, as an illustration of the importance of this play, and the force and power which it still conveys to this day.[41]

In an advertisement published by Associated-Rediffusion in newspapers such as *The Guardian* and *The Times*, this three-part production of *Medea* was showcased alongside ten other programmes – including the 1962 modern Greek *Electra*, Harold Pinter's *The Lover*, and others on sport and current affairs – as examples of 'good television'. 'What is good television?', the advert asks, and discusses:

> It is the attitude of the people who create the programme. If they know their profession, respect their public, and can unite the majority of their audience in a satisfying common experience, then each individual viewer will respond at once, and will become sympathetically involved with the programme.

# Tragedy for Teens

Figure 4.4 Barbara Jefford as Medea. Teachers' leaflet for *Theatre and Temples* (1963).

This is illustrated by a quotation from a schoolgirl viewer who had written in following the transmission of *Medea* to say that 'the fine and overwhelming performances of *Medea* has had the deepest effect'.[42] Perhaps the most striking thing here is that an educational programme made by a commercial television company would be allocated a place in a 'top ten' listing of representative examples of 'good television'. Certainly, this emphasis on the seriousness and weight amongst its programme offerings can be read as an implicit response to the report of the Pilkington Committee, which, reporting in June 1962, famously criticised – as noted above – commercial television's output for triviality.

## CONCLUSION

From the late 1950s, schools television enabled huge numbers of schoolchildren to experience theatre plays in performance, in mediated, age-appropriate contexts that were designed to be accessible and broadly enriching. By the 1960s, the majority of schoolchildren given access to these programmes were not in the most academic streams, which suggests that these programmes may have presented many children with a rare opportunity to experience theatrical works both in performance and as a stimulus to think through the relationship between self and society. Drama is just one example of the many potentially enriching 'off-syllabus' topics that schools were, thanks to the advent of schools television, able to offer pupils.

The BBC had since the 1920s been producing radio programmes for broadcasting in educational contexts, but the energy and vigour with which the independent television company Associated-Rediffusion embarked on the production of television programmes for schools in the late 1950s set the bar high for audiovisual schools programmes, and the following years appear to have been a particularly rich moment for theatre televised for schoolchildren. Both the BBC and Associated-Rediffusion were ambitious in the range of drama offered, and were considered and reflective about the contextual information and paratextual resources that would best serve their young audiences. Although there is a wealth of archival evidence for schools television, such a focused comparative study as this reveals that sources available at the micro level are varied and incomplete. Nevertheless, the small sample of Greek tragic programmes televised in the early 1960s reveal some differences in the pedagogic motivations and priorities of the BBC and Associated-Rediffusion, which larger studies in the future may be able to confirm as characteristic.

The material examined here suggests that the BBC maintained a traditional interest in plays as texts, with the focus on how they may be variously interpreted and made sense of as psychological studies with relevance to the modern world. Here the power of oratory and the suspense of the dramatic action are key to the experience offered, with the discussion by a moral philosopher serving as a significant way in to a thorough exploration of the moral landscapes of Greek drama. Whereas the modernity and topicality residing within the traditional theatrical canon were seen to offer fertile ground for the BBC's discussions of such crucial matters as morality and justice, and how these played out in the relationship between self and society, when Associated-Rediffusion's Greek tragic programmes of the early 1960s explored themes such as guilt and retribution, they were anchored more firmly in the original social and cultural contexts which gave rise to them, with viewers strongly encouraged first of all to consider these plays as products of a particular moment in time. This social and cultural contextualisation drew on documentary techniques to encourage viewers to imagine themselves in the original society, which, it is important to note, was not presented as an unproblematic 'classical' ideal. The aspiration here inclines more towards encouraging empathy and exploring ethics, leading to a deeper sense of humanity and appreciation, possibly, of the humanities.

This perceived difference in emphasis, with the BBC seeming to be more focused on highlighting the modernity and modern 'readings' of the theatrical canon and Associated-Rediffusion concerned primarily with the imaginative and emotional engagement of the viewer, appears to be borne out by an internal BBC report which stated that 'ITV programmes were more successful in that they communicated more realistically with the secondary modern audience at which they were aimed.' This report was written by Kenneth Bird, the BBC Midland Region Publicity Officer, who had given a lecture to the Worcester branch of the Schools Library Association. He was struck by how unanimously the view was held that 'either the [British Broadcasting] Corporation does not know how secondary moderns talk or else it uses people who are out of touch with their audience' and reported that this view, expressed by the headteachers, was 'whole-heartedly supported by the entire meeting'.[43] Teachers were considered by both the BBC and Associated-Rediffusion as vital to the communicative process in schools television programmes: to this end, leaflets for teachers were detailed and helpful, though the BBC quickly realised that not all teachers had the resources to do the 'prep' themselves or with pupils, and experiments revealed that integrating background and context into programmes was overall more successful than relying on overstretched teaching staff to introduce and mediate the experience. Thus the address to the viewer within programmes, and the ways that contextual and historical information was integrated, were crucial to perceptions of a programme's success or failure.

The differences between the motivations and programming of the BBC and its independent rivals are a topic ripe for further exploration, but the most significant finding here is simply that so much Greek drama – and, of course, so much Shakespeare, so much Edwardian drama and (in time) so much contemporary theatre work – was made accessible to the teenage audience in the 1960s classroom. The 'army of eavesdroppers', too, valued schools output. In 1958, in her book on broadcasting, Mary Crozier noted how often schools programming attracted this other audience:

> It is not uncommon for the housewife, or the worker kept at home for a few days, to enjoy following lessons about Chaucer's England or some great novel like *War and Peace*, or about how people live in distant lands.[44]

A *Radio Times* article suggested that parents who are at home in the day could tune in to schools programmes as a way of sharing a valuable experience with their children, and the *TV Times* published a letter from one who considered that schoolchildren were immensely privileged to have access to such drama in performance as the 1963 ITV *Hamlet*. As the broadcasting historian Bernard Sendall has written:

> There can be few clearer demonstrations of the power of television to give an added, live dimension to classroom studies than the presentation of television studio productions of drama, especially of Shakespearian and other classical drama. Very many schools are still without easy access to the live professional theatre; and even where there are theatres within reach the chances of their giving performances of such plays are not great. For some children seeing the *Producing Macbeth* series [in 1958] was their first experience of Shakespeare in performance. 'They were gripped and listened and watched intently', said one report.[45]

## PROGRAMMES DISCUSSED

*The Angry Gods*. 8-part series. Dir. Pat Baker. Associated-Rediffusion. ITV.
Episode 1: 'A Sacred Offering'. Wednesday 18 January 1961, 3.15–3.45pm.
Episode 2: 'The Crimson Path'. Wednesday 25 January 1961, 3.15–3.45pm.
Episode 3: 'The Black Furies'. Wednesday 1 February 1961, 3.15–3.45pm.
Episode 4: 'The Judgement'. Wednesday 8 February 1961, 3.15–3.45pm.

*Philoctetes* by Sophocles. Prod. Ronald Eyre. BBC Television.
'An Introduction to *Philoctetes*'. Tuesday 19 September 1961, 2.05–2.35pm.
The play in two parts: Tuesday 26 September 1961, 2.05–2.35pm; Tuesday 3 October 1961, 2.05–2.35pm.

*Bacchae* by Euripides. Prod. Ronald Eyre. 'For Sixth Forms' series. BBC Television.
'An Introduction'. Monday 8 October 1962, 11.30am-12.00pm.
The play in two parts: Monday 15 October 1962, 11.30am-12.00pm; Monday 22 October 1962, 11.30am-12.00pm.

*Theatres and Temples: The Greeks*. 10-part series (including a production of *Medea* by Euripides over 3 parts), from Tuesday 15 January 1963. Dir. Pat Baker. Associated-Rediffusion. ITV.

## NOTES

1 Scupham (1961).
2 'Notes for the Teacher: Drama', Autumn 1961, p. 3 (BBC WAC).
3 School Broadcasting Council, 'A Second Public Report on School Television, 1962', p. 13 (draft typescript, BBC WAC R16/776/2); henceforth SBC Report, 1962.
4 SBC Report, 1962, p. 13. See also Postgate and Weltman (1966: 59).
5 Cain and Wright (1994) offer an accessible survey of the first seventy years of educational broadcasting in Britain. Briggs' five-volume history of broadcasting in the UK (e.g. Briggs 1995) and the first four volumes of *Independent Television in Britain* by Sendall (1982, 1983) and Potter (1989, 1990) anchor educational strands within wider broadcasting activity.
6 Statistics in Postgate and Weltman (1966: 59, 75–6).
7 'BBC School Television Broadcasts: Twentieth-Century Drama, Spring 1960', p. 3 (BBC WAC).
8 'BBC School Television Broadcasts: Twentieth-Century Drama, Spring 1960', p. 3 (BBC WAC). Schools television productions of near-contemporary plays on social issues began to be transmitted in the second half of the 1960s: e.g. Arnold Wesker's *Roots* (Rediffusion for ITV, 1966) and Shelagh Delaney's *A Taste of Honey* (BBC, 1971). See Moseley (2007) for valuable discussion of the BBC's long-running television drama series *Scene*, which, from 1968, focused on social issues relevant to teens. Interestingly, the February–March 1960 *About the Theatre* series (broadcast in the Children's Television *Focus* magazine strand on Mondays at 5.10pm) set out to 'explore the theatre of today' and was not 'too deeply concerned with history': see Neville (1960).
9 The producer Rosemary Hill herself is credited with the translation.

10 On which see Wrigley (2015b).
11 See Wyver (2014c) for discussion of a 1965 BBC schools version of *Serjeant Musgrave's Dance*, directed by Michael Simpson, and Wyver (2012a, 2012b) for, respectively, a 1961 Associated-Rediffusion five-part production of *Hamlet* for schools, directed by Tania Lieven, and a 1960 BBC schools production of *Julius Caesar* by Ronald Eyre. (Eyre, who produced the *Philoctetes* and *Bacchae* discussed in this chapter, was considered to be 'a pioneering and brilliant figure in bringing the study of television as a dramatic art form into the country's classrooms' by the prominent headteacher and Honorary Professor of Education at Warwick Michael Marland [1992].) See Wrigley (2014b, 2015c) on schools television productions of Synge's *Riders to the Sea* and *The Wakefield Shepherds' Play* respectively. Crook (2007) offers a useful survey of school broadcasting in the UK.
12 Stray (1998); Hall (2004); Wrigley (2015a).
13 On this translation of *Philoctetes*, Cavander's agent wrote to Martin Esslin, head of drama at BBC Radio, stating that the translation had been 'specially done for BBC TV Schools and [it] got most awfully good notices' (letter from Margaret Ramsay to Martin Esslin, 19 October 1961, Scriptwriter file, Kenneth Cavander, 1: 1954–62, BBC WAC). Cavander's published translations of Greek plays were often produced on BBC radio and television in the 1950s and 1960s; later successes include *The Greeks*, the ten-play cycle drawing on Greek tragedies which he wrote together with John Barton for performance by the Royal Shakespeare Company, 1980. On the life of his translations on radio, see Wrigley (2015a).
14 In the years before the establishment of the National Curriculum in 1988, curricula in secondary moderns were influenced by a number of criteria, but, generally, English, geography, history, mathematics, science, domestic subjects and physical exercise were covered over the four years. In the 1950s, an increasing number of pupils stayed on to complete the General Certificate of Education (GCE), and the less academic Certificate of Secondary Education (CSE) was introduced in 1965.
15 SBC Report, 1962, p. 32.
16 For a discussion of another schools production by Ronald Eyre during this year, the 'intelligent, pacey, handsomely shot modern dress production' of *Julius Caesar*, see Wyver (2012b).
17 'Notes for the Teacher: Drama', Autumn 1961, p. 4 (BBC WAC).
18 Scupham (1961). On the mystery play, see Wrigley (2015c: 578–9).
19 The 1944 Butler Education Act had developed the tripartite system whereby children were streamed into grammar, secondary modern and technical schools at the age of eleven. The ~25 per cent of (overwhelmingly middle-class) children who achieved the highest scores in the 11-plus examination were able to go to selective, well-resourced gram-

mars which offered an academic education beyond the age of fifteen, advanced qualifications and easier progression to higher education. The majority of the other ~75 per cent of (mainly working-class) children went, until they were fifteen, to secondary moderns, which were less well resourced, focused on practical skills and offered fewer opportunities to pursue advanced qualifications; others went to the small number of technical schools which focused on mechanical and scientific subjects. See Lowe (1988) on British schooling, 1945–64.

20 SBC Report, 1962, pp. 4–5 and Table 12. Figures relate to schools in England, Wales and Northern Ireland; Scottish schools, along with other schools under the 'Special' heading, totalled 9 per cent (39 schools); a further 9 per cent are listed as 'Miscellaneous'.
21 A typical complaint from teachers is that a drama programme ideally required three lessons, with one for introductory work and one for follow-up: SBC Report, 1962, p. 24.
22 SBC Report, 1962, p. 13.
23 SBC Report, 1962, p. 32.
24 'Notes for the Teacher: Drama', Autumn 1961, p. 4 (BBC WAC).
25 SBC Report, 1962, p. 14.
26 SBC Report, 1962.
27 Dodds (1960), quoted in '*For Sixth Forms*: BBC Television for Schools, Autumn 1962' (leaflet in BBC WAC), p. 8. Dodds was an Irish classical scholar whose 1944 edition of *Bacchae* (2nd edn 1960) was published by the Clarendon Press, with introduction and commentary which engaged with the psychological and theatrical dimensions of the text. See also his landmark *The Greeks and the Irrational* (Dodds 1951).
28 'BBC School Television Broadcasts, Autumn 1962: Drama', p. 3 (BBC WAC).
29 'BBC School Television Broadcasts, Autumn 1962: Drama', p. 5 (BBC WAC).
30 'BBC School Television Broadcasts, Autumn 1962: Drama', p. 8 (BBC WAC).
31 'Television for Schools: Spring Term 1961', *The Times*, 3 February 1961, p. 5, lists the other Associated-Rediffusion series as *The Farming Year*, *British Isles* (geography), *Science: The Story of Medicine* and *French: Chez les Dupré*. Additionally, Scottish Television contributed *The World around Us*.
32 '*The Angry Gods*. Independent Television Programmes for Schools. Notes for Spring Term 1961. Associated-Rediffusion', p. 4 (BFI Library, ART/48/5).
33 'A Sacred Offering' camera script (BFI Library, ART/48/1). Page references in this paragraph refer to this script.
34 On which see Hobden, Chapter 1, above; Foka, Chapter 9, and Scott and Wilson in interview in Chapter 10, both below; and especially Wyver, Chapter 3, above, for near-contemporary comparands.

35 'The Crimson Path' camera script, p. 1 (BFI Library, ART/48/1). Page references in this paragraph refer to this script.
36 '*The Angry Gods*. Independent Television Programmes for Schools. Notes for Spring Term 1961. Associated-Rediffusion', p. 5.
37 The reason for preserving scripts for episodes 1–4 and not 5–8 may have been related to the fact that the first four were, in 1963, transmitted again as part of the ITV schools series *Theatres and Temples: The Greeks*, on which see below.
38 '*The Angry Gods*. Independent Television Programmes for Schools. Notes for Spring Term 1961. Associated-Rediffusion', p. 3.
39 Aspinall (1961: 10).
40 '*The Angry Gods*. Independent Television Programmes for Schools. Notes for Spring Term 1961. Associated-Rediffusion', p. 4.
41 *Theatres and Temples* leaflet, Associated-Rediffusion leaflet (BFI Library).
42 'Are you interested in good television?', advert published on 28 May 1963 in *The Guardian*, p. 5, and *The Times*, p. 7.
43 Internal report from Kenneth Bird (BBC Midland Region Publicity Officer), 17 February 1959 (BBC WAC T16/64 TV Policy. Education, file 6, 1959).
44 Crozier (1958: 167).
45 Sendall (1982: 277).

# 5 The Serpent Son (1979): A Science Fiction Aesthetic?

Tony Keen

This chapter addresses the 1979 television series *The Serpent Son*. This was an adaptation of Aeschylus' *Oresteia* trilogy, his 458 BC depiction of the return of Agamemnon from the Trojan War and his murder by his wife Klytemnestra (in the first play, *Agamemnon*), the subsequent return of his exiled son Orestes, who together with his sister Electra kills his mother and her lover Aegisthus in revenge (in the second play, *Choephoroi*), and Orestes' pursuit by the Furies, spirits of vengeance, and his subsequent trial and acquittal under the auspices of the goddess Athena (in the third play, *Eumenides*).[1]

*The Serpent Son* was made by BBC Television.[2] It comprised three episodes, each matching the three original plays: 'Agamemnon', 'Grave Gifts' (a variation on the 'jug-bearers' of the Greek title, *Choephoroi*) and 'Furies' (the avenging forces who become the more beneficial 'good spirits' of the *Eumenides*).[3] The BBC had a strong tradition of radio productions of the *Oresteia*, perhaps most famously in a 1956 production of a translation by Philip Vellacott which was published later the same year by Penguin Classics.[4]

## A 'MODERN TELEVISION VERSION'

The script for *The Serpent Son* was 'translated and adapted' by Frederic Raphael and Kenneth McLeish, according to the front page of the camera scripts.[5] McLeish had studied Classics at Oxford, whilst Raphael had taken the same subject at Cambridge, and so they both knew Greek.[6] The text is a translation made by the authors, working from Denys Page's

Oxford Classical Text,[7] and then modified for stage performance, rather than being an adaptation based on other English translations (as is the case, for example, with Seamus Heaney's version of Sophocles' *Antigone*, titled *The Burial at Thebes*).[8] Raphael and McLeish had originally been commissioned to do the translation in 1976, having approached the BBC with a project that had emerged out of conversations with their friend Michael Ayrton.[9] Subsequently, the commission was changed to *Agamemnon* alone, plus Euripides' *Medea* and Sophocles' *Antigone*, before reverting to the original idea of the *Oresteia*.[10]

The programmes were directed by Bill Hays and produced by Richard Broke. They were recorded (out of broadcast sequence) in June to August of 1978,[11] and broadcast in March 1979.[12] It was considered a prestige series, comparable in some ways, if not fully in scope, to the BBC's earlier *I, Claudius* (1976).[13] It was given that week's cover of the *Radio Times* (see Figure 5.1), showing Diana Rigg in the role of Klytemnestra, as well as a four-page feature inside the magazine.[14] Related articles appeared in *The Observer* and *Time Out*, as well as in the BBC's internal staff journal *Ariel*.[15] Immediately after the broadcast of 'Agamemnon' Frederic Raphael appeared on *Tonight* to discuss it. As well as the use of an image from the production on the cover of the 1979 publication of Raphael and McLeish's script, stills from the series were also used by publisher Duckworth as cover images on a series of paperback translations of the individual plays of Aeschylus' trilogy.[16]

However, the broadcasts were not particularly well received, either by television critics or by viewers. Clive James in *The Observer* and Bernard Davies in *Broadcast* were particularly scathing.[17] Letters were printed in the *Radio Times* that were critical of the production.[18] I have not been able to find any contemporary scholarly response to the broadcasts,[19] but when I studied Greek tragedy at university a few years later I got the impression that, when spoken of at all, *The Serpent Son* was not generally talked of favourably. Partly perhaps as a result of these responses, but perhaps also partly due to the incomprehensible vagaries of BBC programme scheduling, *The Serpent Son* was never repeated. A couple of years later, it was eclipsed by Peter Hall and Tony Harrison's masterly 1981 National Theatre production of the *Oresteia*, which was subsequently (1983) broadcast on Channel 4 and released on VHS.[20]

## JUST LIKE *DOCTOR WHO*?

It is now necessary to be solipsistic and anecdotal, in order to contextualise properly my initial response to the production, a response

Figure 5.1 Diana Rigg as Klytemnestra in *The Serpent Son* (1979) on the cover of *Radio Times*, 1 March 1979.

that led to the main thrust of this chapter. I did not see *The Serpent Son* in 1979. As someone embarking at the time on Latin and Greek O levels, I was aware of it – I remember the cover of the *Radio Times*, the programme was discussed in school, and I read *The Observer*. But I was not allowed to stay up to watch the broadcasts and, in the 1970s, if one did not see a programme when it went out, there were no chances to catch up. So no further opportunity presented itself to see the programmes until I accompanied Amanda Wrigley into the BFI archives in November of 2011.

My immediate response to *The Serpent Son* (as documented by Amanda in a blog post)[21] was that it looked just like an episode of *Doctor Who*. I am hardly the first person to spot this resemblance. Many responses at the time commented on a science fiction ('sci-fi', 'sf') element to the visual aesthetic of the three programmes. One of James' criticisms was that Agamemnon was '[d]ressed simultaneously as the Last of the Mohicans and the First of the Martians',[22] suggesting an excessive primitivism combined with an excessive sf aesthetic, whilst a viewer whose letter was published in the *Radio Times*, evidently disappointed with what they saw, complained that 'tragedy isn't sci-fi'.[23] Davies drew an explicit connection with *Doctor Who*, saying that 'Diana Rigg looked like one of *Dr Who*'s galactic vampires.'[24] The question is, to what degree was there a deliberate reference on the part of the creators to science fiction?

First of all, it is necessary to establish what actually constitutes a 'science fiction aesthetic'. The aesthetic which the commentators in the 1970s were probably thinking of came from shows which were primarily studio-bound, largely shot on video tape using multi-camera set-ups, and broadcast from unprocessed video tape. Alien environments would be created within what were often relatively small studios and, for larger-scale vistas, matte paintings and model work would be employed. The lighting often produced, at least in the 1970s, a stark screen image in which there is a strong contrast between the light and dark. The typical example of this aesthetic is, of course, the BBC's long-running children's/family drama series *Doctor Who* (1963–89). The particular aesthetic – white spaces, bright, shining surfaces and brightly lit spaces – can be seen, for instance, in 'The Invisible Enemy', broadcast in October 1977, an episode which I would regard as characteristic of Season 15 of *Doctor Who*, the season broadcast most recently before *The Serpent Son* was made.[25]

However, one must remember that *Doctor Who* also made considerable use of film, both on location – mostly, as the show was famous for, in quarries in the south-east of England – and in the BBC's film studios (and by 1978 it was making some use of location video footage). Film lends a very different quality to the image, appearing less stark, and looking sleeker. Moreover, lighting the set for a single camera, rather than for several different cameras shooting at once, allows for greater subtlety and creation of mood; the drawback, of course, is that it is more time-consuming and expensive.

Furthermore, though *Doctor Who* is the first example of this sort of aesthetic that springs readily to mind, *Doctor Who* was not the only science fiction television programme made in Britain in the mid- to late 1970s. Some of the others used a different aesthetic, which perhaps makes them less relevant here. *Space: 1999* (1975–7), created by producer Gerry Anderson and shown on ITV, though set in alien and futuristic environments, was shot on film, using single-camera and expensive special effects (though it did often, particularly in the second season of 1976–7, make use of small studios). In contrast to *Space: 1999*, the BBC's *Survivors* (1975–7), whilst using the same technical set-up as *Doctor Who* – multi-camera studio work mixed in with location filming – was set in a contemporary rural England, and aesthetically had more in common with the long-running Yorkshire-Dales-based soap opera *Emmerdale Farm* (1972–present) than with *Doctor Who*.[26]

Aesthetically more similar to *Doctor Who* were two series that were still running new episodes over 1978–9, both of which employed similar mixes of studio video work and location film-making, with science fictional sets and costumes. One was *Blake's 7* (1978–81), the BBC's space opera for a more adult audience than *Doctor Who*. Similarities with *Doctor Who* are hardly surprising, as it was made by writers, directors and producers who had previously worked on *Doctor Who*. The other series was ITV's teatime rival to *Doctor Who*, *The Tomorrow People* (1973–9), a series that imitated the appeal of the BBC's series. There is, of course, a degree of cherry-picking taking place here. Not all of *Blake's 7* or *The Tomorrow People*, and especially not all of *Doctor Who*, followed this aesthetic. But this is an aesthetic that seems to have lodged in the public imagination and conditioned them to think that television that employed this form of aesthetic would most likely be science fiction. *Doctor Who* can be used as a typical example, if for no other reason than that contemporary critics such as Davies took *Doctor Who* as the standard.

The visual aesthetic of *The Serpent Son* was the work of Hays, Broke, Designer Tim Harvey, Costume Designer Barbara Kidd and Graphics Designer Joanna Ball (and I will talk little about Ball's post-production effects). There are many things that look familiar to a viewer who has seen a lot of contemporary *Doctor Who*. The production of *Serpent Son* is entirely studio-bound, though all made in the large Studio 1 in the Wood Lane Television Centre.[27] This gives it a larger sense of space than *Doctor Who*, which rarely was allowed to use Television Centre Studio 1, and generally had to settle for smaller studios. Harvey's set design is striking. The courtyard in front of the palace at Argos is rendered in bold white spaces, heavily stylised, with little in the way of detail (see Figure 5.2). The space does not look

Figure 5.2 Aegisthus standing behind chorus members in 'Agamemnon', part 1 of *The Serpent Son* (1979). BBC.

like actual buildings made out of stone or wood, but has a degree of artificiality. This resembles the white walls that mid-1970s sf often imagined characterised the interiors of spaceships, such as can be seen in the *Doctor Who* story 'The Ark in Space' (1975). It is definitely a step away from the aesthetic that is often found in productions of Greek tragedy, on either film, television or stage, and that is probably what an audience would have been expecting, which is one based on some combination of classical architecture and/or ruins.

Agamemnon and Menelaus appear clad in armour that is based on the look of the eagle (reflecting a line in Raphael and McLeish's text describing them as 'twin eagles') – hardly the look one might expect for Agamemnon if used to a more traditional Greek hoplite aesthetic. The Argive palace guards are clad in armour resembling beetles. This might be seen as resembling *Doctor Who* monsters, such as perhaps the Ice Warriors.[28] The Furies in the final part of the trilogy certainly employ the kind of make-up effects that had previously been employed in sf. The Chorus in 'Agamemnon', as Clive James rightly observed,[29] are dressed in 'rags ... *designed* as rags' (original emphasis), as can be seen in Figure 5.2: this is perhaps reminiscent of 'primitive' tribes (usually regressed colonists) encountered in such *Doctor Who* stories as 'Planet of the Spiders' (1974) and 'The Face of

Evil' (1977). The sf aesthetic is further heightened by the use of some of the typical tricks of the sf television programme, such as colour separation overlay,[30] employed in, for instance, the opening scene of the original, un-broadcast version of *The Serpent Son*, when Apollo appears to Orestes.[31] And one might also note the maze set which transforms into a brain, intended to indicate the confused nature of Orestes' thoughts, something surrealistic and expressionistic.[32]

This aesthetic in *The Serpent Son* may be contrasted with that on display in *Of Mycenae and Men*, an original play by McLeish and Raphael broadcast two days after the final episode of *The Serpent Son*.[33] Though this also used video tape and a multi-camera, studio-bound set-up, the costume and set design was much more 'traditionally' classical (by which I mean it was more what a general audience raised on portrayals of Greece on television would expect).

There are creative personnel linking *Doctor Who* and *The Serpent Son*. Crew members such as Soundman Ray Angel and Lighting Technician John Treays had worked on *Doctor Who* in the 1960s, and make-up artist Jenny Shircore had worked on one story in 1975. This is unsurprising: in 1978 these were all BBC employees, expected to work on whatever programmes needed their talents. The most significant cross-over is Barbara Kidd, who designed costumes for *Doctor Who* from 1973 to 1975,[34] and was fêted for it.[35] At the time of the production of *The Serpent Son* she was also working on *Blake's 7*. Kidd's unusual costumes are certainly a contributing factor in the weird visual effect of the adaptation, and they came in for particular criticism.[36] However, Harvey's set designs are at least as responsible for the visual effect.

How intentional was the sf aesthetic? It seems unlikely that the creative team were aiming at people who watched *Doctor Who* and *Blake's 7* as their prime audience; *Doctor Who* was aimed at a family watching together, and while *Blake's 7* was intended to be more adult, it was still shown before the 9pm watershed, at a time when viewers were expected not to be exposed to violent or sexual themes. And both were shown on BBC1, the more entertainment-orientated channel, as opposed to BBC2, which had a more 'intellectual' and experimental approach. Rather, the production team for *The Serpent Son* were probably most interested in capturing the audience for antiquity that the success of *I, Claudius* (on which Harvey had previously worked) suggested was out there, although Raphael and McLeish's initial idea for *The Serpent Son* preceded the broadcast of *I, Claudius* by some years.[37]

It is fairly clear, both from the appearance of the episodes, and from things that Bill Hays said at the time, that the production was attempting to get away from what people might imagine a 'typical' production of a Greek play might look like. In part, this was achieved by rejecting design elements drawn from classical Greece. Instead, inspiration was taken from the Bronze Age (second millennium BC) civilisation of Minoan Crete. Female costumes in the first two parts are clearly intended to imitate those found in the archaeological evidence from Knossos, with a thin gauze covering to avoid the attention of Mary Whitehouse, campaigner for 'decency' on television, that would have followed actual baring of the breasts. *Doctor Who* had taken similar inspiration a few years earlier, in a story called 'The Time Monster' (1972), where the costumes had been designed by Barbara Lane. Any similarity between the costumes for 'The Time Monster' and *The Serpent Son* is, however, as likely to be because they are drawing upon the same sources as any direct influence from one to the other.[38] Elsewhere, design elements in *The Serpent Son* drew upon later Greek imagery, but it was archaic (i.e. prior to 500 BC) rather than classical (500–323 BC): for example, the statues of Apollo and Athena seen in 'Furies' are based on archaic models.

And it is quite clear from things Hays said that he wanted to be experimental, and wished to get away from any sort of 'realistic' approach. Hays wanted the production to be 'primitive, barbaric, [...] exotic and ritualistic'.[39] The production team were certainly seeking for a mythic quality to their production, if not an overtly science-fictional one. It is evident, from both observing the series and reading statements made by the production team, that they desired to distance the audience from the people portrayed on screen, to demonstrate how little they actually resembled the audience in cultural terms.[40] In this, they were clearly supported by Raphael and McLeish, whose translation sought to reveal the 'barbaric splendour' of Mycenae.[41] In this *The Serpent Son* is the polar opposite of the 1965 BBC Television adaptation of Plato's *Symposium* as *The Drinking Party* (as discussed in the Introduction, above).

## CONTEXT

*The Serpent Son* needs to be seen, also, in the context of other Greek plays screened on television. Viewer Arthur Pritchard wrote, in a letter to the *Radio Times* that criticised *The Serpent Son*, that '[y]ou can make *Agamemnon* work on TV if it looks like something that could actually have happened'.[42] However, the predominant trend in Greek plays on television seems to have been away from this interpretation of 'realism'. There are, of course, the 1972 BBC *King Oedipus* and the 1974 BBC version of Sophocles' *Electra*, which go so far along the route of 'realism' as to set the play in modern 1970s dress and sets, but these seem very much the exception. If one looks at some of the other productions of Greek drama that predate *The Serpent Son*, one can see similar distancing effects to those used by Broke and Hays. The 1962 ITV production of Sophocles' *Electra* features enormous stylised sets (that, in true *Doctor Who* fashion, wobble when the cast bump into them). The 1977 *Oedipus the King* made for the OU has highly formalised dancing, and half-masks, covering the eyes but not the face. Even the 1958 BBC *Women of Troy* allows some stylisation to creep in, especially in the male costumes.[43] Nor can one claim that Peter Hall's fully masked *Oresteia* is 'realistic' in the way in which a television audience would understand the term: the use of masks acts as a distancing device. It almost seems as if the idea of attempting a 'realistically' costumed and designed version of one of these plays, either in a Bronze Age or fifth-century Athens setting, is shied away from in a way that it is not for plays written in the sixteenth century and set a few centuries before, such as Shakespeare's history plays,[44] or even for a Roman-set production such as *I, Claudius*. And this applies equally to the movie versions of Greek tragedy made by Michael Cacoyannis or Pier Paolo Pasolini, neither of whom were trying to recreate a wholly 'authentic' Bronze Age in their movies.[45]

Indeed, Pasolini's work provides a very clear comparison with *The Serpent Son*. Like Hays, Pasolini was interested in producing a version of Greek myth that stressed primitivism and ritualistic elements. And he emphasises that in *Medea* (1969) through the use of some bizarre costumes, especially for the population of Medea's home of Colchis. What is worn by Aeetes in *Medea* is not that far removed from the costume worn by Terrence Hardiman as Aegisthus in *The Serpent Son* (see again Figure 5.2), and neither costume makes any attempt to replicate what might have been worn either at the play's dramatic date or at its date of performance.[46]

Moreover, it could be argued that it is not merely screen versions of Greek tragedy that take such a 'non-realistic' approach. Having been going to productions of Greek drama since the early 1980s and writing about them since the 1990s, I find it hard to recall a stage production of Greek drama that has adopted Bronze Age or fifth-century Greek costumes without some significant stylisation, other than those which have also adopted masks. Of course, I have no doubt that such productions existed, but that I cannot recall any suggests that they are in the minority. It seems as if portraying Greek drama in its ancient aesthetic context is something that is seen as 'all or nothing': if one uses fifth-century Greek costumes then one must use masks, and if one does not use masks then there is no particular interest in using fifth-century Greek costumes.

*The Serpent Son* is an extreme example of this way of portraying Greek tragedy, especially in the costumes, but I would argue that it is not wholly *sui generis*. This is not a completely left-field production. Moreover, I would argue that it is, almost of necessity, more extreme than other productions, because of the nature of the characters in the story, specifically the active roles played throughout by gods and goddesses. In the Sophoclean plays that television seems to love, the Theban plays and *Electra*, there are no gods on stage.[47] (Indeed, the only god on stage in extant Sophoclean tragedy is in *Philoctetes*.) Euripides' *Iphigeneia in Aulis*, in the form in which we have it, has no gods (though a *deus ex machina* scene may have been lost from the manuscripts).[48] The prologue in Euripides' *Trojan Women* that features Poseidon and Athena is often dropped: the 1958 BBC production does this, as does Michael Cacoyannis' 1971 movie. Don Taylor's 1990 version, written for television, includes this scene in the published text,[49] but since Taylor's planned television production was never made,[50] it is impossible to be sure that he would have retained it in the final production; Katie Mitchell certainly dropped this scene in her 2007 production of Taylor's text at the National Theatre.[51]

In the *Oresteia*, however, the gods are there, especially in the final play, and they cannot be removed.[52] This demands a more fantastical, less realistic approach. Inevitably, such an approach creates something that looks like *Doctor Who*, or any other studio-bound sf series. This does not mean that the programmes were attempting to appeal to an sf audience. Rather it seems that they were targeted at an audience used to approaching Greek tragedy in a stylised form, one that emphasised the differences between ancient dramas and more recent theatre, instead of promoting a continuity.

In conclusion, it seems that the resemblances between *The Serpent Son* and television sf such as *Doctor Who* are not deliberate, but a result of decisions taken about trying to achieve a ritualised aesthetic, in combination with production factors that arise from the ways in which television drama was produced in-house at the BBC in the 1970s. Similarities between *The Serpent Son* and BBC science fiction shows were, at least in part, the product of the BBC's corporate nature, where technicians worked on a wide variety of shows, and could be employed on *Top of the Pops* one week and *Doctor Who* the next. Moreover, to a degree it is simply the case that any sufficiently 'non-realist' television production inevitably ends up looking like *Doctor Who*. However, it is worth noting that the production team, many of whom had worked on television science fiction, and all of whom would have been aware of it, if for no other reason than that is was being made elsewhere in Television Centre, would know that an audience would see *The Serpent Son* and think of it as looking like science fiction. The choice of a 'non-realist' aesthetic such as this in itself makes a clear statement about the producers' view of the connection between a modern audience and the ancient Greek texts.

The result remains, as Amanda Wrigley says, 'striking'.[53]

## PROGRAMMES DISCUSSED

*The Serpent Son.* 3-part series. Prod. Richard Broke. Dir. Bill Hays. BBC2.
Episode 1: 'Agamemnon'. Wednesday 7 March 1979, 9.25–11.00pm.
Episode 2: 'Grave Gifts'. Wednesday 14 March 1979, 9.25–10.50pm.
Episode 3: 'Furies'. Wednesday 21 March 1979, 9.25–10.40pm.

## NOTES

1. Spellings of character names follow Raphael and McLeish (1979). Further on the *Oresteia*, see Howatson (2011), *s.v.* 'Oresteia'.
2. The IMDb entry for the series (<http://www.imdb.com/title/tt0078666>, last accessed 18 August 2017) credits it with the title *Oresteia*. However, whilst the camera scripts give the series title as *The Oresteia of Aeschylus*, this does not appear to have been used in the broadcast: the *Radio Times* (e.g. 7 March 1979, p. 55) bills it as *The Serpent Son*. The IMDb entry also confuses *The Serpent Son* with the later Peter Hall/Tony Harrison version of the trilogy which was broadcast by Channel 4 in 1983.
3. The new titles for the last two plays were added in post-production; the individual camera scripts use the original Greek names: *Agamemnon*, *Choephori* and *Eumenides* (BBC WAC).
4. Vellacott (1956). On radio productions of the *Agamemnon* and *Oresteia*, see Wrigley (2006, 2015a: 221–46).
5. Camera scripts in the BBC WAC.
6. Unwin (1997); Raphael (2015: 4).
7. Page (1972). Raphael and McLeish (1979: 137) also state that several editions were employed, in addition to Page, but the only other one mentioned is Thomson (1938).
8. Heaney (2004); for Heaney's lack of Greek, see Open University (2011: Track 12, 'Interview with Seamus Heaney').

9 BBC WAC T48/487/1: 'Commissioning Brief', 24 February 1976, Drama Writer's File: Frederic Raphael; Fenwick (1979: 72–3). For most of the following I am indebted to Wrigley (2017b). See also Jones (1979: 2).
10 Raphael and McLeish's revised text was published as Raphael and McLeish (1979). *Antigone* was made by the BBC seven years later, as part of Don Taylor's *The Theban Plays* (1986), on which see Fotheringham, Chapter 6, below.
11 'Grave Gifts' was recorded 14–17 June, 'Agamemnon' 16–18 July, and 'Furies' 9–13 August: *Agamemnon*, *Choephori* and *Eumenides* camera scripts (BBC WAC).
12 Unfortunately, little survives in the BBC's WAC in relation to this production, beyond the camera scripts and the 'Commissioning Brief', 24 February 1976 (Drama Writer's File, Frederic Raphael: BBC WAC T48/487/1).
13 On which see now Harrisson (2017).
14 Fenwick (1979).
15 Anon. (1979b); Hodgson and Wyver (1979); Anon. (1979a).
16 Lloyd-Jones (1979a, 1979b, 1979c). These were reissues with new introductions of translations Lloyd-Jones had originally published with Prentice Hall: Lloyd-Jones (1970a, 1970b, 1970c).
17 James (1979); Davies (1979). On the other hand, Rosalie Horner in *The Daily Express* (1979) was much more sympathetic.
18 Letters from Arthur Pritchard of Wakefield and Gladys Hall of Pagham, *Radio Times*, 7 April 1979, p. 79, printed under the heading 'Sci-fi Aeschylus'.
19 The translation is noted briefly in Collard (2002: lxix). Neither television production nor translation is mentioned in Macintosh, Michelakis, Hall and Taplin (2005).
20 For Hall's National Theatre production, see Taplin (2005). For the broadcast of it, see Wrigley (2017b). Having seen the series, I would say that *Serpent Son* deserves a better reputation than it has: it is not better than Hall's production, but it can at least be mentioned in the same breath.
21 Wrigley (2011f).
22 James (1979).
23 Letter from Arthur Pritchard of Wakefield, *Radio Times*, 7 April 1979, p. 79.
24 Davies (1979: 9). It is unclear to me if Davies had any particular *Doctor Who* story in mind. Creatures explicitly identified as vampires would not appear in *Doctor Who* until the story 'State of Decay', broadcast in 1980.
25 The sixteenth season of *Doctor Who* was recorded over 1978, at the same time as *The Serpent Son* was being made; indeed, one recording session for the story 'The Stones of Blood' was in the BBC's Television Centre at exactly the same time as 'Agamemnon' was being made.

26 From 1989 *Emmerdale Farm* became simply known as *Emmerdale*.
27 Television Centre Studio 1 was most commonly employed for large-scale variety and entertainment programmes such as *The Generation Game* (1971–81, 1990–2002) and *The Morecambe and Wise Show* (1968–77), though it was also used for prestige dramas, such as *I, Claudius* (see Kempton n.d.) – hence its availability for *The Serpent Son*.
28 They first appeared in 'The Ice Warriors' (1967), and then reappeared in 'The Seeds of Death' (1969), 'The Curse of Peladon' (1972) and 'The Monster of Peladon' (1974). They were then absent from the series for a long time, before returning in 'Cold War' (2013) and 'Empress of Mars' (2017).
29 James (1979).
30 Colour separation overlay is a technique that allows actors in a specially prepared studio to be superimposed on an image shot separately. It makes possible effects such as gods larger than humans, but tends to look artificial. See Panos (2013).
31 As Amanda Wrigley and I discovered in the BFI's archives, the first episode of *The Serpent Son*, 'Agamemnon', originally featured a seventeen-minute prologue, covering much of the material of Euripides' *Iphigenia at Aulis*: Wrigley (2011f). For broadcast this was reduced to seven minutes.
32 Wrigley (2017b) suggests that this might be intended as a nod towards Michael Ayrton's initial involvement; Ayrton had created many works of art drawing upon the myth of the Cretan labyrinth.
33 On which see Wrigley (2017b).
34 Most significantly for my current purposes, perhaps, on the Egyptological story 'Pyramids of Mars' (1975).
35 It is less important that Maureen O'Brien, who plays Electra, had previously spent time as the Doctor's companion Vicki; ironically, Vicki departs in 'The Myth Makers' (1965), a story set in the final days of the Trojan War, in which she takes on the role of Cressida. On 'The Myth Makers', see further Keen (2010b) and Potter, Chapter 8, below.
36 E.g. from Davies (1979: 9), and some of the letters printed in the 7 April 1979 issue of *Radio Times*.
37 Fenwick (1979: 72).
38 For further discussion of 'The Time Monster', see Keen (2010b) and Potter, Chapter 8, below.
39 Fenwick (1979: 75). Fenwick is not directly quoting, but paraphrasing what Hays said.
40 See Fenwick (1979); Hodgson and Wyver (1979); and Richard Broke's response to the criticisms printed in the 7 April 1979 issue of *Radio Times*.
41 Fenwick (1979: 72). Davies (1979) gets this wrong, admiring the translation but distancing Raphael and McLeish from the finished product.

42  Letter from Arthur Pritchard of Wakefield, *Radio Times*, 7 April 1979, p. 79.
43  For these productions, see Wrigley's articles on the blog of the AHRC-funded project 'Screen Plays: Theatre Plays on British Television' at <https://screenplaystv.wordpress.com> (accessed 18 August 2017): see Wrigley (2011a–f). Further discussion will appear in Wrigley (forthcoming).
44  As generally complied with by the BBC Television Shakespeare project of 1978–85, and expected by at least some of the television audience; a reader's letter, published in the *Radio Times* of 22 March 1979, stated 'It's such a relief *not* to have Julius Caesar in plus-fours, or Romeo and Juliet on motor-bikes.'
45  On the vexed issue of 'authenticity' in productions of Greek drama, see Gamel (2013).
46  On Pasolini's *Medea*, see MacKinnon (1986: 146–54), with discussion of costumes (at 148).
47  Note the various versions of *Electra*, *Oedipus* and *Antigone* mentioned in this chapter, as well as *Steven Berkoff's Oedipus* (Sky Arts 2, 2013) and *Antigone at the Barbican* (BBC4, 2015).
48  As the text currently stands, the miracle of Iphigeneia's replacement by a deer is reported by a messenger. There is reason to believe that this scene in its current form is spurious: see Kovacs (2003a: 161), and Richard Rutherford in Davie (2005: 175, 326–7), but compare Taylor (1990b: xxvii), who argues for the scene's structural integrity with the rest of the play. However, it is possible that Euripides may have included a scene in which the goddess Artemis appeared to report the substitution, giving the play the *deus ex machina* it otherwise lacks; this at least is implied by Aelian, *On Animals* 7.39 (= Euripides, Fragment 857 Nauck), but Kovacs (2003a: 161) raises doubts about whether the language used in the fragment can be genuinely Euripidean. See also Kovacs (2003b).
49  Taylor (1990b: 79–82).
50  On this see Fotheringham, Chapter 6, below.
51  On Mitchell's production of *Trojan Women*, see Keen (2008); Bakogianni (2009a); Cole (2015).
52  Other Greek plays have gods on stage, but with the exception of Tom Paulin's *Seize the Fire* (BBC2/OU, 1989), a version of Aeschylus' *Prometheus Bound*, I am not aware of any being broadcast on British television.
53  In a short piece printed in the *BFI Southbank Guide*, June 2012, p. 36.

## 6 Don Taylor, the 'Old-Fashioned Populist'? The Theban Plays (1986) and Iphigenia at Aulis (1990): Production Choices and Audience Responses

Lynn Fotheringham

On Saturday 21 July 1990, at 8.45pm, BBC2 screened Euripides' *Iphigenia at Aulis* as the last in the fifth season of the anthology drama series 'Theatre Night'. Immediately after the 'TWO' logo faded, a pillar of yellow flame flickered up the centre of the black screen, a gong sounded and the words 'The War Plays of Euripides' appeared in white font over the flame. That plural is the only thing remaining in the televisual record to indicate that director-translator Don Taylor had wanted *Iphigenia* to stand as the first in a series of three televised Euripidean plays (with *The Women of Troy* and *Helen*), standing as a parallel to his earlier production of three Sophoclean plays: *Oedipus the King*, *Oedipus at Colonus* and *Antigone*. These three had been broadcast as a stand-alone series under the title *The Theban Plays* over three nights of a single week in 1986.[1] But the parallel 'trilogy' was never to be completed. Far from being a beginning, *Iphigenia* would turn out to be the last 'Theatre Night' (there was no sixth season), the last time Taylor worked for television, and the last British television broadcast of a production of Greek tragedy for almost twenty-five years.[2]

Despite this irony, Taylor's *Iphigenia* made him the most prolific director of Greek tragedy on British television (with a total of four plays), and the only one to tackle the genre more than once;[3] his wish to direct a second trilogy on television reflects his firm belief that the medium was 'merely the latest extension of a dramatic tradition that reached more or less unbroken back to Aeschylus'.[4] His significance for Classicists interested in the twentieth-century reception and dissemination of Greek tragedy is assured. His significance in the broader history of British television drama has been identified as lying in his eloquent protest against mainstream developments in the field: he represents a range of people and approaches ultimately left behind by those developments.[5] Although most of his television oeuvre in fact consisted of material written for the medium, his productions of Greek tragedy can be seen as exemplary of his determination to make what he considered quality drama available to a mass audience, whatever their origins. A study of these productions is therefore a suitable point of entry into the study of this relatively neglected but important director.

I will begin with a brief survey of Taylor's career and opinions before attempting to convey an introductory impression of his television productions of tragedy; these sections will cover key features of his methodology and contextualise these features in terms of television history. I will then consider evidence for how the productions were received in the form of newspaper reviews and the BBC's 'Television Audience Reaction Report' for *The Theban Plays*. All four plays (henceforward referred to as *King*, *Colonus*, *Antigone* and *Iphigenia*) are treated together, although there is more information available about responses to *The Theban Plays*. The fact that there is a strong stylistic continuity across the four productions, and that the small number of critical responses to *Iphigenia* show no marked difference from those to the earlier productions, makes it reasonable not to separate the analysis of this play from the other three. What will emerge from the study of these documents is a wide variety of opinions on these productions as a whole, on individual aspects of them, and on the very act of putting ancient Greek tragedy on the modern mass medium of television. This variety highlights the impossibility of arriving at a straightforward conclusion about these productions as either artistic successes or failures; and this emphasis on variety seems an appropriate note on which to close a chapter on a man who argued passionately for more variety both in the way television drama was made and in the types of drama put on television.

## DON TAYLOR

The existing brief accounts of Taylor's life and works tend to be influenced by his memoir *Days of Vision. Working with David Mercer: Television Drama Then and Now*, published by Methuen in the same year as the first volume of Mercer's collected plays.[6] Mercer was the best-known of the new writers whose television work dramatising the lives of the working class, and of those educated out of the working class, Taylor directed in his first few years at the BBC (1960–5); the memoir focuses on these early days, though they are explicitly viewed from a later perspective. Born in a working-class London family in 1936, Taylor was in the first generation to benefit from the 1944 Butler Education Act. He developed an enthusiasm for drama and poetry at grammar school, and came to view the upper classes' monopoly on education and culture as perhaps the greatest injustice they had committed against the working class.[7] As a theatre enthusiast starting work at the BBC in 1960, he saw in the wide reach of broadcasting the opportunity to make available to the working class not only 'classic drama' (a term encompassing not just ancient Mediterranean 'Classics' but the entire Western theatrical canon), but also new works of – in his opinion – equally high quality, presenting a left-wing perspective on contemporary issues without descending into mere propaganda.[8] Unlike some others we shall encounter below, he saw no incompatibility between the modern medium and the ancient material, or between television's mass audience and the Western literary canon.

A *Radio Times* article promoting *The Theban Plays* in 1986 describes Taylor as 'not so much an élitist as an old-fashioned populist with a mission to liberate great literature, great drama, great opera from the preserve of the ruling or moneyed cliques';[9] the phrasing suggests concern that Taylor's enthusiasm for Greek tragedy might be misunderstood as 'élitist', typical of a 'public-school housemaster' (which the article carefully explains that Taylor is not). Taylor's approach can be described as 'populist', but as a type of populism it has become 'old-fashioned'. The tone of Taylor's own quoted statement, 'I have resisted the temptation to put Oedipus on a motor bike or exaggerate lurid aspects', hints at his contempt, expressed more explicitly elsewhere, for a different brand of populism: that which sets out to attract the largest possible audience. *Days of Vision* narrates the events which in Taylor's view led to the triumph of that kind of populism on British television, zeroing in on the arrival of Sydney Newman as Head of the BBC Drama Department in 1963. Newman's reorganisation of the Department and fostering of new approaches to drama have often been described as launching a 'Golden Age'; to Taylor, he was an uneducated upstart.[10]

Taylor's attacks on Newman can make uncomfortable reading; Caughie has called them 'naked snobbery' and 'very unpleasant'.[11] *Days of Vision* was written after twenty-five years of fighting a losing battle for something Taylor sincerely believed in, starting with his failure to be given any work by the BBC Drama Department between 1965 and 1972. He blamed the introduction of commercial television (and capitulation to the commercial principle on the part of those running the BBC) for the destruction of his cherished ideals, and excoriated anyone, like Newman, who acknowledged attracting the audience as a goal. He also believed he had been 'blacklisted' by Newman (although Newman left the BBC in 1970);[12] it seems more likely he was not a particularly congenial collaborator for many of those who worked happily under the new regime. He found refuge in the Documentary Features Department; much of his activity there has been described as 'smuggling' drama about historical literary figures on to the screen;[13] his own plays also began being produced in the theatre at this time. The majority of his output as a director for the Drama Department in the 1970s was also self-penned.

There is no doubt that Taylor was in favour of the democratisation of culture (bringing works perceived to be 'the best' to a mass audience) as opposed to cultural democracy (encouraging everyone to create their own art in their own way) – a debate about which, despite Crace's characterisation of Taylor's position as 'old-fashioned', was still going on in the 1980s and indeed beyond.[14] Taylor wrote negatively about popular entertainment more generally, and would not allow the term 'popular culture'.[15] His personal experience led him to reject suggestions that 'élite culture' had nothing to say to working-class people.[16] He generalised too broadly from his personal experience: he believed for a long time that exposure to the 'quality' material that had enthused him would create enthusiasm and demand for that material in a wide section of the population; by the time of *Days of Vision*, he had learned otherwise, and expressed his disillusionment with great bitterness.[17] He failed to recognise the extent to which his value judgements were shaped first by individual as opposed to universal preferences, and then by an extensive education of a particular sort.

His conviction that exposure would create demand recalls the BBC's first Director-General, John (later Lord) Reith. Reith was paternalistic – as evidenced by his notorious comment that 'few know what they want, and very few what they need' – but not elitist, in that he passionately wanted to broaden the audience for the very best of cultural expression in its many forms via broadcasting.[18] Taylor expressed admiration for Reith, and nostalgia for earlier days when a single television channel unified the nation's viewing experience;[19] in the *Radio Times*, he is quoted describing television as 'the whole nation's medium', as if the old monopoly, which would have compelled viewers to watch either Greek tragedy or nothing, was still in force. Instead his productions were broadcast on one of four channels, achieving viewing figures of no more than 0.6 million, while 12.1 million watched detective series *Taggart* on ITV.[20] While Taylor acknowledges that telling people what to do (or watch) on the grounds that it is good for them as 'a political principle ... has ominous overtones', he also admits that 'as a cultural credo it lurks behind the whole history of the BBC, and indeed to a certain degree behind my own work'.[21]

In 1977 he began to turn some of his attention to producing 'classic drama' for television with Granville Barker's *Waste*; in 1981–90 he directed nine such works by twentieth-century playwrights Mikhail Bulgakov, Arthur Miller and Edward Bond as well as by Sophocles, Shakespeare and Sheridan; non-theatrical material at this time was limited to two new self-penned plays and three episodes of the drama series *Maybury*.[22] Shortly after the broadcast of *Iphigenia*, as he was to write later:

> I heard from a member of the production team that Alan Yentob [Controller of BBC2] had announced there would be another Greek tragedy on BBC2 only over his dead body.
> His body is still in the way.[23]

Taylor stopped trying to get work in television, but continued to work in theatre and radio until his death in 2003. He did not attempt to explicate Yentob's reasons for taking this position. In contrast, Simon Curtis, who was brought in by Yentob from the Royal Court to helm the new anthology series 'Performance', spoke warmly in a 1998 interview of Yentob's support for studio productions of theatre plays other than Greek tragedy.[24] Yentob could have taken a stronger position against such material. Early television drama had been dependent on the theatre for material and personnel, as well as wishing to claim some of the older medium's cachet; an understandable desire to establish an identity of its own for the new medium as well as the gradual expansion of the pool of practitioners led to more material being created directly for television, and to celebration of this fact. Theatre and theatricality became representative of the past, of what television was trying to escape: 'the theatrical, the stagy, has been a term of abuse – formally, culturally and politically – at least ... since the late 1950s in television'.[25] The number of productions of theatrical material dropped, decade on decade, from an admittedly very high start. It must be acknowledged, however, that the number of productions of Greek tragedy was never very high – although higher than some other categories, such as medieval plays.[26]

## TAYLOR'S TRAGEDIES

The four plays are presented in new versions written by Taylor himself, working from literal translations provided by Geoffrey Lewis of the University of Edinburgh, who had been a fellow student of Taylor's at Pembroke College, Oxford, and acted as Classical Adviser on the productions. The compositions are verse: unrhymed lines of regular length for the dialogue, and rhyming, irregular lines for the choral song. They stay very close to the originals in terms of structure and content, although the English dialogue sometimes elaborates on the plainer language of the Greek. The plays are largely uncut, despite the enormous length of *Colonus* and scholarly doubt over the authenticity of several portions of *Iphigenia*. The Choruses deliver their lines spoken rather than sung, but accompanied by specially composed orchestral music. There is no space to discuss Taylor's interpretations of the plays here; but they do not stand out as unusual. The translations were published by Methuen, and Taylor's introductions make an interesting case for the value of performance as a hermeneutic tool.[27]

From the point of view of television technique, the productions not only are studio-bound but record the actors' continuous performance over the (between 115 and 140 minutes) running time of the plays, captured as if live by switching from one to another of the studio's cameras as required. This was the technique Taylor had learned as a trainee director on his arrival at the BBC in 1960, when all drama was broadcast live and there were no other methods available;[28] it enchanted him with its ability to enhance the best aspects of theatre through the camera's ability to alter the viewer's perspective on the action: 'in a TV play the cameras had to be inside the story, not merely watching it'.[29] He remained devoted to the technique, which was by this time so infrequently used for drama that he laments the risk that the skills required to employ it were disappearing.[30]

*Mise-en-scène*

Each of the four productions opens with a dialogue-free scene, underscored by orchestral music, which establishes the setting and some aspect of the characters. They represent the gathering of the Theban crowd before the palace (*King*), Oedipus and Antigone wending their weary way on to the set (*Colonus*), sinisterly helmeted guards raising enormous banners depicting Creon's face within a palatial chamber (*Antigone*), and Agamemnon writing his letter while elsewhere soldiers patrol the Greek camp (*Iphigenia*). It is quickly apparent that the sets are not attempting to look like the real world; the effect may be least marked in the interior space of *Antigone*, most marked in *Colonus* with its necessarily stylised representation of a wild place, including a grove represented by green-lit net and fairly neat rows of jagged rocks like corridors lined with broken columns. The space before the palace in *King* includes an enormous gateway in a wall that simply ends, and so requires no gate; the palace facade (not immediately revealed) has sloping, mirrored surfaces.

When the lights come up to reveal the Greek camp in *Iphigenia* clearly, the sets of tidily arranged stone steps and the curving wooden palisades create the overall impression of an acting space where small numbers can enter, interact and depart, rather than a mustering place for a vast army. The impression may be enhanced by the fact that the steps form areas reminiscent of the audience's seating area in an ancient theatre, here frequently occupied by the internal audience constituted by the Chorus. In addition, the central space of the studio is paved in blocks that create a circular pattern and so perhaps recall the (usually) circular *orchestra* of the ancient theatre, where the Chorus danced; the paving of the courtyard in front of the palace of *King* creates a similar although less marked effect, a visual allusion to the ancient theatre rather than an attempt to replicate it. Arrangements of steps and other, shallower variations in the height of the ground are prominent features of all four sets, enabling Taylor to provide some visual interest in these text-dominated plays by having the actors move up and down them: numerous characters take the high ground, as it were, before speaking to the rest of the cast.[31]

In *King* and *Iphigenia*, the wordless opening scene confirms that the productions are not set in a specific, real historical time frame, through the combination of costumes and props from different periods. In *King*, the citizens of Thebes slowly gathering to plead for aid wear costumes from a wide range of centuries; the *Radio Times* article mentions 'sources as varied as Bruegel and the Blitz'. In *Iphigenia*, the cameras shift between Agamemnon, writing a letter with a dip-pen and sealing it with wax by candlelight, and the soldiers patrolling the Greek camp, whose uniforms could plausibly belong to 1990. The effect is not as marked in *Colonus* or in *Antigone*, but these productions, designed to be viewed subsequent to *King*, do not have such a strong need to establish the ahistorical setting.

The costume design overall creates a vague impression of the past. Formal wear and military wear both tend to be conservative and therefore difficult to date; the aristocratic characters – the bulk of the speaking characters – are dressed formally, and many of the men's costumes have military overtones. The constantly present Choruses all come across as roughly nineteenth-century: the Theban senators in their cloaks with a froth of white lace below upright collars and bow-ties (*King*), or tail-coats and identical grey cravats (*Antigone*); the well-to-do farmers of Colonus in their tweeds, gaiters and array of different hats. The outfits of the female Chorus of *Iphigenia* evoke *Little House on the Prairie* more than Queen Victoria; no realist production would put twelve women in identically tailored dresses, each in a different solid colour with no patterning (see Figure 6.1). Some of the humbler speaking characters, such as the Messenger who describes Oedipus' self-blinding in *King* and the Soldier who announces Polynices' burial in *Antigone*, and some silent attendants for the aristocratic characters, are dressed in solid blocks of colour which seem symbolic of uniforms without representing a specific livery or evoking a specific time period.

Every now and then, characters wearing costumes suggestive of different eras (including the contemporary soldiers in *Iphigenia*) reinforce the impression that the action is not taking place in a specific historical period. Characters with religious affiliations who are presented positively, such as the prophet Teiresias and the unnamed

Figure 6.1 The Chorus of *Iphigenia at Aulis* (1990). BBC.

# Don Taylor, the 'Old-Fashioned Populist'?   131

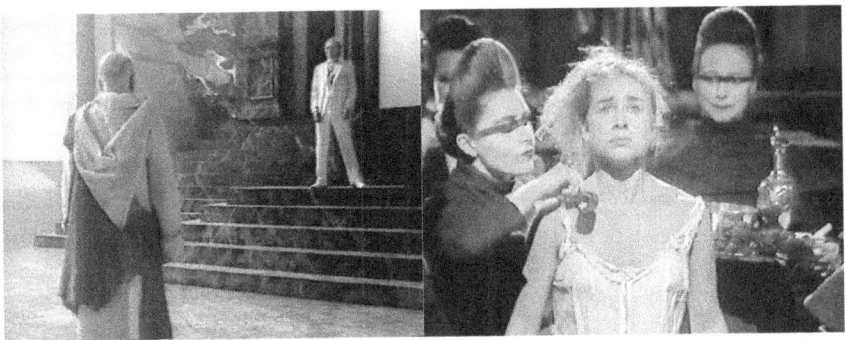

Figure 6.2 Religious figures: Tiresias and Oedipus in *Oedipus the King* (1986); Iphigenia and priestesses in *Iphigenia at Aulis* (1990). BBC.

Theban Priest, are dressed in more medieval-looking outfits: long robes with a homespun appearance, conveying perhaps an unwordliness. In contrast, the silent priestesses who prepare Iphigenia for the dreadful sacrifice are otherworldly and sinister: front-hair pulled into a beehive, back-hair into a bun; faces dead white except for red lips and a stripe of black across the eyes (see Figure 6.2). The sinister helmets of the silent Theban soldiers in *Colonus* may evoke Darth Vader or other *Star Wars* military outfits.

Although there are specific reasons to avoid a real-world setting in a fixed historical time period for the mythological world and highly stylised form of ancient Greek drama, such an approach was in any case congenial to Taylor, who was explicitly opposed to realism as an artistic mode, and who blamed the market-driven triumph of 'location film-making, naturalistic dialogue and journalistic style' in drama for the disappearance from the screen of his own, different aesthetic.[32] Given the wide range of approaches and techniques which can be described as or opposed to 'realism' and 'naturalism' – the terms can even be used as opposites, although Taylor is far from the only writer to use them in reference to practices that are closely aligned if not actually identical – it is necessary to identify what Taylor's opposition involved.[33] It was rooted in his preference for explicit literary artistry, for poetry and metaphor; he argued that these can express and explore the complexity of the world more effectively than a visually or verbally convincing representation of its surface detail. Positive words in his vocabulary include 'artistic', 'aesthetic' and 'stylised' – even, on one occasion, 'artificial' (in relation to language); the terms 'illusion of reality', 'reportage' and 'pictorial record', used in relation to drama, are negative. Taylor's goal in avoiding realism can be compared to the Brechtian *Verfremdungseffekt*: 'The aim [of television] must [be] ... to shatter the audience's film-based visual expectations, to startle them into moments of perception by presenting them with pictures that *do not* look like the real world.'[34] As this quotation suggests, Taylor equated realism and cinema, and thus he was able to exploit the rhetoric of the search for the 'purely televisual' in defence of his preferred alternative: the studio-bound play. Films are shot in 'real' locations; the artificial (or as Taylor put it, 'created') environment of the studio allows realism to be resisted: 'A film is always real, unless you make an enormous effort that it should not be so. A studio television play never is, unless you make an enormous effort that it should be so.'[35] Here, and elsewhere, Taylor seems to fall prey to the assumption that the camera presents an unmediated version of what it is pointed at.[36] Perhaps he aimed at exploiting his reader's tendency to fall prey to it. Unfortunately for him, the association of the camera with television has led audiences to a preference for this kind of realism in that medium as well as in cinema, and to the dismissal of studio-bound drama as 'artificial', 'theatrical' (used in a negative sense) and 'old-fashioned'.[37] When technological developments, especially in the portability of cameras and the editability of video tape, gradually made the enhanced 'realism' of location-shooting more possible and more affordable for television, many directors were happy to escape the studio and give the audience what they wanted. The original attraction of television was precisely its ability to bring moving images of one part of the 'real' world (including the studio) to another (the living room), and in 'real' time.[38] The lack of mediation in 'realist' film and television may be an illusion, but it is an illusion that the audience appears to have bought into with enthusiasm.

*Actors and cameras*

The first principal actors appearing on the screen include Cyril Cusack as the Priest in *King*, Anthony Quayle as the elderly Oedipus and Juliet Stevenson as Antigone in *Colonus*, and Roy Marsden as Agamemnon in *Iphigenia*. Notable figures appearing later include John Gielgud as Teiresias (*King* and *Antigone*), Claire Bloom as Jocasta (*King*), and Fiona Shaw as Clytemnestra (*Iphigenia*). The list features some of the brightest luminaries of the British stage, many of whom would also have been known to the television audience; the Choruses too are full of faces which would have been familiar to viewers, even if they might not be able to name every one. The sheer size of the casts is an indicator of the expense and effort that went into the productions: in each play there are eight speaking parts, twelve Chorus members, and a number of non-speaking extras – most strikingly in *King* (twenty-nine 'Theban Citizens' and 'Theban Children' listed in the credits) and *Iphigenia* (thirty-eight 'Greek Soldiers', some of whom act briefly as a subsidiary Chorus, and twelve 'Priests and Priestesses'). It is in scenes involving a large number of actors and/or extras, including the choral odes, that the elaborate interaction of performers and camera operators required by Taylor's use of the multi-camera, continuous-performance technique is most impressive. This can create a wide variety of effects. The movements of the Choruses are often stylised, as they move around the set in order to group themselves in their different configurations. Although it is no less artfully put together – and much more complex from the point of view of the number of performers and shots – a less stylised impression is created by the opening silent scene of *King*, involving around thirty extras trickling gradually on to the set, over around three minutes.

In the case of the choral odes, the movements of both performers and cameras add visual interest to a feature of ancient drama which is alien to modern audiences in serious drama, although it is used in the popular form of the 'musical'. Both visual and aural interest are also added by shifting between different modes of delivering the lines, sometimes divided among the twelve actors speaking individually, sometimes delivered by the whole group in unison, or in sub-groups of two, three, four or six; the cameras cut or pan to maintain focus on the current speaker(s). Such productions have been described as 'choreographed';[39] the cameras play as vital a role in the 'dance' as the actors, and the director acts as the 'caller' by instructing the vision-mixer to prioritise the feed from this camera or that. The younger, female Chorus and the occasional joyful odes in *Iphigenia* sometimes give the impression of an actual dance; the older, male Choruses of *The Theban Plays* perform movements expressive of solemnity. At the end of the fourth ode of *King* after the terrible revelation, they raise their cloaks one by one to cover their eyes; in *Antigone*, when Antigone ascends the staircase to her death, a line consisting of ten members of the Chorus, shot from above, moves with precision from the vertical through the diagonal to the horizontal across the floor of the darkened set (see Figure 6.3).

Long speeches delivered by single actors tend to involve less frequent shifting between cameras, although they are broken up with reaction shots from the other actors. There is, perhaps, surprisingly little use of the Chorus for such shots except in *Antigone*, which includes several scenes where one character is alone with the Chorus.

Figure 6.3 Chorus movement in *Antigone* (1986): Antigone ascending the staircase, with Chorus below. BBC.

But even keeping the focus on the speaker need not result in a static or simple presentation; to take one example from early in *King*, it takes some effort on the part of the camera operators to maintain the close-up on Michael Pennington in Oedipus' response to the Priest, as he runs down and up the palace steps and moves among the crowd. There are seven separate shots here, from long shots to close-ups, probably involving three cameras; three of the shots involve moving the camera to track Pennington while ensuring that he is not blocked by the extras. The extras, who respond to Oedipus's words, are nevertheless captured in the frame, reducing the need for cutaway reaction shots.

Taylor's long takes focusing on the speaking actor may be particularly long in the tragedy productions due to the length of the speeches. Even so, both his dedication to capturing continuous performance and some of the ways he went about doing so reflect his prioritisation of the actor's performance and of the script as the key elements in television drama: 'There are times when the best possible thing a director can do is to point a camera at an actor and watch him act good words.'[40] It would be unfair, however, to suggest that Taylor was uninterested in visuals, although he did love words. It is clear from a number of anecdotes that in order to achieve specific visual effects he was interested in pushing at the limits of the technology, in terms of number of shots used or the swiftness with which the cameras had to be moved across the floor, or exploiting the latest dollies and cranes to get the camera as high as possible.[41] He continues to be fond of crane shots in his tragedy productions, again exploiting the variations in ground level built into the sets. In the same article that recommends watching the actor 'act good words', he has interesting suggestions for 'the use of unrelated film and the divorcing of the picture from the sound'. But his strongest visual interest is in 'obsessive close-up'. He associates this technique, sometimes combined with whispered dialogue to convey 'a kind of passionate, interior monologue', with the intimacy of television as a medium.[42]

Intimacy and 'liveness' have been seen as integral to the television viewing experience by many creators and analysts, but have been repeatedly redefined over time as increasing screen size and picture quality have reduced the need to huddle close to the set with the curtains drawn (a powerful factor in the early descriptions of intimacy, and one which Taylor clings to), and as drama has increasingly been transmitted as pre-recorded rather than being broadcast live.[43] For example, the casting of well-known actors might be seen as creating an impression not only of quality but of intimacy: the viewers recognise 'old friends'. Taylor's preferred form of intimacy, and his rhetoric on the topic, recalls the earliest days of television. In 1937, for example, producer George More O'Ferrall stated that, with regard to television drama,

> We should regard fine acting as our chief asset and use the cameras to show it to its best advantage and, where possible, to heighten its effect. The value of the close-up is immeasurable.... There is a peculiar intimacy that belongs to television alone.[44]

## RESPONSES TO THE PRODUCTIONS

These four productions received comment in the nation's broadsheets at least twenty times, in a mixture of previews, evaluative comments in listings and post-broadcasting reviews:[45] seventeen times for *The Theban Plays* in 1986, by eleven writers working for six publications (four newspaper groups);[46] three times for *Iphigenia* in 1990, by three writers working in three publications (two newspaper groups).[47] *The Theban Plays* also received two substantial reviews in *The Listener*, the BBC's own magazine: one before broadcast and one after.[48] Table 6.1 shows my evaluation of these comments

Table 6.1 Evaluative comments on Taylor's television productions of Greek tragedy in the press.

| Date | Newspaper group | Writer | Type of notice | Words | Response |
|---|---|---|---|---|---|
| 1986 | The Times | Celia Brayfield | 1 review | 377 | Mixed |
| | | Martin Cropper | 1 review | 108 | Negative |
| | | Peter Waymark | 1 preview, 1 listing | 100, 212 | Neutral? |
| | The Daily Telegraph; The Sunday Telegraph | Robin Stringer | 2 reviews | 360, 115 | Positive |
| | | Philip Purser | 1 review | 735 | Positive |
| | | Peter Knight | 2 listings | 162, 105 | Negative |
| | | Rosemary Say | 1 preview | 162 | Positive |
| | The Guardian; The Observer | Jennifer Selway | 1 preview | 95 | Positive |
| | | Hugh Hebert | 1 review | 545 | Negative |
| | | Alan Rusbridger | 1 review | 560 | Negative |
| | The Financial Times | Christopher Dunkley | 1 review, 3 listings | 347, 113, 100, 31 | Positive |
| | The Listener | Al Senter | 1 review | 714 | Positive |
| | | Peter Lennon | 1 review | 825 | Positive |
| 1990 | The Daily Telegraph; The Sunday Telegraph | Richard Last | 1 review | 629 | Negative |
| | | Sean Day-Lewis | 1 preview | 203 | Mixed |
| | The Guardian; The Observer | Nancy Banks-Smith | 1 review | 203 | Positive? |

as positive overall (though potentially including acknowledgement of negative features), negative overall, mixed or neutral. This variety confirms the significance of individual preferences even in professional evaluations of drama; there is no consensus among the critics on the viability either of the attempt to bring Greek tragedy to television in general, or of these productions in particular. There is also disagreement on individual aspects of the productions and even on individual moments. A varied response likewise appears in the BBC's internal 'Television Audience Reaction Report' for *The Theban Plays*, although the majority opinions reported are positive. This together with the positive reactions from critics indicates that however old-fashioned Taylor's approach to television drama had become by the mid- to late 1980s, that approach had not yet lost the entire audience, who were still prepared to tolerate or even enjoy a variety of types of drama.

The audience report provides viewing figures and summarises the results of a questionnaire which included questions that could be answered yes/no or on a 'strongly agree ... strongly disagree' scale, for which a quantitative analysis can be provided, and space for the respondents to write more discursively about their reactions; a reader's impression of overall tendencies in these comments, occasionally illustrated by quotation of a representative or particularly striking remark, is also offered. Whereas the critics choose what to comment on, the audience reactions recorded here are to some extent shaped by the questions asked by the BBC, and the quotations preserved have been part of a process of institutional selection. In addition to such questions as whether respondents had video taped the plays and what they thought of the decision to broadcast all three in one week (on which opinion was more sharply divided than on the other questions), the questionnaire asked:

- whether the audience found the plays easy to follow, entertaining, attention-holding, too long, or still 'relevant today';
- whether the Chorus 'helped [the audience] to understand the meaning of the plays';
- opinions of the acting, the costumes and the sets.

While some questions are generic, those about length, contemporary relevance and the Chorus may give an insight into anxieties felt about the productions at the BBC.

Viewing figures for *King* and one of the programmes broadcast at the same time have already been mentioned; these confirm that the audience was small and probably consisted of those already interested in or curious about Greek tragedy. This must be borne in mind when noting that a majority of those surveyed not only welcomed the opportunity to see the plays, but said that they were easy to follow, entertaining (slightly fewer), and held the attention; a relatively small number found them too long. The responses to the questions about relevance and the Chorus were slightly less good. The sets and costumes were generally evaluated positively (with sets having perhaps a slight advantage), achieving similar scores to the questions about comprehensibility and entertainment value. The most positive response of all, statistically speaking, was to the acting. The summary of the open responses notes particular appreciation for Juliet Stevenson as Antigone.

The summary provides a little more detail and some reactions to other features of the productions, especially the translation. Opinion on this was divided:

It was described as having 'brought the plays to life' and the use of modern colloquialisms helped to bring out the relevance of the plays to today.... There were also a few complaints about the modernity of the translation.

Similarly, while some found the 'style of presentation ... "fresh and original"', and thought that the *mise-en-scène* 'add[ed] to the plays' messages', others found the staging 'confusing', the 'sets and costumes "hideous and irrelevant" or "weird"', objecting in particular to the mixture of periods or to 'modern dress'. It is also noted that 'some commented on the "clever use" of different levels of the acting areas, which they found very effective' – suggesting that the sets, and the way Taylor directed the action to exploit them, were appreciated. Although some were ultimately unconvinced that the plays remain relevant today, others were enthusiastic about their 'timelessness' and their status as 'masterpieces'.

In the press, the most frequently commented-on aspects of the productions overall were the costumes (mentioned by nine people), the acting or casting (ten) and the translation (eleven); there are also a few comments on the music, the sets and various aspects of the camerawork. There is very little comment on two of Taylor's major concerns: the democratisation of culture and continuous performance. Only Rusbridger picks up on the claim in the *Radio Times* article that Taylor aims to bring tragedy to the working class; Rusbridger makes no serious evaluation of the attempt, but his later comment that the plays 'will doubtless have been videoed by a thousand and one grateful classics masters the length of the land' may imply that he thinks the actual audience is precisely the constituency from which Crace was attempting to dissociate Taylor. Two people mention continuous performance. Stringer believes the technique has been successful; Cropper, on the other hand, writes that 'it was hard to see how the transmission gained thereby'. The process does not seem to have put people off, but it does not seem to have engaged many of them either.

Three specific quotations from reviews of *King* provide a useful introduction to the different attitudes to the project as a whole:

> It is strangely unnerving when the emotional concentrate of ancient Greek tragedy comes flooding down the centuries and bursts through the confines of the box in the corner of the living room. Not the sort of thing you expect. ... Directed by Don Taylor in his own new translation, it carried a conviction that was hard to resist. (Stringer)

> What very nearly sank this version early on, though, was that the production design is a mess, and that Taylor chose to do it as theatre, as opera, not as television. (Hebert)

It is an interesting experiment but the impression at the end is that a great classic tragedy has been scaled down and diminished in the effort to make it more accessible to present day audiences. (Knight)

Stringer's response was extremely positive, but he opens his review with these words, which reveal some concern about the compatibility of tragedy as material and television as a medium – concern which in this case has been overcome. The potential incompatibility is expressed in a contrast between 'emotional concentrate' and 'the confines of the box', which suggests that Stringer may be thinking of the intimacy of the television medium as potentially inadequate to the content of tragedy. The review goes on to list a number of aspects which contribute to the production's success, but continues to mention problems posed by the enterprise, such as the fact that the story is so well known and the Chorus as a dramatic convention. Stringer seems rather more concerned than Taylor himself about the difficulty of the undertaking.

Hebert and Knight, in contrast, are both negative about the way the production has negotiated the question of compatibility, but for rather different reasons: Hebert, prioritising the medium, feels that not enough has been done to adapt the material to television; Knight, prioritising the idea of 'a great classic tragedy', concludes that the effort made to adapt the material for a modern audience is already excessive. Knight's other comments may explain what he means. He focuses on the 'infelicities in the dialogue' resulting from the contemporary tone of the translation; he finds these incompatible with the 'length of the speeches', the 'declamatory style of acting' and the content (the horrors described). To identify these three elements as what Knight himself would associate with 'a great classic tragedy' may be to over-interpret what is of necessity a highly compressed comment appearing in the day's television listings, but that contemporary language contributes to the 'diminishing' effect seems likely. It is implied that the audience lacks some education or experience which would enable it to cope with an undiminished version, presumably involving a linguistically less accessible translation, and although the point is expressed in terms not of intermediality but of the gap in time between tragedy and today ('present day audience'), he may in fact have in mind the mass audience of television, whose level of education cannot be guaranteed. It is not impossible long speeches and declamatory acting seem to him un-televisual, although he does not say so.

What Hebert means by describing the production as 'not television' must likewise be deduced from his other comments. His description of the delivery of the Chorus, 'every voice round and on the breath, not to say bellowing', seems similar to Knight's 'declamatory' and can easily be associated with the theatre; his opinion of the translation is lukewarm at best, but it is not his main concern. Unlike Knight, he identifies Taylor's translation as verse, but does not seem to find this in itself un-televisual. Immediately after the theatre/opera comment, he mentions the mixed periods of the costumes and describes the set as 'a mixture of symbol and pure marbled Melamine'. The combination of the word 'symbol' and the reference to an artificial material indicates that what is here associated with theatre and opera rather than television is the non-realism of the production. Cropper's adverse comment on the 'Sword and Sorcery set' of *Colonus* may also indicate a distaste for non-realism; Day-Lewis, Rusbridger and Last express concern about 'incongruities', 'contradictions' or the like – in the costumes, in the language or between the two – which suggest they would have approved more of a production set in a single coherent historical period.

Waymark's comment that 'there has been no attempt to adopt television's forte of naturalism' makes the most explicit connection between the medium and the mode. Numerous critics do not mention the medium at all, making it difficult to be certain how much they have considered whether the features they comment on favourably are 'televisual', those they view negatively 'un-televisual'; they may simply be talking about their own taste within 'television'. But at least nine raise the question of whether the material is compatible with the medium, however briefly; for Selway and Stringer, incompatibility has been overcome or shown not to exist; for Cropper, Hebert, Last, Rusbridger and Waymark, it is a problem; Banks-Smith and Brayfield are unclear on this point.[49] For Cropper, Hebert and Waymark the compatibility of theatrical material with televisual presentation appears to be in question; the others focus on something other than theatre per se as the thing which may or may not be compatible with television, although all could be seen as focusing on a type of theatre or an aspect of theatre: for Brayfield, Last, Rusbridger and Stringer, the specific genre of Greek tragedy; for Selway, 'great, grand drama'; for Banks-Smith, the 'size' of Fiona Shaw's performance as Clytemnestra. These last two critics may be using the words 'great, grand' and 'size' in opposition to the old idea of the 'intimacy' of television.

Three of the critics who do not raise the issue of televisuality do mention specific difficulties of producing modern productions of Greek drama (Dunkley, Purser, Senter); two more comment on problems relating to 'classic tragedy' or 'the revered classics' (Knight, Lennon). Together with Brayfield, Last, Rusbridger and Stringer, this makes a total of nine critics who focus on tragedy as a genre or on a combination of antiquity and canonicity rather than on the theatre–television polarity; Hebert and Waymark do both. This may suggest that the chronological and cultural gap between ourselves and the tragedians is more of a problem for the critics than the theatre–television polarity, which is only explicitly mentioned by three and perhaps implied by Banks-Smith. But that would beg the question of what aspects of tragedy/'the revered classics' is conceived as causing a problem. Dunkley, Last, Lennon and Purser comment on specific cultural differences between us and the Greeks, such as belief in the gods. Hebert, Purser, Rusbridger and Stringer all comment on the Chorus, an ancient theatrical convention; Rusbridger adds other problematic aspects of ancient theatricality: the reporting rather than presentation of action, lengthy speeches, the unchanging location. Senter's focus combines the cultural with the theatrical.

I close by returning to Hebert and the question of the televisual:

> in the most memorable image of the night, we saw [Oedipus] emerge from the palace with a white cloth over his head, like a ghost in charades, till slowly the two blood stains appear from the empty eyes. I'd have liked more of that kind of thinking, a more sustained attempt to adapt to television.[50]

Oedipus appears at the top of the steps, the object of the fascinated gaze of the Chorus; a Messenger has just narrated his self-blinding. The cloth he holds over his head by a crooked right arm is the train he wore on his first appearance, which Hebert had derided earlier in his review. This spectacle is not a visual revelation of new information, and if Oedipus' action were taken as naturalistic, his generation of this 'memorable image' for the Chorus (and by extension the audience) is more easily read as self-dramatisation than as the instinctive act of a man driven to despair. By first concealing his face, then allowing the bloody image of eyes to appear on the cloth before finally showing his own sightless eyes, Oedipus here presents what he has suffered vividly or even as 'theatrically' as possible (see Figure 6.4). The scene would work well in a theatre, even if television allows it to be enhanced by the use of close-up. Pennington's pose is very similar to a nineteenth-century engraving of French actor Jean Mounet-Sully as Oedipus, in a Comédie Française production of the play, emerging from palace doors at the top of a flight of steps, draped in a bloodstained white cloth which he holds in front of him, although not over his head, by an extended right arm. This theatrical analysis

Figure 6.4 The blinding in *Oedipus the King* (1986): Oedipus in the doorway; close-up on blood stains. BBC.

of the moment Hebert considers an 'attempt to adapt to television' suggests room for disagreement about what 'television' is. The critics overall are not united on the importance of televisuality as a key feature in judging the artistic success or failure of the productions, or on a definition of televisuality. The audience report focuses on specific production decisions rather than on judging the productions 'as television'. Looking at the evidence as a whole, it is clear that responses to this attempt to put Greek tragedy on television vary because individual opinions and preferences vary.

## CONCLUSION

This chapter describes some aspects of Don Taylor's four television productions of Greek tragedy and sets them in the context of (1) Taylor's own writings about his artistic and political goals and (2) the existing evidence for responses to the productions by press critics and members of the viewing public. The result is a snapshot of attitudes to the democratisation of culture, as applied to the material of Greek tragedy and the medium of television drama, at what turned out to be the last occasion for some time on which this material and medium were combined. The conditions of broadcasting in 1986 and 1990 – the fact that other, more popular programmes were available to be watched, and were being watched, at the same time as Taylor's productions – mean that his desire to bring Greek tragedy to all must be seen either as unsuccessful or as untested: the opportunity to reach the audience he wished to did not exist. But although the entire nation did not watch, an audience of 0.5–0.6 million per play is still substantial – a production in a 1,000-seat theatre would have to run for well over a year to capture the same size of audience. We cannot know the motivations that led these people to watch the productions, but we do know a little about how they judged them. There were negative judgements, but the substantial number of positive responses show that however unusual, even old-fashioned, various aspects of Taylor's approach might have been, there was still an audience – including an appreciative audience – for Greek tragedy and for studio drama in 1986 at least. More interesting than the evidence for both positive and negative judgements is the evidence that those who came down on the same side of this division were not necessarily in agreement about the reasons for their conclusion. The variety of opinions reflects the complexity of the issues at stake: social, aesthetic and political questions about the nature of broadcasting, drama, entertainment and culture, and the desirability of various forms of these. When we have the amount of evidence that is extant for *The Theban Plays*, for example – from reviews to the BBC's survey of audience opinion – the variety of opinion amongst contemporary viewers is underscored. With his televised tragedies, the 'old-fashioned populist' Taylor certainly succeeded in engaging a mass audience.

## PROGRAMMES DISCUSSED

*The Theban Plays*. 3-part series. Prod. Louis Marks. Dir. Don Taylor. BBC2.
Part 1: *Oedipus the King*. Tuesday 16 September 1986, 8.30–10.40pm.
Part 2: *Oedipus at Colonus*. Wednesday 17 September 1986, 8.50–11.00pm.
Part 3: *Antigone*. Friday 19 September 1986, 9.00–10.55pm.
The Sophoclean trilogy was preceded by an 'unrehearsed discussion about acting Sophocles and his meaning to the modern world' (*Radio Times*, 11 September 1986, p. 37): *Speaking to the City: Sophocles Then and Now*. Prod. Louis Marks. Dir. Don Taylor. Sunday 14 September 1986, 8.40–9.05pm.

*Iphigenia at Aulis* by Euripides. 'Theatre Night'. Prod. Louis Marks. Dir. Don Taylor. BBC2. Saturday 21 July 1990, 8.45–10.45pm.

## NOTES

I would like to thank the editors for their boundless support, including extremely helpful criticism, and especially Amanda for help in locating the BBC audience report; Matt Brooker for help with image-processing; and most of all, the late Geoffrey Lewis and his wife Sheila for introducing me to Taylor's *Iphigenia at Aulis* in 1990 and providing the video tapes which have greatly facilitated my work on all four productions.

1. The opening gong-sound and the font of the initial title were repeated from *The Theban Plays*. For the planned second trilogy, see Taylor (1998b) and the back flap of the dust jacket of Taylor (1990a).
2. The next broadcasts of Greek tragedy on British television were both of theatrical productions of Sophoclean plays: *Steven Berkoff's Oedipus* (Sky Arts, 2013) was the product of post-performance editing; Ivo van Hove's *Antigone* (BBC4, 2015) was broadcast live from the Barbican.
3. The runner-up is Bill Hays, with his 1979 version of Aeschylus' *Oresteia* (see Keen, Chapter 5, above; Wrigley 2011f, 2017b).
4. Taylor (1990a: 30).
5. See Macmurraugh-Kavanagh and Lacey (1999); Bignell, Lacey and Macmurraugh-Kavanagh (2000: 161, 187); Caughie (2000: 75–6, 86); Wake (2014).
6. Taylor (1990a). Other accounts: Anon. (2003); Hayward (2003); Purser and Billington (2003); Purser (2007); Wake (2014).
7. Taylor (1990a: 47–9).
8. Taylor (1990a: 86–90).
9. Crace (1986: 82).
10. For the 'Golden Age', see Cooke (2015: 70); Caughie (2000: 57–8). For various negative comments on Newman, see Taylor (1990a: 105, 160–1, 169–70, 184–93, 199–204, 221–4, 238).
11. Caughie (2000: 75–6).
12. Taylor (1990a: 221–4). The accusation had been reported in Appleyard (1982); see Newman (1982) for response.
13. Purser and Billington (2003); cf. Purser (2007).
14. See Kershaw (1992: 183–95; cf. 134–6).
15. Taylor (1990a: 5, 19–21, 45–7, 95–6, 200–1).
16. Taylor (1990a: 63).
17. Taylor (1990a: 235–40).
18. The statement, from Reith's *Broadcast over Britain* (1924: 34), is frequently quoted, e.g. in Crisell (2002: 35). For Reith and television, see Cooke (2015: 11–13); for Reith in the context of the interwar generation's resistance to the commercialisation of culture, see LeMahieu (1988: 3–4, 138–9, 141–54); for Reith more generally, see Caughie (2000: 25–9); Bailey (2007: 99–103).
19. Taylor (1990a: 238, 1–2; cf. 237, 243–5 on commercial television).
20. Viewing figures for the evening that *King* was broadcast are taken from BBC Broadcasting Research: Television Audience Reaction Report TV/86/104: *The Theban Plays* by Sophocles, 1 (BBC WAC).
21. Taylor (1990a: 37).
22. On this production of *Waste*, see Wyver (2014b) and Smart (2016). For

23 Taylor (1998b: 38).
24 Ridgman (1998a: 199).
25 Caughie (2000: 219). These developments are traced by Cooke (2015: 12–14, 17–18, 40–3, 56, 68). Macmurraugh-Kavanagh and Lacey (1999) explore and problematise the view that television moved naturally and inevitably from being more theatrical to being more filmic/cinematic.
26 See Taylor (1998); Wyver (2011). On medieval mystery plays on British television, see Wrigley (2015c).
27 The volumes were originally entitled *Sophocles: The Theban Plays* (1986) and *Euripides: The War Plays* (1990). Taylor's Euripides translations were subsequently divided between *Euripides: Plays II* (1991) and *Euripides: Plays III* (1997). The introduction and translator's note to the Sophocles volume were retained in the currently available 1998 edition, *Sophocles: Plays I*, but repaginated following an additional introduction by series editor J. Michael Walton.
28 He gives an admirably lucid account of the studio process at Taylor (1990a: 11–14).
29 Taylor (1990a: 22).
30 Taylor (1990a: 264, 267).
31 The visual echo of ancient theatre seating in *Iphigenia* and the movement of the actors up and down steps in *King* and *Iphigenia* are noted by Wrigley (2012a, 2012d).
32 Taylor (1998b: 39); cf. (1981: 33) and (1990a: 258–9). For other practitioners opposed to realism, not acknowledged by Taylor, see Cooke (2015: 113–20, 129–34); Caughie (2000: *passim*, esp. 152–78).
33 See Cuddon (2013: 462–3, 590–3, 664) for various uses of the terms; Cooke (2015: 27, 51, 81, 104, 108) for the terms used in opposition and (2015: 101, 109, 129) for the terms used in alignment; Caughie (2000: *passim*, esp. 69) for the flexibility and evolution of realism.
34 Taylor (1990a: 264); there are occasional brief references to Brecht elsewhere in the book, and in Taylor (1996), but no sustained exploration of his ideas.
35 Taylor (1990a: 258).
36 The most extended description of the camera as operating on its own occurs at Taylor (1981: 32).
37 Macmurraugh-Kavanagh and Lacey (1999: 66–7, 70–2) discuss the audience's increasing dissatisfaction with studio drama from the mid-1960s.
38 See Caughie (2000: 99–101) for the 'rush of the real' and the aesthetic of immediacy.
39 Cooke (2015: 8).

Taylor's other television productions of theatre plays see *Screen Plays: The Theatre Plays on British Television Database* at <http://bufvc.ac.uk/screenplays> (accessed 25 August 2017).

40 Taylor (1964: 207).
41 Taylor (1964: 152) and (1990a: 25–8, 126–8).
42 Taylor (1964: 206).
43 For intimacy as a property of the medium and an aesthetic value in early discussions of television, see especially Jacobs (1998) and (2000).
44 O'Ferrall (1937).
45 The barer listings that confine themselves to statements that the plays were to be broadcast, summaries of the action and/or extracts from the press pack have not been included in the count.
46 Reviews: Brayfield (1986); Cropper (1986); Dunkley (1986b); Hebert (1986); Purser (1986); Rusbridger (1986); Stringer (1986a, 1986b). Previews and listings: Dunkley (1986a, 1986c, 1986d); Knight (1986a, 1986b); Say (1986); Selway (1986); Waymark (1986a, 1986b).
47 Reviews: Banks-Smith (1990); Last (1990). Previews and listings: Day-Lewis (1990).
48 Lennon (1986); Senter (1986).
49 Four more critics mention the medium (positive are Dunkley 1986b, Purser 1986, Say 1986; neutral is Day-Lewis 1990); not all reviews of television programmes feel the need to point out that the programme is on television, so these may still be significant.
50 In contrast to Hebert (1986), Dunkley (1986b) describes this moment as Taylor's 'sole glaring error'.

# 7 The Odyssey *in the 'Broom Cupboard'*: Ulysses 31 *and* Odysseus: The Greatest Hero of Them All *on Children's BBC, 1985–1986*

Sarah Miles

This chapter explores two television programmes, *Ulysses 31* and *Odysseus: The Greatest Hero of Them All* (hereafter *Odysseus*), for the ways that each retells the myths about Odysseus, with their origins in Homer, for a television audience of children in the 1980s. These two television series merit discussion because they offer individual responses to the myths that were contemporary with one another and aimed directly at children. *Ulysses 31* was a Franco-Japanese production and animation, while *Odysseus* was a live-action, story-to-camera BBC production. Both programmes were initially transmitted in the UK (1985–6) as part of the BBC's newly created Children's BBC on BBC1, and each reconfigured the hero Odysseus and his myths by drawing on different aspects of 1970s and 1980s film and television culture in order to contemporise the classical material.[1] The chapter shows how this was achieved through a combination of innovative storytelling techniques and creative use of the mode of television and televisual animation coupled with a detailed knowledge of the myths of Odysseus. Moreover, these two programmes provide contemporary examples of localised (British) and international (Franco-Japanese) production contexts so that it is possible to compare how these local and international contexts shaped the format and creativity of each programme. Ultimately this study highlights the way that *Ulysses 31* drew on popular film culture and Japanese techniques in animation, framing Odysseus' heroism via cinematic appeal in order to make the stories of Odysseus resonate with new audiences, whereas *Odysseus* adapted the BBC's *Jackanory* story-to-camera format and so constructed an anglified Odysseus that contemporised the character and his setting for British audiences of the 1980s while still evoking the wit and wiles of the Homeric Odysseus.[2]

For viewers in the UK both programmes were seen within the same transmission context when they first aired on Children's BBC, 1985–6. Therefore, although the genre and mode of production are points of divergence between the two programmes, they do share a context of transmission at the very start of the BBC's new programming format, Children's BBC, created by Pat Hubbard, Head of Presentation at the BBC in 1985. This was itself an innovation in children's programming since it included for the first time a presenter live in a small studio, which earned the name 'Broom Cupboard', from where the presenter introduced and reacted to each programme. Children's BBC was set up as a direct response to Children's ITV, which had launched in 1983 with a presenter in a studio. The new BBC format encouraged audience responses in the form of letters, postcards, drawings, birthday cards and sing-alongs, all of which were inspired by the television shows, and this provided a means of response from the child audience to the television programmes. Therefore, the context of transmission for *Ulysses 31* and *Odysseus* was at a point of change in the culture of children's television on the BBC that shaped the programmes' reception by young audiences in the UK.

The discussion of these two television programmes contributes to an understanding of children's programme-making and programming culture on local and international levels, on which there has been a growth in scholarship during the twenty-first century. This can be seen particularly in the work of Máire Messenger Davies and Jeanette Steemers, alongside the launch in 2007 of the *Journal of Children and Media*,[3] and wider public interest in the touring exhibition 'The Story of Children's Television from 1946 to Today' (2015) at a time when UK children's television is under threat.[4] In addition, *Ulysses 31* was not just a children's television programme, but also a children's animation, and this art form has long been undervalued for its aesthetics and narrative power, particularly animation aimed at the younger viewer.[5] This chapter, therefore, adds to the increasing interest in the importance and significance of animation, and here specifically animation as a medium for children's television and classical adaptations.[6] In animation, we are drawn into a world of imagination and seemingly endless possibilities, although always ones that reflect the contemporary contexts in which that animation was created. In the case of *Ulysses 31*, the contexts of future time, a setting in space and the presence of gods allow a freedom of creativity in responding to the stories of Odysseus that produces an artwork not constrained by the need for physical actors, models and cameras, but one that engages with contemporary science fiction/fantasy film and television in order to draw children into the stories of Odysseus. By comparison, Tony Robinson's performance in *Odysseus* used his power of storytelling set in the context of real-world 1980s Cornwall and south-west England to help feed the imagination without presenting the fully dramatised version with multiple actors, sound effects and music.[7]

The narrative modes of these two programmes are of particular interest because children's media, including television and film, are some of the first ways through which people experience Greek myths and events of the Graeco-Roman past. As such, they can play an influential, formative role in shaping attitudes to the classical world in childhood and adulthood. The adult creators of children's television are aware of the ability to educate as well as entertain their audiences, and this is something within the remit of BBC programming for viewers of all ages.[8] The BBC's attitude at the launch of Children's BBC was to create a child's version of adult television, as can be seen from its news release, which speaks of '"Jonny Briggs", the first soap opera for five to eight year-olds; "Galloping Galaxies", the first sitcom set in outer space'.[9] As Steemers neatly puts it: 'the BBC was focused from the start on providing a public schedule in miniature for its young audiences, based on their perceived needs with a varied diet of drama, information programmes, and some animation that protected them from commercial exploitation'.[10] Children's television is defined by its audience, but created by adults whose level of concern with child development and learning is reflected in their modes of production. Some, and by no means all, 1980s adaptations of the myths of Odysseus reflect detailed knowledge of these and other classical sources, as we shall see is the case with *Ulysses 31* and *Odysseus*. This is a choice made by the programme-makers. Sheila Murnaghan notes, 'children's versions of the classics can help us to think about popular versions of the classics more generally, about why they exist and what they accomplish'.[11] These two programmes serve as examples of the diverse ways that children's television can respond creatively and freely to the stories of Odysseus, while maintaining a close knowledge of the ancient sources as the basis for their creative adaptation, in order to reconfigure classical works for new audiences of children.

## 'BY THE GREAT GALAXIES!' ANIMATING ODYSSEUS IN *ULYSSES 31*

*Content and cultural influences*

*Ulysses 31* was a twenty-six-episode animated television series for children which provided a fusion of space adventure, Homer's *Odyssey* and wider Greek mythology, set in the thirty-first century and carefully interweaving characters and stories derived from these ancient Greek sources. It tells of Ulysses' wanderings through space and his efforts to save his companions and return home to earth and his wife Penelope.[12] The father–son dynamic is as central to the narrative as it is in Homer, but in contrast to the Greek epic, Ulysses travels with his son Telemachus, as well as Yumi from the planet Zotra and the robot Nono (see Figure 7.1) and with guidance from the on-board computer Shyrka, whose name is a Japanese corruption of Circe. In Homer, Circe is the sorceress who directs Odysseus homewards, and Shyrka's role as a navigation computer neatly incorporates this Homeric role.[13] The spaceship in *Ulysses 31*

Figure 7.1 Yumi, Ulysses, Telemachus and Nono in *Ulysses 31* (1985). DiC Entertainent and Tokyo Movie Shinsha.

is notably called the 'Odyssey', acting as a constant reminder of one of the classical influences for the series. The divine element is kept alive in Ulysses 31, but there is no Athena to aid our hero, as found in Homer and other versions of the Greek myths. Instead Ulysses battles directly against the will of Zeus throughout the series, and there is continual reference to 'the gods', who are represented mainly by a masculine voice, visually inspired by classical Greek sculpture (and depicted as if they were stone with no facial or physical movements), and whose emblem is the trident. The foregrounding of a male voice for divine power and the removal of the female voice of Athena are in keeping with the marginalisation of female roles in mainstream science fiction/fantasy television and film of the 1970s–1980s.[14]

Throughout the series numerous narrative elements which have their roots in Homer's Odyssey form part of the animated action, which are re-set within a futuristic space age of robots and computers. The order of narrative events loosely follows that of Odysseus' journey homeward in Homer's Odyssey, except that the series ends with Ulysses' escape from Hades rather than after his return home to Penelope. However, Ulysses 31 deftly uses a time-travelling episode in order to depict the reunion between the original Ulysses of ancient Greece (the ancestor of Ulysses 31) and his Penelope.[15] The series starts with the blinding of the one-eyed Cyclops (a giant bio-mechanical creation of the god Poseidon); then other familiar characters appear including Aeolus king of the winds, the Laestrygonians (although they are not cannibals), Scylla and Charybdis (depicted visually as two planets encircled by an infinity loop representing fire and ice), the Sirens, Circe (including Hermes' appearance as Ulysses' guide and protector, just as he appears in the Odyssey[16]), Calypso (a love-interest for Ulysses) and the lotus-eaters (represented as stereotypical hippies); then comes the battle against the suitors (uniquely set in ancient Greece) and finally the journey to Hades. In addition, elements of wider Greek mythology recur within the series: Ulysses battles Medusa, meets Sisyphus and nearly swaps places with him, solves the riddle of the sphinx, outwits Cronus, meets Theseus and Ariadne and kills the Minotaur, helps Atlas, sees the three Fates, and travels with Orpheus in search of Eurydice on the way to Hades. The series engages closely with the rich resource of Greek mythology as well as episodes in Homer's Odyssey.

However, the journey of this Ulysses is not just one of Greek mythology in space, and the breadth of cultural material beyond ancient Greece incorporated into this series is equally wide: episode fifteen 'Before the Flood' involves Ulysses giving an ad hoc lesson to the children on Inca culture and the shifting poles of prehistoric earth, and episode twenty-two 'The City of Cortex' considers the effects of an evil super-computer on a society. Meanwhile stories deal with themes of love, loss, family unity, slave labour, gender inequality (as Ulysses helps Hypsipyle free women from enslavement by men) and even drug addiction (via the lotus eaters). In addition, there is a notable mix of science fiction/fantasy references, including to Stanley Kubrick's film *2001: A Space Odyssey* (1968) for the visual conceptualisation of the animation set in space. Episode twelve 'Trapped between Fire and Ice' even sees the characters find an abandoned ship from earth with an astronaut in suspended animation who is said to be from 2001 specifically.[17] A second significant cinematic influence on *Ulysses 31* is George Lucas' films *Star Wars* (1977) and *The Empire Strikes Back* (1980). Many aspects of *Ulysses 31* in terms of the orchestration of space-battle scenes, thematic music and the style of sound effects recall those of the Star Wars universe (including light-sabre sounds for Ulysses' weapon and noises reminiscent of R2D2, X-wings and TIE fighters). There is even a snippet of music from the scene of The Battle of Hoth where Luke Skywalker destroys an AT-AT with a grenade in *The Empire Strikes Back*.[18]

The animated world of *Ulysses 31* affords us visual, live-action depictions of imagined pasts and futures with musical soundtracks and special effects from contemporary popular culture used to communicate and reshape the stories of Odysseus for its intended child audience. The stories, characters, artwork and overall story arc in *Ulysses 31* show an acute awareness of the ancient sources in episodes that are, nonetheless, as creative with Greek myths as they are knowledgeable about their workings. One example of this occurs in episode twenty-four ('Strange Meeting', 'Ulysse rencontre Ulysse'[19]) when the Ulysses of the thirty-first century is forced to travel back in time to help the Ulysses of ancient Greece regain Penelope and his throne. Only if the future Ulysses succeeds can he continue to exist in his own time, and so the Ulysses of past and of future are here explicitly linked by their genealogy. The two Ulysses characters meet, and their conversation is at times metatextual, including the revealing line: '5,000 years lie between us but our stories appear to be linked.' Linked they are, and the writers here openly declare it to their audience. In Homer's *Odyssey*, when Odysseus slowly moves towards his final act of vengeance on the suitors, who are trying to gain the hand of his wife Penelope, the narrator intervenes with this passage:

> While they [the suitors] were talking Odysseus, master of stratagems, had picked up the great bow and checked it all over. As a minstrel skilled at the

lyre and in song easily stretches a string round a new leather strap, fixing the twisted sheep-gut at both ends, so he strung the great bow without effort or haste. Then with his right hand, he tested the string, and it sang as he plucked it with a sound like a swallow's note. The suitors were utterly mortified; the colour faded from their cheeks.[20]

The great bow mentioned here was used in the contest to decide which of the suitors would marry Penelope in the absence of Odysseus. However, all the suitors failed to string the bow, and in the passage above the narrator slows down the narrative time to focus on the precise moment when Odysseus strings the bow, adding the musical simile to emphasise the sweet sound of the bowstring in stark contrast to the slaughter of the suitors that is to follow. The parallel scene in *Ulysses 31*, as the suitors fail to string the bow, clearly owes something to peplum movies of earlier decades, including the successful *Ulisse* (dir. M. Camerini, 1954), starring Kirk Douglas, Silvana Mangano and Anthony Quinn.[21] However, in this key moment of suspense *Ulysses 31* is alone in retaining from Homer's narrative both the distracted suitors and Ulysses plucking the bowstring which scares the suitors. The key change is that in *Ulysses 31* the sound is of a low acoustic guitar string rather than a swallow or lyre. No other television or cinematic adaptation of Homer's *Odyssey* of which I am aware employs this musical moment. The cinematic and dramatic qualities of Homer's *Odyssey* remain effective in twentieth-century media. Therefore, amid the myriad of contemporary and historical cultural influences, *Ulysses 31* recreates a scene from its Homeric forebear, imitating this moment of tension from the ancient epic, but updating the acoustic reference so that the bow in *Ulysses 31* resonates not like an ancient lyre but like a popular contemporary instrument, the guitar.

## Production and transmission

*Ulysses 31* was in the unique position of being the first Japanese–French co-production split between the French television production company DiC Entertainment and Japan's Tokyo Movie Shinsha (now TMS Entertainment). Jean Chalopin and Fujioka Yutaka were the producers, and Chalopin was co-writer of the screenplay and script with Nina Wolmark.[22] It first aired on FR3 in France and RTL in Luxemburg in 1981, entitled *Ulysse 31*, but in Japan only parts of the series were shown in 1988 under the title 宇宙伝説ユリシーズ 31 *Uchū Densetsu Yurishīzu Sātīwan (Space Legend Ulysses 31)*.[23] *Ulysses 31* was redubbed in order to reach audiences in the UK, Spain, Italy,

Germany, Poland, Sweden, Greece, Portugal, Australia, Canada and the USA, including rebroadcasts from the 1980s to the 2000s alongside VHS and DVD releases.[24] In France in the early 2000s *Ulysses 31* was shown as part of 'Soirées Gloubiboulga' at which thousands of adults gathered to watch cartoons from their childhood, indicating its continuing appeal to adults.[25] Amanda Potter's research into British adult viewers of *Xena: Warrior Princess* included a question about their prior knowledge of Odysseus, and five out of twenty-five responses cited *Ulysses 31* as contributing to this knowledge, demonstrating how these viewers had made a connection between the animated *Ulysses 31* and a broader understanding of Greek mythology.[26]

The creation and production of this animated children's series represented a key point in the global spread of anime (Japanese animation), which has a unique narrative form and cutting-edge visuals. In *Ulysses 31*, moreover, we see an early stage of this fusion of Japanese and European artistic forms and genres taking place. This co-production contained an impressive list of figures in anime including the director Nagahama Tadao, who sadly died before the series was completed,[27] and Araki Shingo, famed as a character designer for anime, whose most internationally successful work, *Saint Seiya* (1986–2003), was inspired by Greek mythology. Araki had previously worked in the studio of the great Tezuka Osamu, whose name is perhaps better known in the UK and who in 1963 created *Astro Boy*, 鉄腕アトム (*Tetsuwan Atomu*), the first animated Japanese television series, based on his manga (Japanese comics). Notably, Araki designed characters for the pilot episode of *Ulysses 31* with distinctive anime characteristics, but these were then altered to create more American-styled characters, which also meant the gods were depicted to recall classical Greek sculpture, again adding an air of classical art to this self-styled space opera. *Ulysses 31* also employed the artistry of Kawamori Shôji, the famous designer of mecha anime (creator of *Macross* and involved in the design of Optimus Prime in *Transformers*).[28] Kawamori was in charge of designing the spaceship, the 'Odyssey', which incorporated the logo of FR3, the French television channel that broadcast the series.

*Ulysses 31* represented a huge leap forward in animation: the production time for each episode was increased from one week to two; whereas the standard of anime at this time was four to six frames per second, *Ulysses 31* was twelve frames per second.[29] These factors allowed for a level of detail and fluidity in animation that defined the series. Early examples of wire-frame model 3D animation also appeared scattered throughout (its usage was limited by budget and computer processing time). Therefore, this was not a cheap, quickly produced animation but rather one in which much time, talent and innovative animation were invested from both France and Japan. This also created a unique aesthetic for the series, drawing on conventions distinctive of Japanese manga and anime. Scott McCloud has discussed the difference between Japanese manga and American comics that he observed as an artist in 1982, noting that manga contained iconic characters, wordless narrative style, choice of shots, a sense of place and emotional intensity.[30] Meanwhile Ledoux and Ranney note that 1970s Japanese animated television series 'absolutely overflow with tracking shots, long-view establishing shots, fancy pans, unusual point-of-view "camera angles" and extreme close-ups', whereas US animation 'tends to thrive in an action-obsessed middle distance'.[31] The techniques mentioned by McCloud, Ledoux and Ranney are apparent in *Ulysses 31*, and marked it out as distinct from other animation available to non-Japanese audiences at the time. For example, the reunion of father and son in episode one ('Vengeance of the Gods') employs a mixture of changing shots and perspectives, wordlessness, music and silence to create a powerful moment in the cartoon; in episode eleven ('The Seat of Forgetfulness') the visualisation of the power of the Fates is abstract and detailed, in a wordless sequence representing a myriad of tiny black-and-white figures working the loom that weaves the thread of the Fates. One of the directors of *Ulysses 31*, Bernard Deyriès, similarly acknowledged the unique aesthetic at work in children's anime in the 1970s–1980s: 'The Japanese offered a breath of fresh air compared with Disney … I was disillusioned by the USA. The concepts there are often the same, too simplistic/black-and-white' (my translation).[32]

The mixture of techniques of anime, influences of contemporary science fiction/fantasy, and stories from Homer and Greek mythology meant that *Ulysses 31* appealed widely, as evidenced by the number of countries that aired it. This point has been noted by Jason Bainbridge, who considers that these Franco-Japanese animations are 'fascinating examples of convergent media texts, convergent not only in terms of their *production*, but also in terms of their *content*' (emphasis in original).[33] However, the picture is complicated when one looks more closely at the localised cultural variations in the way *Ulysses 31* was broadcast in different countries. This can be seen by comparing the various dubbings of *Ulysses 31*: France kept the Greek names and mythological topics in the foreground for all their episode titles, while the English dubbing played down these elements (see Table 7.1), and the French character 'Thémis' becomes the English 'Yumi'.[34] Although there is no attempt to imitate the

Table 7.1 *Ulysses 31* (1985): a comparison of English and French episode titles.

| English | French |
| --- | --- |
| 1 'Vengeance of the Gods' | 1 'Le Cyclope' |
| 2 'The Lost Planet' | 2 'La planète perdue' |
| 3 'The Black Sphere' | 3 'Hératos' |
| 4 'Guardian of the Cosmic Winds' | 4 'Éole' |
| 5 'The Eternal Punishment' | 5 'Sisyphe' |
| 6 'Flowers of Fear' | 6 'Les fleurs sauvages' |
| 7 'Mutiny on Board' | 7 'La révolte des compagnons' |
| 8 'Secret of the Sphinx' | 8 'Le Sphinx' |
| 9 'Cronus, Father of Time' | 9 'Chronos' |
| 10 'Temple of the Lestrigones' | 10 'Les Lestrygons' |
| 11 'The Seat of Forgetfulness' | 11 'Le fauteuil de l'oubli' |
| 12 'Trapped between Fire and Ice' | 12 'Charybde et Scylla' |
| 13 'Phantoms from the Swamp' | 13 'Le marais des doubles' |
| 14 'Song of Danger' | 14 'Les sirens' |
| 15 'Before the Flood' | 15 'La deuxième arche' |
| 16 'The Magic Spells of Circe' | 16 'Circé la magicienne' |
| 17 'Lost in the Labyrinth' | 17 'Le Minotaure' |
| 18 'At the Heart of the Universe' | 18 'Atlas' |
| 19 'The Hidden Truth' | 19 'Nérée ou la vérité engloutie' |
| 20 'The Magician in Black' | 20 'Le magicien noir' |
| 21 'Rebellion on Lemnos' | 21 'Les révoltées de Lemnos' |
| 22 'The City of Cortex' | 22 'La cité de Cortex' |
| 23 'Calypso' | 23 'Calypso' |
| 24 'Strange Meeting' | 24 'Ulysse rencontre Ulysse' |
| 25 'The Lotus Eaters' | 25 'Les Lotophages' |
| 26 'The Kingdom of Hades' | 26 'Le royaume d'Hadès' |

distinctive language of Homer (filled with epithets, stock phrases and similes), *Ulysses 31* develops an individual style of language through the oaths which the characters swear (for example, 'By the Great Galaxies!', 'Quivering Quasers!', 'Quarks and Charms!' and countless more), which marks it out as clearly a separate time and culture from that of its audience.

Animation is an internationally understood form of popular culture, which travels very readily around the world due to the ease of dubbing the sound tracks and voices. *Ulysses 31* arrived in the UK in 1985, when all twenty-six episodes were broadcast in the first year of the new Children's BBC programming format (weekly at 4.30pm, 7 November 1985 to 8 May 1986). In 1981 animation made up only 9 per cent of the BBC children's schedule, compared to 35 per cent in 1996 (on ITV the leap was similarly from 9 per cent to 40 per cent).[35] Therefore, animation on Children's BBC was still in itself a novelty in 1985. The success of *Ulysses 31* with UK-based children is evident from the bountiful stream of pictures and drawings which was sent into Children's BBC and displayed in the 'Broom Cupboard'.[36] There was even a mimed sing-along of the theme music to *Ulysses 31* which presenter Philip Schofield conducted, and copies of lyrics were sent out to children for *Mysterious Cities of Gold* on request, suggesting a degree of audience participation. As a later presenter, Andi Peters, acknowledged, 'Singalongs were part of the Children's BBC tradition.'[37] Indeed, the internationally produced and transmitted *Ulysses 31* was made to fit into the BBC's programming format with Canadian voice actors speaking in English. The Franco-Japanese collaboration that was behind the success of *Ulysses 31* was not made clear to its intended audience beyond the names in the end credits, and yet it is the distinctive aesthetics and creativity of this collaboration that contributed to the programme's success.

## TONY ROBINSON AND STORYTELLING IN *ODYSSEUS: THE GREATEST HERO OF THEM ALL*

In contrast to the international collaboration involved in the creation of *Ulysses 31*, *Odysseus: The Greatest Hero of Them All* was a more home-grown affair. This twelve-part series was produced by the BBC's Children's Department, but only two episodes of *Odysseus* are accessible to researchers in the BFI National Film and Television Archive; the status of the remainder of the series in the BBC archive is unknown.[38] The main extant source for the series lies in the two books closely adapted from the television series and published by BBC and Knight Books (1986, 1987), and audiobooks of Tony Robinson reading out these books unabridged. Both the written and audio formats preserve the use of comic-book-inspired sound effects which also characterised the television series (doors shut with a 'GUDUNG!'; Charybdis bursts forth with a 'SPLUUUUME!'). This gives a sense of the character of the series, but does not capture the energy and visual aesthetic of the television version.

*Odysseus* was created by leading British comedic talent of the 1980s: Tony Robinson wrote and performed *Odysseus*, and Richard Curtis was a co-writer. Curtis had already written a book for children in 1982, *The Story of Elsie and Jane*, and in the *Odysseus* books Curtis is described in the 'About the Author' section as someone who studied 'Classics at Papplewick and Harrow School, and Greek at Oxford'.[39] The choice to include this information adds an authorising tone to this retelling of Odysseus' adventures in its relationship with classical sources. This is all the more notable since Curtis in fact studied for an English degree at Oxford, but here emphasis is put on his study of Greek as part of his degree, although, as we shall see below, Robinson's role in the reworkings of classical sources is just as important to the television series. *Odysseus* adopted the simple technique of storytelling to camera, as had been used in *Jackanory*. *Odysseus* was filmed on location in Cornwall and south-west England – indoors, outdoors and in public, with Robinson constantly on the move creating a lively, real-time atmosphere for the retelling of these stories of Odysseus in contemporary Britain. Robinson's storytelling employed frequent jokes, wordplay and contemporary humour: for example, there is a touch of political satire through the inclusion of an unnamed female prime minister, in the role of Laocoön, who is swallowed by the sea monster outside Troy; and the Cyclops, upon seeing the Greek sailors (and before eating some of them), declares, 'I like Greek food.' But the narrative could also change to a more sombre mood when required: for example, when describing the death of Odysseus' dog Argos or Telemachus' reunion with Odysseus. This variety of tone was coupled with endless enthusiasm and energy in performance to bring the stories of Odysseus to life.

Both Robinson and Curtis had been involved in *The Black Adder* (1983) for the BBC, and by spring of 1985 *Blackadder II* was in pre-production. Meanwhile, *Odysseus* was first broadcast as part of Children's BBC twice a week from 13 November to 22 December 1986. *Odysseus* clearly came at a time of great creativity for Curtis and Robinson. However, *Odysseus* was also Curtis and Robinson's second work together, following the four-part *Theseus the Hero*, which was made for *Jackanory* and broadcast from 11 to 28 January 1985. The programme used the same to-camera style as *Odysseus*, and it was filmed on the streets around Bristol. Although no known television recordings survive, the *Radio Times* summary of the first episode gives a flavour of the humour which would be further developed in *Odysseus*: 'Theseus was a hero from the word go. Well he had to be, didn't he, with enemies like Pinebender and the Great Tosser to contend with. But most villainous of all was his treacherous Uncle Leos – and he was unspeakably nasty.'[40] This summary also reveals that amid the humour Robinson and Curtis were acutely aware of the mythical tradition involving Theseus and his labours. For example, Pinebender (*pituokampte*) was the Greek epithet for Sinis, who killed his victims by tying their arms and legs to bent pine trees before letting the trees go and tearing their bodies apart. Moreover, Robert Graves' popular book *Greek Myths* employs this very epithet,

Pinebender, as he tells the story of Theseus and Sinis. This book had been in wide circulation in the UK since its first edition in 1955,[41] and the dedications in the first *Odysseus* book accompanying the television series contain the words 'and written in memory of Robert Graves', again indicating his influence on the work of Robinson and Curtis.[42] Therefore, *Theseus the Hero* contained a mixture of humour and erudition, which at least suggests the dual concerns of its creators to educate while providing entertainment for children about Greek mythology. This approach is continued and developed with *Odysseus*, as the episode descriptions in the *Radio Times* listings illustrate (see Table 7.2).

*Theseus the Hero* was produced by Angela Beeching and directed by David Bell, and both worked with Robinson and Curtis soon after to create *Odysseus*. However, this time the storytelling was not a part of *Jackanory*, but rather Robinson approached Beeching, the producer of *Jackanory*, with the idea for *Odysseus*. *Jackanory* was a blend of children's literature and television that was created by the Children's Department at the BBC in 1965 and ran until 1996. The key point in *Jackanory* was the direct address to the audience of the storyteller, who made direct and continual eye contact with the imagined viewer, while the voice, face and gesture told the story, sometimes accompanied by props and illustrated or performed inserts.[43] By 1985 the *Jackanory* format had been running for twenty years, and *Jackanory* had developed its own traditions in televisual storytelling for UK children. Therefore, by adapting the *Jackanory* format, the makers of *Theseus the Hero* and *Odysseus* were speaking in a commonly held form of televisual language; children were familiar with the concept of a story to camera, and so they already knew how to 'read' the programme. However, as the producer Beeching put it, 'Tony took it a huge step further.'[44] Robinson had already developed his own approach to storytelling on television, as seen in the popular *Fat Tulip* (1985) for Children's ITV, written by Debbie Gates and Robinson, which spawned further series and books. In *Fat Tulip* Robinson narrated stories to camera, putting on an array of voices and moving around as he narrated while the camera slowly followed his movements. The manner of filming and narrative techniques from *Fat Tulip* were used and adapted further in *Odysseus* by the director Bell and Robinson, who also employed filming techniques from *The Tube*, a Channel 4 live music programme produced by Tyne-Tees Television and presented by Jools Holland and Paula Yates (1982–7). As Bell noted, 'we used their innovative to-camera style that we felt was very cheeky and off-the-wall.'[45] The makers of *Odysseus* were experimenting with filming techniques in order to

Table 7.2 Episodes of *Odysseus: The Greatest Hero of Them All* (1986)

| Episode | Title | Description in *Radio Times* |
|---|---|---|
| 1 | 'The Golden Slagheap' | 'Odysseus takes a tip from both his wily Grandpa and Penelope's chamber-pot. He falls in love, and the adventure begins.' |
| 2 | 'The Burly Nun' | 'Who is the sinister one-eyed man? Why is Achilles dressed in women's clothes? And where is Troy?' |
| 3 | 'The Colour of Birds' Eggs' | 'The siege of Troy starts well enough – until the Greeks get bored and begin to quarrel.' |
| 4 | 'Achilles' Heel' | 'Achilles is niggled when Trojan spears make a six-foot hedgehog out of his best chum. Odysseus persuades him to take revenge.' |
| 5 | 'Revenge of the White Goddess' | 'The Greek army chooses a new hero, and Odysseus takes Diomedes down a sewer on a secret mission.' |
| 6 | 'Getting In' | 'Odysseus develops a brilliant new weapon, and the prime minister makes her last, fatal, mistake.' |
| 7 | 'The Fat Batsman' | 'The Cyclops traps the Greeks in his cave and gets ready for a tasty kebab. But it's one in the eye for him when his sheep are stolen.' |
| 8 | 'The Wind and the Wallabies' | 'With half their colleagues eaten by cannibals, the men decide to turn vegetarian. But they still eat like pigs . . .' |
| 9 | 'The Faces of the Dead' | 'Odysseus meets old friends, and listens to the world's most dangerous music.' |
| 10 | 'The Pirate Queen' | 'On the way home Odysseus loses his clothes but finds some friends.' |
| 11 | 'Beggar in the Rubbish Heap' | 'After 20 long years, Odysseus returns home. But no welcome awaits him . . .' |
| 12 | 'The Showdown' | 'If Odysseus wants to live happily ever after, one final heroic deed remains to be done.' |

influence the way the narrative was perceived by children. Overall, it added an improvised air to proceedings, so that Robinson's storytelling appeared genuine, without an autocue. However, this off-the-cuff effect was an illusion, and the scripting and filming had of course been carefully planned in advance. Bell acknowledges that the on-location

Figure 7.2 Tony Robinson narrates episode 10 of *Odysseus: The Greatest Hero of Them All* (1986). BBC.

shooting in Cornwall was intended to mirror in a contemporary way the historical locations of the story.⁴⁶ For example, Odysseus' departure from the young princess Nausicaa and the Phaeacians is shot on a small, idyllic Cornish quayside, against a background of a dry-stone building and rocky outcrop (see Figure 7.2).⁴⁷ In contrast, Robinson narrates Odysseus' approach to the suitor-infested palace of Ithaca from the site of a demolished building which is strewn with bent metal, broken concrete and an old traffic cone, while cars pass in the background. This visual variety aided children in interpreting the scene of Odysseus returning home to his dilapidated and downtrodden Ithaca while grounding this Odysseus in a contemporary English setting.

*Odysseus* provided a chronological narrative of Odysseus' adventures, starting from his childhood and the boar-hunt where he receives the scar on his thigh through the Trojan War to his return home and reunion with Penelope. Therefore, the flashback narrative of Homer is not retained but instead a linear structure is used that was easy for children unfamiliar with the adventures of Odysseus to follow. Whereas *Ulysses 31* presents its lead character as a hero whose manly stature and perfect physical features mark out his heroic status and cinematic appeal, Robinson and Curtis' *Odysseus* conjures up a more intelligent, tricky and deceitful character, more reminiscent of the Homeric Odysseus, which they mixed with a sense of humour and colloquial tone that make him instantly accessible to UK children. The visual setting too, of English towns, countryside and seaside locations, grounds this Odysseus firmly within UK space and culture. This is a truly anglicised Odysseus.

*Odysseus* garnered critical attention at the time. Messenger Davies' article for *The Listener* declares that 'Libraries would do well to stand by for a rush on Homer', although as Robinson's comments (below) reveal it is Homeric tradition rather than Homeric epic that *Odysseus* recasts for its child audience.[48] Notably, Messenger Davies attempts to contextualise *Odysseus* for the reader by contrasting it with Hollywood's 'Sword and Sandal' movies, a form of popular culture through which many children and adults may have experienced a visual depiction of the classical world. Messenger Davies outlining *Odysseus* through what it is not indicates how much it was breaking with convention in representing Homeric epic on screen. Indeed, the innovations of *Odysseus* may have contributed to it winning the Royal Television Society's award for Best Children's Programme, 1986.

Throughout the twelve episodes the narrative draws on a wide range of ancient and modern accounts of Odysseus' travels, not only Homer's epic poems. Indeed, the programme nowhere claims to be adapting Homer's *Odyssey*, although the book that followed the television series contains the following phrase amid the publishing details: 'The original stories are of course by Homer.'[49] This is perfectly true, and it gives prominence to the name 'Homer', but in fact a range of sources contributed to *Odysseus*, as Robinson himself explains in an article for *Books for Keeps: The Children's Book Magazine*:

> As well as the *Iliad* and the *Odyssey* we've used the play *Philoctetes*, and the *Oresteia*, Robert Graves, *The Anger of Achilles*, and the *Little Iliad* – about ten different sources in all. I don't think I've made anything up but I've run some characters together and sometimes I've trade[d] an explicit contemporary reference. Some scholars may get cross about that but for me that is what storytellers do and my retelling is part of a long cultural tradition.[50]

It is clear that Robinson's interest in storytelling is coupled with an interest in retelling the stories which originate in Homer, but Robinson goes on to acknowledge that changes must be made to make them accessible and inspirational to a child viewer of 1980s television:

> if in my telling I can make them a bit more accessible, democratising the references, finding contemporary resonances to illuminate things which were different 'then' but are related to 'now', then maybe there is a chance to open up the whole thing to more people.[51]

The child audiences of *Odysseus* were engaging with Homeric epic via Robinson's retelling in a way that touched the storytelling roots of Greek epic, which was performed to ancient audiences by a solo artist: the audiences were experiencing Homer as oral poetry, and Tony Robinson was playing the bard.

## CONCLUSION

*Ulysses 31* and *Odysseus* used their unique generic forms to contemporise Odysseus' adventures for young audiences and to push their respective television formats into new uncharted space. The manner in which this occurs also indicates how both programmes worked equally hard to engage closely with their Homeric sources and wider Greek mythology, reflecting the cultural significance that Homer's *Odyssey* was seen to possess. The makers of *Ulysses 31* crafted a hero using popular film culture and Japanese techniques in animation to frame Ulysses' heroism in a way that held international appeal. By contrast, Robinson and Curtis made their Odysseus accessible to UK audiences using colloquial English language and humour, and the BBC's format of *Jackanory*, familiar to UK viewers. This was set in recognisably English towns, countryside settings and seascapes that created a localised and anglicised Odysseus.

The tension between fidelity and innovation can be particularly fierce for the creators of children's television because of the concern among some programme-makers to inform and educate children about their own cultural heritage while creating enjoyable and inspiring works in their own right. *Ulysses 31* and *Odysseus* aspire to this. The freedom of animation for visualising fictional space (past or future) is apparent in *Ulysses 31* in its attempt to bring the stories of Odysseus to life, whereas in *Odysseus* Robinson takes on the role of the bard, employing the lively performance and innovative take on *Jackanory* to reanimate Odysseus with an English town and country setting as the backdrop. The creative approach of each programme was shaped by their divergent contexts of creation and production, by the different genres within which they worked, and by appealing to international (cinema and anime) and localised (BBC TV) conventions in visual media. Both programmes appeared on the screens of children who viewed Children's BBC in 1985–6, itself a new, more interactive format for children's programming. This provided first contact, or at least early contact, for children with the medium of television, animation and the adventures of Odysseus.

## PROGRAMMES DISCUSSED

*Theseus the Hero.* 4-part series for *Jackanory.* Prod. Angela Beeching. Dir. David Bell. BBC1. From Friday 11 January 1985, 4.15–4.30pm.

*Ulysses 31.* 26-part series. Prod. Jean Chalopin and Fujioka Yutaka. DiC Entertainment, France, and Tokyo Movie Shinsha, Japan. BBC1. From Thursday 7 November 1985, 4.30–4.55pm.

*Odysseus: The Greatest Hero of Them All.* 12-part series. Prod. Angela Beeching. Dir. David Bell. BBC1. From Thursday 13 November 1986, 4.20–4.35pm.

## NOTES

1. *Ulysses 31* was first broadcast on Children's BBC from 7 November 1985 to 8 May 1986 and *Odysseus* was first broadcast twice a week from 13 November ro 22 December 1986, and repeated from 11 October 1987 to 24 January 1988.
2. The term 'anglified' is used to highlight the choice of setting, performer and idiom used in the series, but the series was broadcast to audiences throughout Britain, which only serves to highlight the complex overlap of British and English identities.
3. E.g. Messenger Davies (1989, 2001, 2010); Steemers (2010, 2013, 2016).
4. E.g. the work of The Children's Media Foundation: <http://www.thechildrensmediafoundation.org> (accessed 6 July 2016), formerly Save Kid's TV; Home (2011) raises concerns about the quality of UK television output for children.
5. The notable exception to this is Hodge and Tripp (1986), who provided a theoretically informed, audience-based analysis of the children's cartoon *Fangface* (1978), arguing that such cartoons are complex structures which engage the child viewer on multiple levels as the viewers decode the cartoon visually, verbally and aesthetically. More recently Wells (2007: 201–2) has summarised his approach to theorising animation, which was first developed in his seminal 1998 monograph. The recent three-volume history of world animation by Bendazzi (2016) is another important step in scholarship on animation. On other forms of animation see Moseley (2016), who provides the first academic discussion of UK stop-frame animation 1961–74.
6. As Lindner (2008: 39) notes: 'The children's animation film may be among one [*sic*] of the most lucrative genres for studios worldwide, but so far this genre has been widely ignored in academic research dealing with classical topics.' See also Lindner (2017) and Castello and Scilabra (2015), who survey the connection of anime and classical antiquity but

play down the importance of *Ulysses 31* within this tradition. Even Ray Harryhausen, the animator on the films *Jason and the Argonauts* (dir. D. Chaffey, 1963) and *Clash of the Titans* (dir. D. Davis, 1981), was involved in an unrealised version of animating the stories of Odysseus: *The Story of Odysseus* (1996–8) for Carrington and Cosgrove Hall Productions. See Marciniak (2016) for an important volume on the growing scholarly interest in children's literature and classical antiquity.

7 Wrigley (2015a: 173–4) discusses Homeric storytelling on BBC radio, which also appeals to the audience's imagination although without the visual stimulus of television.

8 The BBC, a public service broadcaster, was created with the aim to 'inform, educate and entertain', and these words still form the BBC's mission statement at the time of writing in 2016: <http://www.bbc.co.uk/corporate2/insidethebbc/whoweare/mission_and_values> (accessed 6 July 2016).

9 News release for the launch of Children's BBC: <http://web.archive.org/web/20141106183544/http://www.thebroomcupboard.co.uk/page2.html> (accessed 6 July 2016).

10 Steemers (2016: 107).

11 Murnaghan (2011: 340).

12 'Ulysses' is the Latin name for the hero Odysseus, and the French is 'Ulysse', which, given the French origins of *Ulysses 31*, offers a plausible reason as to why the name Ulysses is maintained in the English-language versions, whereas the German and Greek version is retitled: *Odysseus 31*.

13 Homer, *Odyssey* 10.488–540: Circe explains the tortuous route home to Odysseus. Circe is more famous for turning Odysseus' men into pigs, an aspect which both *Ulysses 31* and *Odysseus* preserve when their hero meets the sorceress Circe.

14 In the case of cinematic film it is common to cite Lt Ellen Ripley (*Alien*, dir. R. Scott, 1979) or Sarah Connor (*The Terminator*, dir. J. Cameron 1984) as counter-examples; however, Conrad (2011) surveys the marginalised roles of female characters in the majority of science fiction film. As King and Krzywinska (2000: 40) note in their overview of female roles in sci-fi films: 'Space may offer an escape from many terrestrial limitations, but the "glass ceiling" usually remains in place.' On television of the 1970s–1980s the story is little different; the sci-fi series *Star Maidens* (1976, UK/West Germany) was notable for replacing patriarchy with matriarchy, but as a means to critique the contemporary feminist movement of the 1970s, as discussed by Sharp (2008). In British sci-fi television the dominance of male characters is reflected in Wright (2005), who surveys British sci-fi television while noting its engagement with contemporary political and social debates, but gives no consideration to feminist or gender debates, and mentions *Star Maidens* only in passing as 'a less successful SF-comedy series' (Wright 2005: 300).

15 Episode twenty-four 'Strange Meeting'. This episode is discussed below.
16 Homer, *Odyssey* 10.275–306.
17 During episode twelve, Telemachus looks at the ship containing the man from 2001 and says: 'I think I saw a model identical to this one in a museum on the exploration of the solar system.' Later we see Ulysses' reflection in a lens-like computer screen which immediately evokes HAL 9000.
18 Internet rumours circulate that a legal dispute resulted, but no evidence of this is forthcoming.
19 The French title ('Ulysses meets Ulysses') highlights the connection between the two Ulysses characters in the episode.
20 Homer, *Odyssey* 21.404–13; translation from Rieu (1991: 327).
21 On peplum movies see Aziza (1998) and Boschi and Bozzato (2005). Verreth (2008: 65) provides a survey of films about Odysseus, and he counts 'more than eighty titles from 1905 to the present'. Paul (2013b: 139–40) discusses the initial box-office success of *Ulisse*.
22 *Ulysses 31* also brought together Jean Chalopin and Bernard Deyriès, whose collaborations with Japanese animators produced defining cartoons of the 1980s. Best-known in the UK would be perhaps *Mysterious Cities of Gold* (also shown on Children's BBC), where Araki Shingo was again involved, as were the writers of the popular title music of both animations (except in Japan), Haim Saban and Shuki Levy.
23 The full series was not broadcast in Japan until 1991.
24 In the UK *Ulysses 31* was broadcast on BBC 1 (1985–6, at times between 4.10pm and 4.35pm), Channel 4 (1993, 6.30am), The Children's Channel (1994–5), The Disney Channel (1998–9), Fox Kids (1999), Jetix (2005–) and Toon Disney (2005–). Knowledge of rebroadcasts in other countries varies, but some information can be found currently on two websites, which also contain detailed records of the worldwide merchandising connected to *Ulysses 31*: <ulysse31.saitis.net/verse trang.htm#Index> and <simonin.pagesperso-orange.fr/Ulysse31> (both accessed 6 July 2016).
25 Krémer (2002). A DVD of one Soirée Gloubiboulga, including *Ulysse 31*, was released in 2003: *Gloubi Boulga Night* (Universal Pictures). Examples of Soirées Gloubiboulga include: 4 May 2002, Lille; 5 April 2003, Bordeaux; 14 June 2003, Grand Rex, Paris; 15 November 2003, Geneva.
26 Potter (2014). My thanks to Amanda Potter for allowing me to see the data underpinning her doctoral research. The five respondents comprised two female general viewers (i.e. not classicists), one fan of *Xena*, one female classicist (BA and MA in Ancient History), and one male 'partner of a classicist'. The data was collected between 2006 and 2011.
27 Nagahama is renowned for his work on the 'Romance Super Robot Trilogy' in the 1970s, but he was also a director on famous anime including *Versailles no Bara* (*Versailles Rose*, 1979) and *Star of the*

*Giants* (1968). Clements (2013: 143–4) discusses *Star of the Giants* for the ways that Nagahama and his animators employed new technologies in xerography: 'to transfer foreshortening, deformation, impressionistic speed lines and other artistic effects directly to their cels' (where a 'cel' is a transparent celluloid on which animators draw). These techniques were deployed in *Ulysses 31*.

28 Mecha anime focuses on robots and machines and involves detailed models of each, often related to toy manufacture.
29 Drouin (1981).
30 McCloud (2006: 215–23).
31 Ledoux and Ranney (1997: 3).
32 In Faviez (1996): 'Les japonais apportent un nouveau souffle par rapport à Disney ... j'ai été déçu par les USA. Les concepts y sont souvent les mêmes, trop manichéens.'
33 Bainbridge (2010: 78).
34 The French 'Thémis' is a transliteration of the Greek 'Themis', a goddess of ancient law and order.
35 Broadcasting Standards Commission survey. See Messenger Davies (2001: 233).
36 E.g. on 24 April 1986 a variety of *Ulysses 31* drawings are visible behind the presenter Debbie Flint, who also holds a further pile of pictures: <http://www.thebroomcupboard.co.uk/page2.html> (accessed 6 July 2016).
37 'Interview with Andi Peters', *Broom Cupboard: An Unofficial History of Children's BBC Presentation*: <http://www.thebroomcupboard.co.uk/page7.html> (accessed 6 July 2016).
38 Episode two 'The Burly Nun' and episode seven 'The Fat Batsman' are held on VHS by the BFI.
39 Robinson and Curtis (1986: 2, 1987: 4).
40 *Radio Times*, 3 January 1985, p. 91.
41 Graves (1981: 91).
42 Robinson and Curtis (1986: 2).
43 Home (1993: 80–5).
44 Author's interview with A. Beeching, 17 April 2015.
45 Author's interview with A. Beeching, 17 April 2015.
46 Author's interview with A. Beeching, 17 April 2015.
47 Homer, *Odyssey* 6.186–315: Nausicaa, daughter of King Alcinous, helps the shipwrecked Odysseus in gaining access to Alcinous' court, from where our hero finally manages to secure safe passage home to Ithaca.
48 Messenger Davies (1986: 30). In interview in 2015, Beeching acknowledged that *Jackanory* books encouraged children to obtain books from the library or to buy them.
49 Robinson and Curtis (1986: 2).
50 Robinson (1986).
51 Robinson (1986).

# 8 Greek Myth in the Whoniverse
## Amanda Potter

One of the first aims of *Doctor Who*, the iconic British science fiction television series targeted at children and family audiences, which aired on the BBC from 1963 to 1989 before going back into regular production from 2005, was to 'teach history' to young viewers.[1] Early serials from 1964, for example, included 'Marco Polo', 'The Aztecs' and 'The Romans'; episodes set in the past have continued, but the series soon moved away from these straightforward 'historical' episodes (where the only change to historical events was the presence of the Doctor and his companions), in favour of episodes where aliens have already intervened in the historical past, and the Doctor and his companions arrive to put things right.[2] No episode has featured a historical event or historical characters from ancient Greece, in the way that 'The Romans' features the Emperor Nero and the fire of Rome. Rather, Greek mythology has proved to be a more interesting prospect for *Who* writers, perhaps because its monsters (such as the Minotaur) can be reused and its heroes (such as Jason and Theseus) reinterpreted.[3]

In this chapter I examine all *Doctor Who* serials and episodes before 2016 based to some extent on Greek mythology, including episodes in the spin-off series *The Sarah Jane Adventures* and *Torchwood* that form part of the wider 'Whoniverse'. I discuss how different approaches have been taken over time by the creators of the series: for example, myth treated as history, as in 'The Myth Makers' (1965), where the Doctor travels back in time to the city of Troy; the use of mythic plotlines transposed into space, as in 'Underworld' (1978), where the voyage of Jason and the Argonauts is rewritten as the story of Jackson and his crew of the R1C spaceship; and the use of mythic monsters removed from their classical context, such as the appearance of a Siren on board a pirate ship in 'The Curse of the Black Spot' (2011). These episodes have not all been analysed together before, and the ensuing discussion traces shifts in the tastes of both producers and audiences over time. Although none of the episodes require background knowledge of Greek mythology to understand the *Doctor Who* stories, some knowledge is anticipated in the earlier episodes, and this knowledge greatly enhances the viewing experience, as certain plot twists and nuances would be lost on those without it. In later episodes less knowledge is expected, but those viewers who do have knowledge of the myths will still benefit from this in being able to compare ancient and modern treatments of monsters. I use feedback from viewers, obtained from BBC Audience Research Reports and from my own online research, to illustrate how viewers engage with the myth within the episodes.

## 'THE MYTH MAKERS': HOMERIC MYTH AS GREEK HISTORY

The first *Doctor Who* serial featuring Greek myth is 'The Myth Makers' (1965) from season three.[4] Written by Donald Cotton and featuring William Hartnell as the Doctor, this four-part serial, which has been described as a 'historical',[5] sends the Doctor and his companions back in time to the Bronze Age city of Troy. There has been popular interest in proving that the city made famous by Homer's *Iliad* actually existed since Heinrich Schliemann first excavated at Hisarlık in Turkey in the late nineteenth century.[6] By 1965 there was ample archaeological evidence to support Troy's existence: for example, in the early 1960s the findings were published of Carl Blegen's excavations in the 1930s.[7] The BBC archives hold a document entitled 'Historical Facts Surrounding the Trojan War', which includes a list of 'books of reference used' and notes 'gleaned from the various works': the writer is interested in the origins of the names used by Homer, geography, customs and potential motivations for war.[8] Although the document has no name attached to it, the author is likely to have been Cotton himself. The ten books listed include Chester G. Starr's *The Origins of Greek Civilisation* (1961) and M. I. Finley's *The World of Odysseus* (1954), both important books of their time (still in print today), drawing on archaeological and historical evidence of Bronze Age Greece. Before working on *Doctor Who*, Cotton had written radio plays based on Greek myth for BBC

Radio's Third Programme, so 'The Myth Makers' is in keeping with his broader interests, but in this serial he is working in a different tradition: that of emphasising the historicity of Troy.[9]

All four episodes of 'The Myth Makers' are lost, but fans have reconstructed the serial using an audio recording, stills and found footage. The Doctor and his companions Vicki and Steven travel to Troy ten years into the Trojan War (the moment when Homer's *Iliad* is set) and the Doctor witnesses Hector's fight with Achilles. On stepping out of the TARDIS the Doctor distracts Hector, who, having just denied the existence of Zeus, king of the Olympian gods, believes the Doctor himself to be the god. This provides Achilles with the chance to run Hector through with his sword. Thus, in this version, the Doctor inadvertently causes Hector's death. The Doctor quickly adopts the guise of Zeus, referring to the TARDIS as his travelling temple. In the *Iliad* a god (Athena) did intervene to help Achilles kill Hector;[10] in 'The Myth Makers' the story is rationalised, with an alien (the Doctor) taking the place of a god. The Doctor participates in the mythological action. Under house arrest and attempting to secure his release, the Doctor, undertaking an advisory role, as illustrated by one of the surviving stills (see Figure 8.1), suggests to Odysseus that he should build a wooden horse to allow the Greeks to enter the enemy city, a stratagem that was initially rejected by the Doctor when his companion Steven proposed it: 'the whole story is obviously absurd. Probably invented by Homer as some good dramatic device. No, I think it would be completely impractical.' The Doctor thus becomes the architect of the device he was initially dubious about and brings an end to the Trojan War.

In the 'Historical Facts' document, the writer grapples with what is perceived to be the lack of historicity in the wooden horse story:

> The wooden horse is almost certainly complete myth... However I feel that it is legitimate that Doctor Who himself could suggest the idea of the wooden horse (i.e. a forerunner of the siege engine) to the Greek armies, so long as he lets them know that in years to come somebody will write about just such an incident.[11]

The problem of what to do with the Trojan Horse arises out of the requirement to rationalise the Trojan War story, making this more plausible for viewers, within the fictional world presented. The writer wants to bring in the Trojan Horse as a narrative detail that the viewer familiar with the story might expect to see, even though he does not believe that the horse actually existed. He uses this as an example of a time-travel paradox: the Doctor suggests it because he read about it in Homer and it appears in Homer because the Doctor suggested it. Cotton therefore blends history and myth together by making the Doctor both the consumer and inventor of the Trojan Horse story.

# Greek Myth in the Whoniverse

Figure 8.1 The Doctor offers advice to the Greek generals at Troy in 'The Myth Makers' (1965). BBC. (<http://whobackwhen.com/c020-myth-makers>, accessed 18 August 2017)

At the end of the serial Priam and Paris have been killed by the Greeks and Odysseus takes Cassandra as a 'personal present' for Agamemnon, as in ancient versions of the story. Vicki, who has taken the name Cressida, stays behind with Troilus, with whom she has fallen in love: a Trojan and a character from the twenty-fifth century therefore become the lovers from the medieval Romance tradition in Chaucer and Shakespeare.[12] When they are approached by Troilus' cousin Aeneas, Vicki realises that 'with your cousin's help we can build another Troy'. The intervention of the Doctor and his companions again results in a scenario that broadly follows the ancient tradition, with Aeneas surviving to found a new city as in Virgil's *Aeneid*. Cotton may well have anticipated some level of pre-knowledge amongst a proportion of his audience: certainly, viewers who knew the *Iliad*, the *Aeneid* and *Troilus and Cressida* (or their stories) are likely to have had an enriched experience.

Historian Matthew Kilburn suggests that Cotton's historical *Doctor Who* serials, 'The Mythmakers' and 'The Gunfighters' (set in the American Wild West, 1966), attempt to 'subvert audience expectations'.[13] However, ultimately expectations are met for viewers who know how the story of the Trojan War traditionally ends. The ending of the serial paves the way for unlikeable characters Cassandra, who wanted to have Vicki burned as a witch, and Agamemnon, who has initiated the war through greed, to meet their untimely deaths in Mycenae. Meanwhile Aeneas and the Trojan survivors, including likeable characters Vicki/Cressida and Troilus, begin a journey that, for viewers who know the *Aeneid*, results in the founding of Rome. Knowledgeable viewers can be satisfied that characters who are shown to be 'bad' in the serial will be killed and the 'good' characters survive (although this is a departure from the tragic ending for Troilus and Cressida in Chaucer and Shakespeare).

The British television audience of 1965 might have been familiar with the Trojan War story from a range of sources, primarily BBC radio programmes broadcast in the 1950s and 1960s, Herbert Wise's film *Helen of Troy* (1956) and children's story books featuring the myths (for example, books by Roger Lancelyn Green published by Penguin).[14] This is in addition to information that, for some, would have been picked up at school, in a period when Greek and Latin was taught in grammar schools.[15] Writers of early *Doctor Who* could tell stories that, according to novelist Daniel O'Mahony, demand a 'previewed familiarity on the part of the audience'.[16]

Two Audience Research Reports exist in the BBC archives covering the first and last episodes of 'The Myth Makers'. The report for 'Temple of Secrets' (16 October 1965, 5.50–6.15pm) finds that it held 'scant appeal for a substantial number of the sample'; the majority preferred science fiction stories.[17] Similar findings were recorded in the report on 'Horse of Destruction' (6 November 1965, 5.50–6.15pm): one viewer considered that 'potted classics and *Doctor Who* do not go together'; but another found the episode to be 'a daring bit of fiddling with history, but surely as informative as it was entertaining'.[18] A schoolboy (who, as a young viewer, was part of the target audience for the series) stated 'these episodes appeal to me because of the Greek-Trojan War'; he found the story 'superb'. Together these comments attest to the prior knowledge of at least some of the viewers, although this led to mixed results. At any rate, the Reaction Index for each episode measured 48 and 52/100 respectively, close to the average *Doctor Who* score of 53.

## MYTHIC FANTASY AND 'PSEUDO-HISTORICAL' SERIALS

Viewer ratings were not greatly worse for historicals than for science fiction stories, but historical serials had fallen out of favour by the late 1960s, and were largely replaced by 'pseudo-historicals' in which aliens infiltrate and manipulate the past for their own gains.[19] An early example is 'The Time Meddler' (1965), where the title character attempts to destroy the Vikings in 1066, preventing the battle of Stamford Bridge and thus helping King Harold and the Saxons to win the battle of Hastings – an important episode from English history that would have been known to many young viewers. This approach to the past is evident in the next *Doctor Who* serials to feature elements from Greek myth: 'The Mind Robber' (1968), a fantasy serial starring Patrick Troughton, and 'The Time Monster' (1972), starring Jon Pertwee and set on earth and in Atlantis.

In 'The Mind Robber', the Doctor and his companions Zoe and Jamie encounter mythic and fairy-tale characters – including Lemuel Gulliver from *Gulliver's Travels*, Rapunzel, a unicorn, a Minotaur and Medusa – in a void outside of space and time.[20] When the trio find themselves in a maze, the Doctor states that a ball of twine is 'the classical way of getting through a maze'. At the centre of the maze a Minotaur starts to attack the Doctor and Zoe, but when they state that 'the Minotaur is a mythical beast', it disappears. Meanwhile, Jamie, who is in a castle, sees a tickertape machine labelled 'work in progress': he reads on it, 'The Doctor and Zoe were face to face with Medusa. One glance from her eyes would turn them to stone.' As Jamie reads, the Doctor and Zoe find a statue of Medusa that is starting to come to life. It is as if an unseen writer is, in the moment, directing the action by writing about it. Zoe is initially afraid of Medusa; the Doctor remembers that Perseus used his 'polished shield' to see the Gorgon's reflection and avoid being turned to stone. When Zoe looks at Medusa's reflection in a mirror, the Doctor says 'there's no danger in the reflection' and Medusa becomes a statue again. The Doctor and his companions finally find out that the fictional world is being created by a kidnapped writer known as the Master of Fiction (not the Master who is the Doctor's arch-enemy in the later serial 'The Time Monster', discussed below), controlled by a computer and enforced by robots. Once the Doctor overloads the computer, the fictional world is destroyed, and the Doctor, his companions and the writer escape to the TARDIS.

The Doctor and Zoe survive because they know their Greek mythology, using twine to navigate the labyrinth and the mirror to vanquish Medusa. On the tickertape, Jamie reads from 'Legends of Ancient Greece', words that are suggestive of children's books featuring the stories of Theseus and the Minotaur and Perseus and Medusa: the sort of book that the young *Doctor Who* audience might be familiar with. According to the Audience Research Report for the fifth and final episode of 'The Mind Robber' (12 October 1968, 5.20–5.40pm) some 'older' children 'welcomed this adventure as "one of the best ideas ever thought of in this series"', perhaps responding to the interesting idea that the characters can write their own stories.[21] However, the report found that many adult respondents thought the episode 'far-fetched' and 'silly'.

'The Time Monster' bears more similarities to 'The Myth Makers' than to the fantasy serial 'The Mind Robber', since the Doctor and his companion travel back to the legendary island of Atlantis that is submerged in the Atlantic Ocean in Plato's *Timaeus* and *Critias*, but in this episode it is treated as a historical place.[22] No reading list survives in the archives for this (or for later episodes featuring Greek myth), but it is clear that research into Minoan culture and archaeology on the island of Thera (modern Santorini) had been undertaken by writers Robert Sloman and Barry Letts and designer Tim Gleeson. The city of Atlantis is decorated with Minoan-style wall paintings and includes a prominent life-sized statue of a snake goddess – a famous Minoan motif since Arthur Evans discovered a small figurine of a bare-breasted woman holding snakes when excavating Knossos in 1903.[23] The episode starts with the Doctor's assistant, Jo Grant, referring to a map of Thera and saying to the Doctor that she has read in the newspaper that the island is 'believed by many modern historians to be all that remains of Plato's metropolis Atlantis'. (Excavations of the Minoan site of Akrotiri on Santorini took place from 1967 to 1974 and around this time *The Times* and *The Guardian* published articles linking Atlantis with Santorini.[24]) For the benefit of Captain Mike Yates, a member of UNIT (United Nations Intelligence Taskforce, a military organisation working with the Doctor), Jo elaborates: 'apparently it was part of the Minoan civilisation. Oh you know, the Minotaur and all that Cretan jazz.' Although both the Doctor and Jo joke that she is not very clever, Jo is actually very bright and educated. When the Doctor says to the Brigadier that 'perhaps a classical education would have helped' him to decipher that the Doctor's arch-enemy the Master is hiding behind the pseudonym Professor Thascalos, it is Jo who picks up the clue, saying, 'Thascalos is Greek for Master.'

The six-part serial finally reaches Atlantis in episode five: there, they meet the Minotaur who guards the crystal that can be used to summon the Chronovore Kronos, a creature who feeds on time. (His name comes from the Greek Titan who was overthrown as leader of the gods by his son Zeus.[25]) The Minotaur is a man with the strength of a bull, yet he is easily defeated by being pushed through a wall, showing that he is an inferior adversary when compared with Kronos or the Master. Atlantis is then quickly destroyed by Kronos with a few flicks of his wings. As in 'The Myth Makers', where the Doctor causes the destruction of Troy, in 'The Time Monster' the intervention of the Master causes the destruction of Atlantis.

The Audience Research Report for the final episode reveals that viewers' reactions were again mixed. As with the reports for 'The Mind Robber' some viewers felt that *Doctor Who* was running out of new ideas (the series had been running for over eight years by 1972 when 'The Time Monster' was broadcast). The continued use, since 1971, of the Master as the evil villain who always managed to escape is likely to have led to the comments that the series had become 'predictable':

> Some, certainly, enjoyed this imaginative and enjoyable fantasy about the possible fate of the fabled city of Atlantis, which had some tense moments, but, on the whole it was felt to reflect the general 'tiredness' of the series, several dismissing it as 'absolute rubbish'.[26]

## MYTHIC THEMES IN SPACE

The late 1970s, when Graham Williams produced *Doctor Who* with Tom Baker as the Doctor, was an era filled with episodes set in space. The serials featuring Greek myth from this period, 'Underworld' (1978) and 'The Horns of Nimon' (1979–80), transpose the stories of Jason and Theseus onto other planets. Both these serials use naming clues to point to the mythical story that is being paralleled. So 'Underworld' features the characters Jackson, Herrick, Orfe and Tala (Jason, Heracles, Orpheus and Atalanta) on a quest to find the spaceship P7E (Persephone), and in 'The Horns of Nimon' a group of young people including the young man Seth (Theseus) from planet Aneth (Athens) are sent as tribute to Skonnos (Knossos) where they will face the Nimon (Minotaur) and Soldeed (Dedelos/Daedelus). Although these names are not direct anagrams of their counterparts in Greek mythology the links are obvious enough for some viewers, at least, to decipher them easily. A third serial, 'The Armageddon Factor' (1979), uses a science fiction take on the Trojan Horse to bring a resolution to a war between two planets, again combining classical names (Atrios/Atreus, Zeos/Zeus) and a myth-inspired plot. Williams justifies the way in which Greek myth is used in these episodes as follows:

For those who knew it, it would mean something; for those who didn't, it wouldn't detract anything. I think if the story had depended on knowing ... the original myth and legend, then it would have been too 'in' – it would have been a bad thing. But as a story I think ['Underworld'] stands up on its own ... Then if you know about the original, you get the bonus of the 'P7E'.[27]

Science fiction and fantasy writer and academic Colin Harvey suggests further that 'the emotional intensity of the episode is likely to be different if the viewer does have prior knowledge of the mythic structures informing the program'.[28]

In 'Underworld', the TARDIS materialises on board the spaceship the R1C and the Doctor and his companion Leela meet the crew of four Minyans, who have been on a quest for 'a hundred thousand years' to find the genetic race bank for their species which was on board the lost spaceship the P7E (Persephone, queen of the ancient Greek underworld). Crash landing on a planet that has formed around the P7E, they find that the Minyans' descendants have been enslaved, and that the golden cylinders containing the race bank are held by the Oracle who has enslaved them, supported by beings called 'the Seers of the realm of Hedas' (Hades, the ancient Greek underworld). The Oracle attempts to destroy Jackson and his crew by giving them bombs disguised as cylinders; the Doctor, deducing that they have been tricked, helps the Minyans to escape to their new home, Minos II (named after the mythical king of Crete).

At the end of the episode, the Doctor refers to Jackson as Jason – just in case the viewer has not understood the connection between the character and the ancient Greek hero. Leela asks why and the Doctor states: 'Jason was another captain on a long quest', 'looking for the Golden Fleece'. Leela asks if Jason found it; the Doctor replies, 'Yes. He found it hanging on a tree at the end of the world. Perhaps those myths are not just old stories of the past, you see, but prophecies of the future. Who knows?' K9, the Doctor's robotic dog, says 'Negative', suggesting that the Doctor is wrong in this assertion. Earlier in the episode the Doctor had told Leela that 'myths often have a grain of truth in them, if you know where to look', a premise that is taken up in more recent episodes of *Doctor Who* and *The Sarah Jane Adventures* (namely, 'The God Complex' and 'Eye of the Gorgon', discussed below), in which a Minotaur and a Gorgon are found to be aliens, transforming Greek myth into reality in the Whoniverse.

In 'The Armageddon Factor', the Doctor and his companion and fellow Time Lord Romana are seeking the sixth and final piece of the Key to Time on planet Atrios, which is at war with neighbouring

Zeos. Beyond the resonances of these names, noted above, and the involvement of a princess who wants to end the war (known as Astra, the Latin word for 'stars', but representing Helen of Troy), further classical allusion is postponed until the sixth and final part of the serial. The Doctor, aided by Time Lord Drax, asks, 'Did you ever get to Troy, Drax? Little place in Asia Minor.' The Doctor and Drax have been accidentally reduced in size, allowing them to hide inside K9 and reach the lair of the evil Shadow, who is also trying to obtain the Key. Undetected within the metal dog, they jump out, restore themselves to full size, retrieve the sixth piece of the Key from the Shadow and escape. The use of the Trojan Horse trick here demonstrates how *Doctor Who* not only re-uses Greek myth, but also re-uses Greek myth as created by the Doctor himself – the inventor of the Trojan Horse in 'The Myth Makers' – although this may only be recognised by long-standing fans with an eye for detail.

'The Horns of Nimon' follows the model of 'Underworld' by setting a story from Greek mythology, that of Theseus slaying the Minotaur, in space. In the *Doctor Who* serial the Doctor and Romana go to the planet Skonnos, where the leader Soldeed is working with the Nimon, a horned monster. The Doctor and Romana find a group of young prisoners, or 'Tribute', who will be sacrificed to the Nimon, a monster that survives by draining the life from those sacrificed, in the labyrinth-like power complex on Skonnos. The prisoners include a girl, Teka, and a boy, Seth, who, according to Teka, 'is going to destroy the Nimon and take us home in triumph. His father is keeping a lookout so that he can have a welcome party ready.' With help from Romana, Seth defeats the Nimon and Soldeed. K9 helps the Doctor, Romana and Teka to find their way out of the labyrinth, a more modern navigation device than the traditional ball of string, and Teka and Seth leave Skonnos on board another spaceship. However, Seth forgets to paint the spaceship white before returning home, meaning that his father will think that the black ship signifies that Seth has been unsuccessful, just as Theseus forgets to change his black sails, mistakenly signifying his death to his waiting father Aegeus, which leads to Aegeus' suicide.[29] Seth's father's suicide is not shown, but those familiar with the myth will understand the implications.

Literary scholar David Rafer identifies a key diversion from Greek myth in 'The Horns of Nimon', in which the Minotaur is the offspring not of Pasiphae and a bull but of an alien.[30] This change is unsurprising for a family television show: in the Minotaur's earlier and later incarnations in *Doctor Who* episodes 'The Mind Robber', 'The Time Monster' and 'The God Complex', the Minotaur is, respectively, a fictional character, a man transformed by the Titan Kronos and an alien; he is never the product of bestiality. For Rafer, the species of Nimon 'symbolise technology and power under bestial control', with the bestial aspect 'translated ... through the Nimon's corruption of human bodies when drawing away the life forces of the sacrifices'.[31] The Nimon species is positioned as a monstrous race to be destroyed. Even though the Nimon's planet is dying, the viewer's sympathy is with the young people being sacrificed.

## GREEK MYTH IN NEW *WHO* SPIN-OFFS: MYTHIC CREATURES IN MODERN CONTEXTS

When *Doctor Who* returned to television screens in 2005, with Russell T. Davies as executive producer and lead writer, the series included a number of 'pseudo-historical' episodes in which the Doctor and his companion(s) travel back in time to combat aliens existing on earth in the past. Notable early examples include 'The Unquiet Dead' (series one, episode three, first broadcast on 9 April 2005), set in nineteenth-century Cardiff, where alien creatures are taking over human bodies; and 'The Girl in the Fireplace' (series two, episode four, 6 May 2006), in which clockwork androids pursue Madame de Pompadour in eighteenth-century France. The ancient world was later visited by David Tennant as the Doctor and his companion Donna in 'The Fires of Pompeii' (series four, episode two, 12 April 2008),[32] but during the Davies era (2005–10) no episodes featured plots or characters from Greek history or mythology. However, during this period Greek myth was used in episodes of spin-off series for children *The Sarah Jane Adventures* and the adult-orientated *Torchwood*. In 'Greeks Bearing Gifts' (*Torchwood*, series one, episode seven, 26 November 2006), an alien likens herself to the marooned Philoctetes in order to gain the trust of a member of the Torchwood team, and in 'Eye of the Gorgon' (*The Sarah Jane Adventures*, series one, episodes three and four, 1 and 8 October 2007) an alien who can turn people to stone is discovered disguised as a nun.

'Greeks Bearing Gifts' mixes two elements from the Trojan War: the Trojan Horse conceit that what appears to be a gift can actually be a curse; and the character of the archer Philoctetes, best known from Sophocles' eponymous tragedy and representative of someone deserted in a foreign place. In this episode, the analyst Toshiko finds love for a brief time in a relationship with an alien in human guise, known as Mary. Approaching Toshiko in a bar, Mary gives her the precious gift of a pendant that allows the wearer to read people's thoughts. This pendant, like the bow of Philoctetes that his former comrades need to end the Trojan War, is something very special. It also recalls the Trojan Horse and the warning from the priest Laocoön that the Greeks should not be trusted, even if they bring gifts (the well-known saying from Virgil's *Aeneid*, 2.49, alluded to in the episode's title). Mary's gift also appears innocent, but she uses it to gain the trust of Toshiko in order to get access to the Torchwood hub where the transportation device that could help her to leave earth is kept. Mary likens herself to Philoctetes: she is an alien marooned on a foreign planet just as the archer was marooned on Lemnos. Toshiko feels empathy for Mary, a 'political prisoner' who was 'just left' on earth, 'forgotten' by her species. But Mary is a murderer who has survived on earth by killing humans and eating their hearts. Rather than returning Mary to her home planet, Torchwood's team leader Jack Harkness sends her into the sun – to her death. Toshiko destroys the pendant, ultimately deciding that it is too powerful: not a gift after all, but 'a curse'.

'Eye of the Gorgon' is an entertaining two-part episode from the first season of *The Sarah Jane Adventures*, originally broadcast in the Children's BBC early evening television slot in 2007. The young protagonists Maria, Luke and Clyde find a Gorgon hiding in an abbey, where nuns protect her. The Gorgon, an alien creature, has the power to turn humans to stone by looking at them. She is trying to bring the rest of her race to earth where they will take human hosts. This is a familiar *Doctor Who* narrative used with a diverse range of aliens, most famously with the cyborg species the Daleks and the Cybermen, but also in 'The Horns of Nimon', discussed above. The Gorgon first needs a new human host for herself and she chooses Sarah Jane, erstwhile companion to the Doctor and mentor to the children. Sarah Jane realises the creature is a Gorgon but, when she explains this to Maria, the girl is initially sceptical:

Maria: A Gorgon, all snakes for hair and turning people to stone just by looking at it? It's a fairy story, isn't it?
Sarah Jane: A myth, a Greek myth. There's a big difference. And incidentally, for future reference, Maria, even some fairy tales have a foundation in fact.

This explicitly replays the theme from earlier episodes of *Doctor Who* that stories from Greek myth are based on fact in the Whoniverse. The appearance of the Gorgons is rationalised within the world of *Doctor Who*, where aliens exist but where fantastical Greek monster and gods do not, by making them into alien beings with the power to turn humans to stone. This idea that stories from Greek mythology (and also the stories from *Doctor Who*) have a basis in fact adds realism to the series. The episode draws on Ovid's *Metamorphoses* in relating the story that the Gorgon Medusa was once beautiful, but omits other information which would be unsuitable for a young audience: for example, that after being raped by Poseidon in Athena's temple Medusa was turned into a monster.[33] Sarah Jane goes to a book rather than to her super-computer, Mr Smith, for information on the Gorgon. Obtaining information about monsters from books is a popular trope in fantasy television series, including *Buffy the Vampire Slayer* (1997–2003) and *Charmed* (1998–2006): in a series aimed at younger viewers it could be interpreted as an encouragement to read more, including the tie-in books written to accompany the series. Later on in the episode a book in the abbey library leads the children to a secret passage, showing that knowledge obtained from books can have a practical application. And Sarah Jane is ultimately saved by Maria, who, like Perseus in the book, uses a mirror to deflect the blue lights from the Gorgon's eyes that would have turned Sarah Jane to stone. The Gorgon is turned to stone instead. This series appears to be teaching the myth to children, returning perhaps to the educational purpose of early *Doctor Who*. The episode writer Phil Ford also wrote the 2007 tie-in novel in which he includes more details of the story of Perseus and Medusa, furthering this potentially educational dimension.[34]

## GREEK MYTHIC CREATURES IN MODERN CONTEXTS

When Steven Moffat took over from Davies as executive producer and lead writer in 2010 – with Matt Smith as the Doctor and Amy and Rory as companions – four episodes across seasons five and six incorporated strands of Greek myth: in 'The Pandorica Opens' (series five, episode twelve, 19 June 2010) and 'The Big Bang' (series five, episode thirteen, 26 June 2010) Pandora's Box is a weapon of mass destruction; 'The Curse of the Black Spot' (series six, episode three, 7 May 2011) features a Siren; and 'The God Complex' (series six, episode eleven, 17 September 2011) includes a Minotaur. These episodes include ancient Greek objects and monsters but are themselves divorced from ancient Greece.

Steven Moffat wrote both 'The Pandorica Opens' and 'The Big Bang', a complicated time-travel story that ends the season story arc about cracks appearing in time. Moffat uses the childhood reading list of the Doctor's companion Amy ('The Story of Roman Britain' and 'The Legend of Pandora's Box') to create the background against which her fiancé Rory becomes an immortal Roman soldier, and the Pandorica (Pandora's Box) is created by the Doctor's enemies as a prison in which to trap him. In these episodes, Pandora's Box has propensity for both evil and good, just as in Hesiod's *Works and Days* (94–8) Pandora opens a jar, letting evils into the world, but hope remains in the bottom. In the *Doctor Who* episodes, the Pandorica is used as a prison for the Doctor, but also as a means to save Amy, who has been shot in the past and must be preserved until she can be restored to life in the present, using a scan of her DNA.

'The Curse of the Black Spot' is a pirate story that includes a Siren, a female monster from Greek mythology (best-known from the *Odyssey* 12.165–200) who lured sailors to their deaths by attracting them with her beautiful singing. The Siren appears from the sea or from other shiny surfaces, charms the sick or injured with her music, puts a black spot on their hands and causes them to disappear. Eventually, the Siren is revealed to be not a monster preying on crew, but a holographic doctor, a sympathetic character who uses music to anaesthetise the sick and injured before treating them in her spaceship's sick room; she leaves a black spot when she takes a tissue sample.

In 2011, I conducted online research to understand fans' reactions to this episode and 'The God Complex'. Via a survey posted on fan websites, I found that many respondents (mostly women, aged 18–35) liked the twist that made the Siren into a good character (90 per cent of the 86 respondents had heard of the Siren before watching).[35] One commented: 'interesting character. We thought she was an evil being, killing men. Instead, she was saving them. This is in complete contrast to the traditional, mythological Sirens who lured men to their deaths on the rocks.' The myth of the Sirens was adapted to create a more positive female character, playing to a feminist agenda, and this worked for some fans. For others, however, the depiction fell far short of reclaiming this female monster for feminism: 'a Siren without a voice – a Siren's defining characteristic? And yet another female character without the ability to speak for herself? ... Badly done.' These views of fans provide an insightful and critical analysis, even if they are not statistically scalable.

If 'The Curse of the Black Spot' is essentially a pirate episode that happens to include a Siren, then 'The God Complex' is an episode about a maze-like hotel that happens to contain a Minotaur. Speaking of 'The God Complex' in *Doctor Who Confidential* (BBC2, 17 September 2011), the writer Toby Whithouse confirms that the Minotaur was not the initial idea behind the story:

I developed [the idea] from a one-line pitch from Steven [Moffat]: 'The Doctor and Amy are stranded in a hotel, and the corridors and rooms keep shifting, so that they're completely lost'. As a kid I loved reading the Greek myths. It's a theme I've alluded to in previous things I've written ... So when we started discussing what monster might lurk at the heart of this maze, I immediately thought of the Minotaur, the monstrous half man half bull from the legend of Theseus. In that story, the Minotaur is presented with tributes, sacrifices, and again that was something I wanted to employ for this story.

The Doctor and his companions are in a hotel in space, full of rooms that contain whatever represents the deepest fears of the guests. A monster hunts the guests one by one. As more fall victim, they begin to worship the monster, saying 'Praise him.' The monster turns out to be a Minotaur, trapped in a prison disguised as a hotel, feeding on people with a strong belief system – including Amy, who has a strong belief in the Doctor. Amy asks, 'Is it a Minotaur, or an alien, or an alien Minotaur?' The Doctor reveals that the Minotaur, a 'distant cousin of the Nimon', was a member of a race that invaded planets: they set themselves up as gods to be worshipped, but were eventually dispelled. The reference to Nimon establishes a continuity between new *Who* and the 'The Horns of Nimon' in the classic series: *Doctor Who* is creating its own mythology by using Greek mythology.

By persuading Amy that he was not worthy of her faith, the Doctor is able to 'sever the food supply', giving the Minotaur 'space to die'. As it dies the Minotaur draws a comparison with the Doctor, who is also an 'ancient creature with the blood of innocents on his hands drifting through space, to whom death would be a gift'. The Minotaur is treated sympathetically, as an isolated being and a reluctant killer that wants to die, and the comparison with the Doctor, as the Minotaur dies in the Doctor's arms, deepens our sympathy, compared with the unsympathetic Nimon in 'The Horns of Nimon'.

Around half of those who completed the survey liked the use of the Minotaur (and 98 per cent of the 100 respondents had heard of the Minotaur before watching).[36] Others thought that the Minotaur 'felt a bit shoe-horned in', 'a bit of an afterthought' and 'could have been any old space monster', or that the Minotaur was under-utilised: 'they could have done so much more with it'. Whithouse had also been the writer of the *Torchwood* episode 'Greeks Bearing Gifts', and the story of Philoctetes there could similarly be seen as 'shoehorned in'. As one respondent in my viewer research commented, 'I didn't feel the allegory contributed at all, it felt layered on for the non sci fi audience'; another considered that 'the myth felt tacked on: a lazy writer's way to make a script look "intellectual"'.[37]

In both 'The God Complex' and 'The Curse of the Black Spot', Greek mythological monsters are made sympathetic or (as with the Siren) cast in a positive light. This strategy is different from the use of the Minotaur in 'The Time Monster' and 'The Horns of Nimon', where it was a thing to be destroyed by the Doctor and his companions. In the preface to a book on *Monster Theory* Jeffrey Jerome Cohen writes that we need monsters so that we can name what we cannot understand and domesticate what threatens us.[38] In *Doctor Who*, the classical monsters are not only named, but rationalised and then either domesticated or destroyed, or both, so that they are no longer a threat. Even Pandora's Box, a potential weapon of mass destruction, can be used to save first Amy and then the universe. In the later episodes, it is noteworthy that all the necessary background information about the monster is included: viewers are not expected to have any previous knowledge of the Greek myths.

## CONCLUSION

Tony Keen has commented that '*Doctor Who* has, almost from the beginning, reflected story rather than history.'[39] At the end of the comedic pseudo-historical episode 'Robot of Sherwood' (series eight, episode three, 6 September 2014), Robin Hood tells the Doctor (Peter Capaldi) that 'history is a burden; stories can make us fly'. What is, or is not, the truth about Robin Hood does not really matter, as long as the story told is a good one. John-Nathan Turner, *Doctor Who* producer (1980–9), considered that 'some of those mythic stories are terrific' and 'if it's a good story, use it'.[40] The use of Greek myth in *Doctor Who* has changed over time, from the historical treatment in 'The Myth Makers' to the use of mythic themes in space in the 1970s and to the treatment in new *Who*, where classical monsters the Minotaur and the Siren are taken out of the ancient Greek world and made sympathetic and (with Pandora's Box) integral to a complex story arc. The Minotaur has been re-used four times, as a fictional monster, as a transformed man, and twice as an alien creature. In 'The Horns of Nimon' Seth is a young protagonist, and in 'The God Complex' Matt Smith is a young-looking Doctor: despite the latter's longevity both stand in for the youthful hero Theseus, a character young viewers would be able to relate to in terms of age.

As my research into fans' reactions reveals, *Doctor Who* fans who responded to the survey tended to have an interest in and pre-knowledge of Greek myth. The new *Who* episodes do not require knowledge of the myths, but this can provide an additional layer of meaning as it did for viewers in earlier decades. Some viewers even engage with *Doctor Who* and Greek myth by writing fan fiction of their own.[41] *Doctor Who* writers, both commercial and amateur, return to Greek myth for inspiration in the creation of entertaining stories and for monsters that can be reinvented for new audiences. With an upsurge in interest in Greek mythology among young readers, thanks to the popular *Percy Jackson* series of novels by Rick Riordan, and to films like *Clash of the Titans* (dir. L. Letterier, 2010) and *Hercules* (dir. B. Ratner, 2014), it is expected that this trend will continue in the years to come.

## PROGRAMMES DISCUSSED

*Doctor Who*. Season 3, serial 2: 'The Myth Makers' (4 parts). Prod. John Wiles. Dir. Michael Leeston-Smith. BBC1. From Saturday 16 October 1965, 5.50–6.15pm.

*Doctor Who*. Season 6, serial 2, 'The Mind Robber' (5 parts). Prod. Peter Bryant. Dir. David Maloney. BBC1. From Saturday 14 September 1968, 5.20–5.40pm.

*Doctor Who*. Season 9, serial 5, 'The Time Monster' (6 parts). Prod. Barry Letts. Dir. Paul Bernard. BBC1. From 20 May 1972, 5.50–6.15pm.

*Doctor Who*. Season 15, serial 5, 'Underworld' (4 parts). Prod. Graham Williams. Dir. Norman Stewart. BBC1. From Saturday 7 January 1978, 6.25–6.50pm.

*Doctor Who*. Season 16, serial 6, 'The Armageddon Factor' (6 parts). Prod. Graham Williams. Dir. Michael Hayes. BBC1. From Saturday 20 January 1979, 6.25–6.50pm.

*Doctor Who*. Season 17, serial 5, 'The Horns of Nimon' (4 parts). Prod. Graham Williams. Dir. Kenny McBain. BBC1. From Saturday 22 December 1979, 6.10–6.35pm.

*Torchwood*. Series 1, episode 7, 'Greeks Bearing Gifts'. Dir. Colin Teague. BBC2. Sunday 26 November 2006, 9.00–9.50pm.

*The Sarah Jane Adventures*. Series 1, episodes 3–4 ('Eye of the Gorgon'). Exec. Prod. Phil Collinson, Russell T. Davies and Julie Gardner. Dir. Alice Troughton. Prod. Matthew Bouch. CBBC. Thursday 1 October 2007, 5.00–5.25pm; Thursday 8 October 2007, 5.00–5.25pm.

*Doctor Who*. Series 4, episode 2, 'The Fires of Pompeii'. Prod. Phil Collinson. Dir. Colin Teague. BBC1. Saturday 12 April 2008, 6.45–7.35pm.

*Doctor Who*. Series 5, episode 12, 'The Pandorica Opens'. Prod. Peter Bennett. Dir. Toby Haynes. BBC1. Saturday 19 June 2010, 6.40–7.25pm.

*Doctor Who*. Series 5, episode 13, 'The Big Bang'. Prod. Peter Bennett. Dir. Toby Haynes. BBC1. Saturday 26 June 2010, 6.05–7.00pm.

*Doctor Who*. Series 6, episode 3, 'The Curse of the Black Spot'. Prod. Marcus Wilson. Dir. Jeremy Webb. BBC1. Saturday 7 May 2011, 6.15–7.00pm.

*Doctor Who*. Series 6, episode 11, 'The God Complex'. Prod. Marcus Wilson. Dir. Nick Hurran. BBC1. Saturday 17 September 2011, 7.10–7.55pm.

## NOTES

1 Tulloch and Alvarado (1983: 40). A single television film was broadcast in 1996. The series features a (so far) male protagonist, the Doctor, a humanoid alien Time Lord who travels through time and space in his time machine (the TARDIS), having adventures and solving problems, with mostly (though not exclusively) human companions. The Doctor has had a number of reincarnations, through a process known as 'regeneration', originally devised when the actor who first played the Doctor, William Hartnell, became too ill to continue in the role. This mainstay of British television is popular worldwide: on 23 November 2013, the fiftieth anniversary episode, 'The Day of the Doctor', was simultaneously broadcast to ninety-four countries, on television and in cinemas (see <http://www.doctorwho.tv/whats-new/article/guinness-world-record-for-the-day-of-the-doctor>, accessed 16 April 2016). See Hills (2010) and Chapman (2013) for overviews of the series.

2 See Kilburn (2007) and O'Mahony (2007), with Keen (2010a, 2010b).

3 On ancient Greece's relative lack of popularity among film-makers, see Nisbet (2008), although Greece was more popular than Rome on radio in the twentieth century: see Wrigley (2015a).

4 The classic *Doctor Who* series (1963–89) comprised individual episodes that made up serials with a single storyline; each series included multiple serials. This practice was not continued in new *Who*, where series comprise mostly discrete episodes.

5 Although 'The Myth Makers' has been categorised as a historical episode, it is also described as a comic or satirical story: see Kilburn (2007: 75) and O'Mahony (2007: 63).

6 Treating the story of the Trojan War as history is not new; ancient writers attempted to rationalise the story (see Danek 2007). On more recent debates see Saïd (2011: 75–94).
7 On excavations at Troy, see Blegen (1963), Rose (1998), Wood (2001) and Korfmann (2007).
8 BBC WAC T5/647/1.
9 On the Third Programme and Classics see Wrigley (2015a: 79–81).
10 Homer, *Iliad* 22.188–360.
11 BBC WAC T5/647/1.
12 Thompson (2004: 154–77) discusses the Troilus and Criseyde/Cressida story in Chaucer and Shakespeare.
13 Kilburn (2007: 76).
14 See Solomon (2007: 532–3) for popular interest in the *Iliad* during this period and Wrigley (2015a) on radio versions of Homer.
15 On classics and grammar schools, see Stray (1998).
16 O'Mahony (2007: 61).
17 BBC WAC VR 65/576.
18 BBC WAC VR 65/627.
19 On 'pseudo-historical' versus 'historical' serials, see Kilburn (2007), O'Mahony (2007).
20 See Burdge (2013: 72–4) on 'The Mind Robber'.
21 BBC WAC VR 68/630.
22 Compare the treatment of Atlantis in television documentaries: see Foka, Chapter 9, below.
23 For the Minoan snake goddess, see Hughes (2005: 313–22).
24 See, for example, Hammond (1969) and Friendly (1970).
25 As briefly narrated in Hesiod, *Theogony* 492–500.
26 BBC WAC VR 72/370.
27 Quoted in Tulloch and Alvarado (1983: 146).
28 Harvey (2013: 29).
29 See Plutarch, *Theseus* 22.
30 Rafer (2007: 132).
31 Rafer (2007: 132).
32 On 'The Fires of Pompeii' see Hobden (2009) and Keen (2010a).
33 Ovid, *Metamorphoses* 4.790–803.
34 Ford (2007).
35 The survey is online at <www.surveymonkey.com/r/LHW379H> (accessed 16 May 2016).
36 The survey is online at <www.surveymonkey.com/r/H8KHYXY> (accessed 16 May 2016).
37 See Potter (2010) for a summary of the findings from this research.
38 Cohen (1996: viii)
39 Keen (2010a: 94).
40 Quoted in Tulloch and Alvarado (1983: 146).
41 See Potter (2016).

# 9 The Digital Aesthetic in 'Atlantis: The Evidence' (2010)

Anna Foka

Over the many centuries since the Greek philosopher Plato committed it to writing, the story of Atlantis, the city destroyed by Poseidon, god of the sea, has captured people's imagination.[1] From the treatises of renowned thinkers to the jingoistic discourses of nation states to the explorations of adventure archaeologists, two questions in particular recur: did Atlantis exist, and where was it?[2] On 2 June 2010, 'Atlantis: The Evidence' (henceforth 'Atlantis'), an episode of the BBC2 historical documentary *Timewatch* series, set out to investigate. As the title suggests, the aim was to gather and evaluate clues: these were to reveal that the Platonic myth referred to the Bronze Age town of Thera, which was destroyed during a massive volcanic eruption towards the end of the second millennium BC. This theory was hardly new.[3] However, in the use of digital technology in the assemblage and display of evidence, 'Atlantis' built a distinctive account of Atlantis-Thera before, during and after the eruption. In this, the programme conformed to the emerging digital aesthetics of historical documentaries on television. However, the scale and diversity of digital tools used for visualisation make 'Atlantis' an illuminating case study not only for the treatment of an ancient Greek myth on British television, but for the impact of digital technologies in the documentary genre.

Across the creative industries, digital tools have become ubiquitous in the production of audiovisual images, especially through CGI, by which means environments and their inhabitants – and therefore historical places and people – can be produced. At the same time, academics today use digital technologies to visualise places distant in time and space via interactive mapping, 3D models and prototypes: techniques that are frequently described as 'cyber-archaeology'.[4] In both cases, digital tools offer new opportunities for representing the past, mimetically and schematically. The application may be for entertainment or for education, or both, but always the result is constructive of the past. So, for example, video games are increasingly analysed as forms of (hi)storytelling, by which players navigate landscapes and engage with narratives that immerse them in, and thereby develop a sense of, the past.[5] Furthermore, as Bettany Hughes, the popular historian and presenter of the *Timewatch* 'Atlantis' programme, notes, the application of digital technologies in the construction of knowledge about the past by archaeologists raises the possibility that 'History ... should be discovered not just *via* TV, but *thanks* to TV.'[6] By this interpretation, transposed onto television, the audiovisual reconstructions facilitated by digital technologies provide opportunities for historical exposition and explanation.

In the light of these trends in the application of digital technologies, it may seem unsurprising that television documentaries – themselves a mode of historical representation crafted out of words and images that combines entertainment with education[7] – follow suit. In particular, for 'Atlantis' a digital approach was facilitated by its co-production with the BBC1 drama *Atlantis: End of a World, Birth of a Legend* (2011), the promotional material for which emphasised its use of cutting-edge technology to '[bring] viewers face to face with one of history's greatest disasters' and 'immerse the viewer in a world they've never seen before, in a brand new, exciting way'.[8] Transported into 'Atlantis', scenes from the historical drama realised in CGI potentially carry forward the immersive effect. Yet this very engagement raises questions beyond those that are sometimes posed regarding the integration of 'fictional' drama into a programme investigating 'fact',[9] as a consequence of assumptions (like those expressed by Hughes) about the capability of digital technologies. As Landesman has argued for 'digital documentaries' more widely, the 'conceptual and theoretical utopias ... repeatedly proposed regarding digital visuals' represented by such claims underplay the challenge posed to viewers by 'digitality'.[10] The digital age is delineated as 'a historic break in the nature of media and representation', emphasising the unprecedented capacities digital technology holds for visual manipulability.[11] For a genre like documentary that is devoted to careful crafting of reality – in this case the reality of Atlantis as Thera – this is particularly pertinent. By examining digital manipulations in the service of presenting evidence for a historical Atlantis, focusing on their character and effects, this chapter considers the challenges of digitality to the depiction of the ancient world.

To this end, the present study thus approaches digital technologies in 'Atlantis' as elements in the documentary's *ekphrasis*.[12] Currently used to mean a 'vivid description' in specific reference to images and art, in ancient Greece *ekphrasis* originally referred to textual narratives 'rich in visual and emotional effects' that offered the reader/audience an immersive experience.[13] Like those oral and written narratives that enact 'a mental representation of that subject', subjects rendered digitally are constructive and affective, as this chapter will show. In what follows I examine the Atlantis documentary as digital *ekphrasis* – an evocative representation on the audiovisual plane facilitated by digital techniques that generate a distinctive aesthetic and contribute to the programme's proposition regarding the relationship between Atlantis and Bronze Age Thera (its demonstration and interpretation of 'the evidence'). From the catastrophic eruption to the physical environment and the Minoan population of Thera, the experimental, interactive and collaborative CGI techniques familiar from television drama and cyber-archaeology construct the events and people of the distant past into a distinctive posthuman world.

## FROM FICTION TO FACT: THE *EKPHRASIS* OF AN ANCIENT CATASTROPHE

When Atlantis appears for the first time in Plato's dialogues *Timaeus* and *Critias*, it is as an allegory of or warning for contemporary Athens as a city that falls out of divine favour and submerges into the ocean. While the story of Atlantis is widely regarded as a fictional tale and a rhetorical construct, what served as its inspiration remains debated.[14] From the first, 'Atlantis' claims to know. For all that the promotional summary describes Atlantis 'as one of the most intriguing mysteries of all time', there are 'geological, archaeological and historical clues' that will enable the presenter, Bettany Hughes, to solve that mystery.[15] These clues are the titular evidence, marshalled over the programme to support the contention that the 'tale' or 'myth' of Atlantis, as Hughes introduces it, was an allusion to the volcanic eruption of Bronze Age Thera. The shift from fiction to reality is reinforced during the programme's introduction. In a montage sequence of modern-day Athens, close-ups on contemporary inner-cityscapes combine with static high-angle and panning camera shots of the Acropolis, while in voiceover, Hughes explains: 'A thousand years before Plato lived, a truly amazing civilization thrived here in the eastern Mediterranean.

But that civilization suffered a terrible catastrophe.'[16] When Hughes utters that final word, three volcanic eruptions ensue. The footage is anachronistic to antiquity: the first low-quality colour clip of an eruption is followed by a close-up of bubbling lava and, in quick succession, a CGI eruption of ash clouds in black and white, giving the impression of film before the advent of 1950s technicolour. This sequence builds upon generic televisual experiences of volcanic eruptions, asserting through analogy what remains as yet unstated: the means by which Atlantis was destroyed.[17] This inference is immediately confirmed: 'Brand new scientific evidence suggests that this catastrophe was at least twice as disastrous as previously thought.' The demonstrative, anaphoric pronoun 'this' links visualised eruptions to the stated destruction of Atlantis as 'catastrophe'. Meanwhile images of underwater archaeology, lava stones, the bronze Poseidon statue from Sounion at Athens' national archaeological museum, plus more CGI lava and tidal waves serve as depictions of science in action and its results. A question closes the introduction: 'Could this tragedy be the basis for Plato's story?' The word 'catastrophe' is here replaced by 'tragedy', in order to encourage an emotional perspective, by inferring a human aspect to events. In large letters, the words 'ATLANTIS, The Evidence' appear on the screen during a long shot of the presenter walking on the beach at sunset. Thanks to visual sequences that combine images edited and in some cases created by computer software, the answer to the question is already apparent.

In so far as the introduction builds suspense towards an appraisal of the evidence, the programme proceeds to its evaluation, engaging with ancient textual sources and artefacts and conducting interviews in settings typical of ancient world documentaries. Thus, the narration begins with a long shot of Hughes standing before unidentified archaeological monuments, carrying a book, Plato's *Dialogues*. The camera closes in on the cover of a standard Loeb edition of the text, with ancient Greek and English facing text. With a side-view camera angle the presenter reads a passage from *Critias*.[18] While the presenter reads, Plato's words are simultaneously visualised via a montage sequence of new media artefacts. Contemporary sounds of waves and seagulls, static photography of waves and CGI lava in close-up illustrate Atlantis' maritime power and wealth and its vanishing following 'portentous earthquakes and floods'.[19] Thus, Plato's narrative is made contingent through analogy. Sounds and images that capture the contemporary world bring Atlantis to life.[20]

In what follows, digital technology contributes to the presentation of evidence that validate the programme's hypothesis in a more direct way. Moving location to Santorini (Thera), where 'fresh scientific evidence buttresses the idea that Plato's story was inspired by a real island', volcanologist Dr Haraldur Sigurdsson (University of Rhode Island) is interviewed by the presenter about his underwater expedition in an attempt to establish that what the presenter claims to be the greatest volcanic eruption in the whole of the ancient world took place there. As Sigurdsson describes the process of the eruption, the screen is filled by images of scientific scans of the sea floor, underwater scanners and the interfaces of computer programmes. Scientific explanations are supported by illustrations of processes inferred to generate the knowledge upon which they are founded. However, these remain at the generic level: up-to-the minute technology and its digital end products demonstrate the tools of archaeological interpretation, contributing allusively rather than directly to the analysis. Strikingly, Sigurdsson further compares the eruption of Thera to that of Vesuvius in AD 79. Now older, archival footage of the Fiorelli casts, human figures covered in volcanic lava, appear on screen. These casts are usually part of the representation of Pompeii and Herculaneum, towns destroyed in that geological event.[21] The famous disaster is drawn into the signification process for the eruption of Thera.[22] Raw scientific data presented in a non-linear manner connect disparate information and events, so that Plato's Atlantis is connected to Thera's eruption, an event that is made comprehensible by reference to the more familiar events of Pompeii. Once again Plato's fiction is positioned as fact, while the digitally inflected visualisation of activities and artefacts in the present substantiates a proposition about the past.

Next, Hughes visits the excavation site in Thera in order to examine geological data. Close-up shots of the area's sedimentary and layered volcanic rocks appear on screen while Dr Floyd McCoy of the Department of Natural Sciences (University of Hawaii) assesses the likely human experience of the eruption. McCoy narrates in voice-over how the volcanic eruption began gradually with small earthquakes and sulphur emerging from cracks in the ground. This time, however, the CGI illustrates not the geological event, but its impact on the human world. CGI-based Theran walls appear to be shaken by an earthquake, while actors in sepia film run about at an eye-level camera angle.[23] The sounds of rolling rocks and actors' screams embellish the visual cues. This is the show's first attempt to digitally reconstruct the city as an architectural, physical and social entity, and it represents a shift in the focus of the story. As Christos Doumas, director of the Akrotiri excavation in Thera, explains in voice-over, after the earthquake people started rescuing things that were needed. Simultaneously a drama reconstruction in sepia depicts the narration: pottery is placed by actors in safe positions, and original footage from the 1960s excavation depicts how pottery was found, thus connecting narration with conservation techniques. This dramatisation at once reiterates the tragic dimension of the eruption and legitimises this version of events, whilst also illustrating what ancient Thera looked like via physical sets and CGI. In fact, the scenes of human settlement and activity are drawn from another televisual interrogation of Atlantis, the BBC docudrama *Atlantis: End of a World, Birth of a Legend*, which illustrated the fate of Thera/Atlantis through extensive dramatisation and limited voiceover (discussed more below). Once again the boundaries between fact and fiction are blurred, this time by the presentation of snapshots from the fictionalised account of Thera's final day as evidence.

## CGI: INVENTING POSTHUMAN MINOANS

In the sequences discussed so far, CGI is integrated into audiovisual sequences that resonate with statements, assertions and arguments elaborated by the presenter and interviewed guests on 'Atlantis'. The images act, therefore, as evidence. However, rendering the built and populated environment of Thera digitally also affects how we see Atlantis. Since the late 1990s, CGI has been utilised by film-makers to recreate populated environments. For the ancient world, *Gladiator* (dir. R. Scott, 2000) was particularly noteworthy. As Winkler has argued, the technological innovations in *Gladiator* incorporate spectacular and impressive artificial components made by CGI (large crowds, reconstructions of buildings and places and realistic instances of violence), thus portraying 'a kind of cyber-Rome'.[24] However, not only did this cyber-Rome act as a setting for the tale of rebellion against an oppressive regime, but its execution also achieved an 'unprecedented scale and detail for their display of the once-buried metaphors of the Roman spectacle'.[25] In the years since, film technology has been recognised as a potential marker of film innovation, often functioning as the main attraction of a film itself.[26]

Since 2000, CGI has become cheaper and more efficient.[27] Beyond blockbusters, the HBO TV series *Rome* (2005–7), created by John Milius, William J. MacDonald and Bruno Heller, for example, used CGI to recreate an artificial ancient city: the 'artistic' sepia filter and moving graffiti in the opening title are a conceptual attempt at an 'authentic' architectural and pictorial representation. Similarly, the fiction-fuelled docudrama *Atlantis: End of a World, Birth of a Legend*

(8 May 2011, BBC1) that offers scenes for 'Atlantis' (as discussed above) adopted CGI so as to impress and 'immerse the viewers in a unique experience'.[28] These artificial details speak to the advent of a digital or posthuman aesthetic in audiovisual media.[29] The boundaries between existence and computer simulation are blurred.[30] 'Atlantis', although relying on typical documentary techniques, also embraces the posthuman turn in media aesthetics through CGI.

In 'Atlantis', CGI is deployed most notably in order to vivify Minoan civilisation during Hughes' visit to the archaeological site in Akrotiri. Before the site's gates, the presenter states that 'Theran Bronze age society is the most beguiling of all civilizations that ever walked the earth.' Regular close-ups on the colour restoration of Minoan paintings and Egyptian art are used as a point of comparison, as the presenter emphasises the 'sophisticated' civilisation of the former. She also pits the societal position of women in Thera (as portrayed in artefacts) against the allegedly secluded women of classical Athens.[31] She concludes that in Thera 'women are conspicuous not by their absence but by their presence'. These elements of 'sophistication', defined as liveliness, individualism and gender equality, are further visualised with the aid of CGI. Again there follows the juxtaposition of ancient artefacts and drama reconstruction by actors in sepia, against CGI backdrops of 'Atlantean' buildings from the Atlantis docudrama mentioned above. The sequence alternates between a CGI backdrop of a port with montaged tracking shots in sepia of actors trading and carrying large pots (see Figure 9.1) and close-ups of restored Minoan pottery. The sequence further includes tracking shots of women, with characteristic Minoan hairstyles as previously shown in original artwork, succeeded by close-ups of their hands using scales to measure saffron, and painting ceramic pottery. Each of these filmed sequences is paired with close-ups of relevant original artefacts, such as scales, murals and pottery. Eventually, the presenter refers to a famous 'fleet fresco', followed by the director of excavation in voiceover discussing how Minoan society and economy had sailing, shipping and trade at their core. A CGI depiction of the harbour followed by static camera shots and close-ups of actors performing the roles of traders and rowers alternates with detailed close-ups of the fresco. Excavated artefacts are thus restored to life, as is the sophisticated Minoan civilisation of ancient Thera.

Finally, towards the end of the programme, the presenter returns to Plato's narrative. A montage sequence of static camera shots of large CGI waves in sepia appears on screen, while the presenter narrates: 'according to Plato, Poseidon was the master of Atlantis, and when its

Figure 9.1 CGI Theran Port: 'Atlantis: The Evidence' (2010). BBC Northern Ireland.

people fell foul of him, their island was swallowed by the sea'. As the narrative progresses, the CGI-montaged sequence incorporates gradually bigger waves that eventually alternate with high-angle shots of actors/Minoans in CGI-reconstructed streets attacked by waves. In the grand spectacle of destruction, the devastation and emotion of the moment for the community whose lives have previously been witnessed are realised.[32] As in *Atlantis: End of a World, Birth of a Legend*, the combination of artefacts and CGI is key to credibility.[33] Drama and digital technology help bring the city of Akrotiri to life and then destroy it, at each moment serving the goal of validation.

CGI represents a new step in the history of visual simulation because it allows the creation of moving images of non-existent worlds. Digital technologies not only create new and imaginative virtual worlds, but also allow human positioning and mobility within those dimensions. As 'Atlantis' well shows, the use of CGI effects, with or without artistic touches, enhances narrative immersion. This combination of live action and CGI 3D has been termed 'synthetic realism'.[34] Achieving synthetic realism means attaining two goals: the simulation of the code of traditional cinematography and the simulation of the perceptual properties of real-life objects and environments. For the first goal, computer codes simulate a virtual camera that has lenses, depth of field, and lighting – the tools of traditional photography.[35] A goal of computer-generated graphics is photorealism, but CGI signifies the posthuman turn in the art of filming, since 'the synthetic image is free of the limitation of both human and camera vision with the potential of unlimited resolution and level of detail'.[36]

In television productions, synthetic images appear to be like traditional film photography; their resolution diminishes their perfection as a way to match the details of the film's images by adding grain or diluting the colour of the image. The use of CGI in enacting Atlantis/Thera renders an 'aged' effect through sepia and grainy filters in order to create a sense of past times. The documentary's style is reminiscent of the mid-2000s landscape of ancient-world film that stresses the imperfection of the image rather than its precision. This is notable in the artistic sepia-grainy filters in, for example, the film *300* (dir. Zack Snyder, 2006) or the thirty-nine-episode television series *Spartacus* (STARZ Networks, 2010–13). The synthetic image then becomes posthuman, since it cannot be seen by natural means. From this perspective, digital technology can be seen to operate as optical digressions in 'Atlantis' that oscillate in a conceptual dialogue between decelerating the unfolding of time and space, and historical narrative. The warranting effect is carried over along with the object, as it moves from 'real-life' settings into digital worlds, placed alongside digital replicas. In this way, the digital aesthetic adds an extra layer of validation for the programme's hypothesis.

## ATLANTEAN LIFESTYLES BROUGHT TO YOU BY CYBER-ARCHAEOLOGY?

Beyond television, digital visualisations have found prominent use within humanities research.[37] For example, the visualisation of raw data can provide historical insights into aspects of urban development,[38] and may also facilitate critical discussions of the application of digital tools within the context of cultural heritage.[39] The majority of scholarly attempts to reconstruct ancient urban sites digitally rely on the visual representation of architecture (buildings, bridges or roads) through 3D and early virtual reality models for archaeology, also known as virtual archaeology (VA). As the present analysis shows, however, the common use of digital tools to represent the past also introduces issues. For example, it has been argued that visualisations, largely synonymous with reconstruction in 3D models, may present a photorealistic, pseudo-ideal vision of the past.[40]

Earlier digital visualisations (1990–2000) intended for research have been criticised as maintaining static and sanitised historiocultural ideals.[41] In the mid-2000s, the evolution of VA, namely cyber-archaeology (CA), has recently challenged these ocular-centric modes of knowledge production by using participatory and interactive designs that enable reflection and cooperative efforts in investigations of sensory engagement with space, architecture and artefacts of the past.[42] CA further promises, through interactive virtual immersion, to deal with the deeper and more difficult questions about the past. While CA is still largely experimental it is the new step in archaeological inquiry.

'Atlantis' adopts digital archaeology, specifically CA technologies which I address and analyse below. The experience of living in Atlantis in relation to architecture and urban planning is one of the central attractions of the programme and it is used to justify the identification of Bronze Age Minoans as the advanced civilisation in Plato's account. On site and during a high-angle long shot that places her among ruins, Hughes explains that 'like the Atlanteans, they [Therans] harnessed the landscape to create an architectural masterpiece in town planning'. She reads once more from the Loeb edition of Plato's *Critias*: 'And of the buildings, some they framed in one single colour, some were a pattern of many colours by blending the stones ... some of them being white, black and red.' The camera changes focus from Hughes to the stones of the Akrotiri site. The presenter continues, now filmed in a long shot, while pointing at the multicoloured stones: 'Just look at the local stone that they still use here at the site of Akrotiri.' She proceeds to show preserved buildings that were buried under up to sixty feet of volcanic ash. The presenter explains that, 'even so, it's been difficult to know what the place must have looked like in its former glory [pause] until *now*' (spoken emphasis). In what follows, digital technology is used as a tool to visualise how Therans may have been the creators of architectural masterpieces, just like the Atlanteans.

Next, Hughes and Professor Clairy Palyvou of the School of Architecture at the Aristotle University of Thessaloniki are filmed in a point-of-view shot before a computer screen. A close-up reveals that they are observing a software program for 3D architectural modelling.[43] Hughes' voiceover states: 'Palyvou has come up with a vision of Akrotiri in its heyday, before the eruption, where the buildings were intact.' While the camera navigates through and inside these generously decorated 3D buildings, Palyvou explains:

> It is a very sophisticated architecture ... not only meeting everyday needs ... shelter or protection ... so many things that are there for the first time in the world ... two, three storey buildings on an earthquake sensitive region ... built in a style of architecture that involves a lot of openings back then ... that [windows] was something very innovative ... the architecture of an affluent society. This prosperity is shared by a large number of the community, it's not something that is kept only for the elite.

The virtual exploration of the 3D reconstructions (as for example in Figure 9.2) grants the viewer a navigable/interactive insight into the society of the Therans as a technologically advanced society. The 3D models used in 'Atlantis' are on a par with recent trends in archaeological scholarship.[44] The 'Atlantis' models could be classified under the CA wave, influenced by theory on human–computer interaction and gaming software that attempts immersive simulation.[45] It includes engagement with the user, in the form of first-person navigation.

Figure 9.2 Inside a Minoan house: 'Atlantis: The Evidence' (2010). BBC Northern Ireland.

It pays more attention to the experience of place and space than to static recreation. In other words, the user's interaction with the model potentially generates further archaeological observations. In 'Atlantis' this interaction between user and cyberspace is ruled by a kinaesthetic approach. Hughes and Palyvou exchange information with the environment by embodied navigation, and interpret the site for the televisual audience collaboratively. CA tools and methodology are then deployed to communicate space, light and quality of lifestyle. The collaborative analysis of the 3D visualisation sheds light on Minoan life via interaction, engagement and feedback, as CA epistemologies dictate.[46] The virtual environment is a simulation space of an archaeological site created by information with the help of software. Through this technologically advanced methodology, informed by current trends in archaeology, the programme validates once more the hypothesis that the architectural expertise of the Therans matches Plato's narration of the Atlanteans.

## CONCLUSION: POSTHUMAN CLASSICAL RECEPTIONS

This chapter showed that while archaeology dominates the discursive techniques of the genre, digital technology is slotted in among more traditional modes of rendering the documentary's subject to justify the hypothesis that Plato's Atlantis corresponds to Bronze Age Thera. In order to legitimise fiction as fact, the programme visualises selected parts from Plato's *Dialogues* and evaluates scientific evidence through the indexical power of images, bringing together archaeological sites, original media footage, specialists and Bronze Age artefacts; it also incorporates digital tools known from popular culture and scientific research, such as CGI and 3D visualisations. This collection and organisation of disparate visual cues blend fiction into fact, narration into experience, and connect up ancient ideas with present epistemologies. The 'evidence' and its additional digital layer are placed to visually validate the ancient Greek narrative in immersively ekphrastic (and perhaps convincing) ways, as the programme's promotional material claims.

Specifically, the digital aesthetic of Atlantis brings to life Plato's tale of a long-lost utopian civilisation, and connects it with a real place: Thera.[47] This connection is made credible as it incorporates scientific evidence in justifying Atlantis' location in the Cyclades. Technology, conceptual art, narrative and science mingle to validate the documentary's hypothesis. In many ways, 'Atlantis' is a prime example of the interdisciplinarity that characterises current historical inquiry. It shows how beyond the 'wow' factor of sophisticated reconstructions of the ancient world, technology allows the aggregation, subsequent extraction and visualisation of information about the past in ways which were previously extremely difficult to achieve due to the large scope and complexity of data. Plato's narrative becomes visualised with the validating authority that science and digital technology allow, and the audience is led from fiction to reality, and vice versa. There are deeper epistemological problems regarding the relative value of the visualisation of the intersections between scientific and humanistic modes of knowledge creation.[48] However, by discussing digital technology as a tool for the visualisation of the mythical Atlantis, this study demonstrates how technology may contribute to the production of knowledge.

'Atlantis' is a particularly rich example of how historical documentary evolves as a cultural form. It combines, at the same time, human and posthuman elements and in so doing, it claims a right to make meaning about human experience, with tools beyond human experience. In documentary, technology is not neutral in the process of knowledge production: it defines the level and aesthetic of conceptualisation and recreation of a given culture and society. Furthermore, it creates affordances for authenticity. Digital tools are therefore central to how the imagined past is both rendered and received. Beyond quality and aesthetics, what we can do with technology decides the specifics of what we may visualise and, in turn, what we may claim about the past.

## PROGRAMMES DISCUSSED

*Timewatch*. Episode: 'Atlantis: The Evidence'. Prod. and dir. Natalie Maynes. BBC Northern Ireland. BBC2. Wednesday 2 June 2010, 7.00–8.00pm.

*Atlantis: End of a World, Birth of a Legend*. Prod. Detlef Siebert. Dir. Tony Mitchell. BBC Northern Ireland. BBC1. Sunday 8 May 2011, 9.00–10.00pm.

## NOTES

1 See Vidal-Naquet (2005).
2 Described by Vidal-Naquet and Lloyd (1992).
3 See Pellegrino (1991) and Friedrich (2000).
4 See, for example, Schreibman, Siemens and Unsworth (2004); Mahony and Bodard (2010: 1–14); Barker et al. (2012). For 3D geospatial

analysis see Landeschi et al. (2016). Cyber-archaeology is introduced more fully below.
5 For gaming as instrumental in mediating the past see Chapman (2016). See also current online initiatives from within and outside the realm of game studies, such as <http://www.playthepast.org> for history and <https://archaeogaming.com> for archaeology (both accessed 20 March 2017).
6 See Hughes (2012: 10), cited by Hobden (2016: 134) (original emphasis).
7 On these qualities of historical television documentary, see for example Makrinos (2013: 368).
8 See promotional material at <http://www.bbc.co.uk/pressoffice/pressreleases/stories/2010/02_february/26/atlantis.shtml> (accessed 20 March 2017).
9 On dramatisation in ancient world documentaries, with references to the wider discussion of its place within the documentary tradition, see Hobden (2017: 503–11).
10 Landesman (2008: 34–5).
11 Rosen (2001: 302), cited by Landesman (2008: 34).
12 On digital *ekphrasis* in relation to tactility see Lindhé (2013) and in relation to immersive sound see Foka and Arvidsson (2016).
13 Theon, for example defines *ekphrasis* as 'descriptive language, bringing what is portrayed clearly before the sight' (Kennedy 2003: 45). Initially used within the practice of rhetoric, the origin of *ekphrasis* is documented in the Hellenistic schools during the first centuries AD in the compositional exercises *Progymnasmata*: four treatises attributed to Theon, Hermogenes, Nikolaos and Aphthonios. Cf. Webb (2009: 5, 128).
14 For the tale of Atlantis and its later reception see Ellis (1998). In terms of what served as the inspiration for the tale of Atlantis see Friedrich (2000) and Vidal-Naquet (2005). For Atlantis as a rhetorical construct see Morgan (1998).
15 A typical ancient world documentary technique. See the programme description at <http://www.bbc.co.uk/programmes/b00sl29f> (accessed 20 March 2017).
16 This is the script recording of the first broadcast, openly available under a presumption of 'fair use' on Dailymotion: <http://www.dailymotion.com/video/xt53x0_bbc-timewatch-2010–atlantis-the-evidence-hdtv-x264–ac3-mvgroup-org_school> (accessed 20 March 2017).
17 Post-processual archaeological theory emphasises the subjectivity and multiplicity of interpretations of the same artefact and events connected to it. See Hodder and Hutson (2003).
18 The BBC sought permission to use the Loeb 1929 edition, translated by R.G. Bury. Hughes simplified the translation herself in order to make the text more accessible to the average viewer (source: personal email correspondence with the author). The Loeb series is a documentary staple.

19 Manovich (2001: 218).
20 This technique is often referred to as database narrative: when visual and narrative are not chronologically linear but an assemblage that may be geographically and chronologically disparate. See Manovich and Kratky (2005), with Murray (1998: 157). On the indexical power of images see Ward (2005: 11) and Hughes-Warrington (2009: 7).
21 See Hales (2011).
22 'Atlantis" survey of catastrophe departs from Mary Beard's *Pompeii: Life and Death in a Roman Town* (Lion TV, 2010) where catastrophe is restaged as archaeology in performance: Hobden (2013a). The docudrama *Pompeii: The Last Day* (2003) and *Pompeii: The Mystery of the People Frozen in Time* (2013) does not deploy digital technology. For science and technology as a rhetorical trope in documentary see Hobden (2016: 131–4).
23 Sepia (the word derives from the Greek for 'cuttlefish') was used in antiquity as a colour and a drawing material; it remained an artist's drawing material until the nineteenth century. The colour connotes the past because it is associated with old-time photography and painting. See the entry for 'sepia' in Maerz and Paul (1930: 179).
24 Winkler (2004: 89).
25 Cyrino (2005: 224).
26 Paul (2010: 20).
27 Belton (1992).
28 See promotional material on the BBC website: <http://www.bbc.co.uk/pressoffice/pressreleases/stories/2010/02_february/26/atlantis.shtml> (accessed 20 March 2017).
29 See Warren (2000) for early work on the posthuman aesthetic in film, and Brown (2013).
30 Hayles (1999: xi).
31 Athens is canonised in documentary as a politically progressive city state: see Hobden (2013b).
32 For the emotional component, compare Hobden (2016: 121–6) on (CGI) spectacles of destruction in the BBC dramatised documentary *Pompeii: The Last Day* (2003).
33 See Hobden (2013a) for the programme as a form of dramatising archaeology.
34 Manovich (2001: 153).
35 Manovich (2001: 91–192).
36 Manovich (2001: 202).
37 Schreibman, Siemens and Unsworth (2004); Forte (2010).
38 Schreibman, Siemens and Unsworth (2004); Mahony and Bodard (2010: 1–14); Nygren, Foka and Buckland (2014); for mapping visualisations especially see Barker et al. (2012).
39 Giaccardi (2012). For an overview on technology and the potential of digital models to reconstruct the ancient space, especially regarding

Roman society, see Earl (2007) and Anderson (2004). For work on 3D geographic information systems and visuality of ancient home space see Landeschi et al. (2016).
40 Forte and Siliotti (1997).
41 Westin (2012); Tziovas (2014).
42 Forte (2010).
43 Mattis Lindmark, a 3D specialist at HUMlab, Umeå University, identified the program as a 2010-version Maya 3D or Max. The way the camera navigates in the virtual environment points towards a pre-rendered movie. This level of technical quality can easily be accomplished by any software today.
44 Forte and Siliotti (1997).
45 Forte (2010).
46 On the basis of the latest full-immersion screens and wearables (Oculus Rift etc.) it is estimated that frames separating cyberspace and reality will give way to augmented reality and so forth: see Forte (2010).
47 For a detailed discussion of the posthuman, see Hayles (1999: 2–33).
48 Smithies (2014).

# 10  *Greece in the Making: From Intention to Practicalities in Television Documentaries. A Conversation with Michael Scott and David Wilson*

On a sunny summer's afternoon in 2015, Fiona Hobden, one of the editors of this book and a specialist from the University of Liverpool in ancient world documentaries, met with the ancient historian Dr Michael Scott, Associate Professor at the University of Warwick, and David Wilson, a director and producer of documentary films, at the Institute of Classical Studies in London.[1] This chapter presents an abridged and edited version of their conversation. In it Scott and Wilson discuss their experiences making documentaries about ancient Greece for television. Having recently worked together on *Delphi: The Bellybutton of the Ancient World* (2010), *Guilty Pleasures: Luxury in Ancient Greece* (2011) and *Ancient Greece: The Greatest Show on Earth* (2013) for BBC4,[2] the pair offer insights into factors that influence the representation of ancient Greece on screen across the production process. From the commissioning stage through to writing and filming, that process is characterised by a continual negotiation between initial intent, the varying goals of television documentaries, the opportunities attendant upon telling a story through an audiovisual medium, and on-the-ground practicalities during filming, with every decision informed by budgetary constraints. As the conversation unfolds, Scott and Wilson also reflect on the characteristics and value of ancient Greece on television.

## GETTING STARTED

Fiona Hobden (FH): What first drew you to making television documentaries about ancient Greece?

Michael Scott (MS): I come at this from the point of view of a university lecturer in a Classics department, focused on studying the ancient Greek and Roman world. For me, being an academic is also fundamentally about speaking to communities outside of the academic world, to explain why I and others spend our time studying that world and encourage more people to learn about it. And that's what drove me from the very beginning, post-PhD level onwards, to always try to find ways of doing that. My particular research focus is ancient Greece, and my PhD focus was Delphi. In 2009/10, having done a number of small host or interview roles for different programmes on the History Channel, including their *Ancient Discoveries* and *Ancient Rulers* series, I heard that the BBC were doing an 'Ancient Greece' season. But you cannot simply go to a channel and say 'This is what I want to do. Clear the decks!' Rather it's much more of a process of discussion, waiting for all the stars to be in alignment: gaps in schedules, necessary funding, thematic links with already commissioned programmes, recent news event linked to topic etc. And if they are, then the BBC may well turn to somebody like me they are interested in working with, and ask 'Well, what do you think would fit here?' And at that point I said, well Delphi's a great topic. Certainly, it seemed to tick all the boxes. It was an extensive physical site with lots of good finds that would make a strong visual impact. It had a story that continued through the whole of ancient Greek history with most of the major known ancient Greek and, indeed, wider Mediterranean historical characters having a role to play. Moreover, that story wove religious practice in with human competition and *polis*-level propaganda and rivalry – ideas that are as modern as they are old. And finally, Delphi offered the opportunity to underline how much the modern world creates an ancient world to fit its priorities as we investigated the changing representations of Delphi through into the twenty-first century. The BBC then linked me up with an external production company, which in this case was Tern Television. And then Tern Television brought David on board as the person to direct and produce.[3]

David Wilson (DW): I'm a freelance director, which means that there's a limit to how much I can specialise. One ends up making the films one is offered. But I have been making films about history and religion – and sometimes both – for about twenty-five years. And I've always been fascinated by ancient Greece. So when the chance came to make a film about it, I was delighted. All I knew at that stage was that it was about Delphi, and it was going to be presented by an academic called Michael Scott. So when I went to see Michael, and we had to decide what the programme was going to consist of, I suggested that the first thing was to identify six big things that he wanted to say. I thought we could get through each of them in ten minutes, in one order or another. When we had those I went away and wrote a kind of argument – what we call in the trade a 'Treatment' – and sent it back to him, and he in turn corrected it and on the basis of that I wrote a draft script which I sent to him, and he rewrote it back to me. When we were more or less happy we sent it to Harry Bell, the Creative Director and Executive Producer at Tern. His job is to be the voice of the viewer, to stand back and make sure the film or series is what the broadcasters want, without getting involved in the details of the story. He of course threw up his hands in horror at the first draft and said 'I don't understand any of it.' And so we went back and rewrote it again so that when we sent it to the BBC commissioning editor he said, 'Yep, just move that bit there and we'll be fine.' And so then we had a script that we could go out and try to film. But of course what we filmed wasn't exactly what we had written, even though it was near enough in argument. Because the main thing is to get an argument through, make your point, tell a story, rather than to stick to a script.

## EDUCATION OR ENTERTAINMENT?

MS: There were three different stakeholders in this programme, as there are in any documentary programme in which an academic is involved: a practising academic who wants to inform and explain why we, in our academic world, find what we do interesting and why it should be interesting to more people. There's the production team, who are looking to make a good film. And there's the BBC channel whose mandate is to inform, educate and entertain, with a hefty eye on their audience figures and reviews.

DW: You have to entertain the audience. Sometimes the audience can be quite highfalutin, and so that's why you get to do ancient Greece: it's not all *Strictly Come Dancing* on the BBC or any of the main channels. But you do have to entertain them.

MS: It's crucial to remember that the BBC's goal is to simultaneously inform, educate and entertain. So entertainment with information, great. But no programme can be purely about teaching people stuff, as if you were making a video to go along with a course book, or a programme directed strictly towards schools. That does not mean a TV doc needs to dumb down the ideas and intellectual content – absolutely not. But it needs to find ways to explain and think about them which are informative, educational and entertaining all at the same time for an audience who may have no or little knowledge of the subject. The litmus test is this: say you are an accountant, or whatever, and you've had a tiring day and you come home and switch on the television, what's on – to be successful – has to be something you are happy to spend your few free hours a day watching and feel like it was worth it afterwards.

FH: So even when you're on BBC4, that's still the imperative behind it?

MS: Each channel offers a different balance between inform, educate and entertain, with BBC4 more towards informing and educating than BBC1.

DW: The balance moves all the time. But it's also important to understand the mechanics of the medium. Film and television are visual media; they work by manipulating the power of images and sounds. And the effect of those is primarily emotional. We want to make the best film we can, so that means moving people, as well as entertaining them.[4] You have to move them. And if you don't move them, you won't inform them either. Neuroscientists believe these days that all the information and sense-impressions in our brains have an emotional component or tag.[5] So there are always these questions. Is it going to be a good film: will it move people? Is the content going to be correct: will it inform them? Is the film going to get the viewers: will it entertain them? These are the three things you have to consider.

FH: What about *Ancient Greece: The Greatest Show on Earth*, which was made in conjunction with the Open University?[6] Did it have a different dimension, because it had that explicitly educational context, or did you work from the same motivating principles?

MS: That series came about as a result of a series of discussions between the BBC4 commissioner, myself, and Harry Bell. It was only really post-commission that discussions were had with the Open University, who were then involved in the process of script generation at different stages, although probably less than usual because an academic was writing and presenting. But critically, even as an OU-associated programme, it is fundamental for the film still to be informative, educational and entertaining at the same time.

DW: This was rather different from what happened with productions like *Coast*,[7] which always had a much more entertaining remit. It's a factual magazine series rather than a through-written documentary, so the OU needed to think very hard about how they were going to use it in education.

## AUDIENCE ADDICTIONS AND COMMISSIONING CONCERNS

FH: Nonetheless, the remit of BBC4 falls firmly within the realm of public service broadcasting. It promises programmes that are 'intellectually and culturally enriching'.[8] That makes some assumptions about the audience and broadens your scope to be entertaining and informative, I'd have thought.

MS: You're right. BBC4 is a haven for producing programmes that shine a spotlight on areas that don't normally get a lot of TV time. Or on particular aspects of a topic that while the general topic gets TV time, they wouldn't. The BBC4 viewer is the person who says 'Ooh, I don't know much/anything about that. I'd love to watch it and find out.'

DW: They're addicted to this kind of thing, in a way. You just have to stick up a programme on ancient Greece, and the ancient Greece audience will watch it, regardless. Half a million of them, consistently. That's more than the readership of any broadsheet newspaper: and BBC4 has other constituencies – science, for instance, or the arts. People come to ancient Greece partly because of the blue sea and white marble, sunshine and cypresses, partly because of the familiar stories, partly because people have been there, and also because people imagine that it's got something to do with them. And you couldn't say that necessarily – weirdly, this being Britain – about the Plantagenets. I did a series on them [*Britain's Bloodiest Dynasty*, Channel 5, 2014]. They have *definitely* got something to do with us in Britain today – our entire constitution and legal system derives from that time, for example – but there's very little recognition here of what the Plantagenets were about. You can say 'Magna Carta' and that's about it, whereas people seem to know a lot more about ancient Greece.

MS: There is a big difference, though, between ancient Greece, ancient Rome and ancient Egypt as topics. My experience of getting shows commissioned is that (especially on BBC Channels other than BBC4) it is two or three times as hard to get a show commissioned about ancient Greece, as opposed to either the Romans or the Egyptians. And partly that has come about because people, the general viewing public, feel they get the Romans. They feel they have a handle on how their society worked.

DW: And there are bits of it all over Britain.

MS: They touched us, they came to us. And it's an empire, there was a ruler – it's a political system understandable to us today. So they get the Romans. On the other hand, the Egyptians are presented as entirely weird and alien.[9] Again we can engage with that and enjoy it, because it isn't us. The Greeks occupy this much more difficult middle ground: they're sort of like us, but not like us. As a result it is fundamentally harder to secure documentary commissions about the Greeks because people aren't sure how to relate to them, or what the big picture of their world really is. For example, 'How did Greek society work?' 'Well, you know, there were all these competing mini-states . . .' Where's the narrative thread, where's the story, where are the charismatic leaders, where's the sense of identity, where are the things that we can see in our world that we can link to? That's why, of the ancient Greece topics that make it onto the screen, it's most often the Athenian empire, Athenian democracy, or Alexander the Great – things that we can more easily relate to (and fall into the model of empire/leaders/political systems we recognise). And a second problem in securing commissions about ancient Greece compared to ancient Rome is people's sense of what the ancient Greek world looked like. We know what Rome looks like. Think Colosseum, think forum, think gladiator, think centurion. But ancient Greece? Think Parthenon, think naked statues, think . . . bearded men talking philosophy? People find it harder to imagine ancient Greece.[10] It's telling that the only mainstream cinematic film about ancient Greece to really grab people's imaginations and become a commercial success has been *300* [dir. Z. Snyder, 2006] – shot in the style of a graphic novel – a fantasy world.

## OLD GREECE OR NEW?

FH: So with your programmes do you feel that you have been contributing to a repetition of ideas about ancient Greece, or have you had an opportunity to really open up and explore other sorts of stories?

DW: We've tried really hard to make sure that it all seemed relevant, that even quite obscure topics seem relevant today. So, with *Guilty Pleasures* the pitch was '*We* worry about luxury, let's see why by examining how *they* worried about luxury.' It turns out the worries about luxury that ancient Greeks and medieval people had – the series dealt with ancient Greece and the Middle Ages – are related to ours. It's either a sin (Middle Ages), or you've got above yourself (ancient Greece). Now getting a commission to explore that in 2011 was quite an interesting project, because it wasn't just a stand-alone series; it was part of a 'Luxury' season. All the other programmes were about how wonderful Lamborghinis are, and so this was coming from a different direction, cutting across the grain of all that.

FH: I thought it was quite an unexpected topic, actually.

DW: Well, at the time it was all about topicality. The 2008 financial crisis and the 'credit crunch' had made the super-rich and their luxuries a prime subject. The BBC proposed a 'Luxury' season and Harry and Michael stepped in and offered a great vehicle for dealing with the contradictions involved. But anyway, in general, you can't get away with just regurgitating the usual stuff; you have to do something new with it. Otherwise you'll bore yourself and the audience too. Don't you agree?

MS: I would say yes, we did offer something new. What have we done? Delphi: an in-depth focus on a particular centre of the ancient world. That hadn't been a topic covered before and certainly not in depth as the sole focus of an entire programme. Luxury, as you say, is a very unusual angle to come at ancient Greece from. A three-parter on theatre. Well, yes, theatre's been talked about before, but it had never been done in that kind of depth across three parts that not only talked about the acme of Greek theatre with Aeschylus, Sophocles and Euripides, but took it into the fourth century, and took the story into the era of Roman theatre as well. So they were unusual topics that, while treating places like Athens and people like Alexander, broke those moulds of being programmes solely about these well-known tropes. What David very cleverly did, when we had those initial discussions about the script, was to say 'We need a frame, we need a thread that we can follow through these stories.' And what worked for us, certainly in *Delphi* and in *Luxury*, was using the traditional thread of Greek history that people *are* familiar with – the highpoints of the Persian Wars, Athenian democracy and empire, going through to Alexander the Great, and indeed beyond – as our tent poles for telling a different, unknown story. This was a way to say 'OK, well, you know about this moment, but what did it look like from the perspective of Delphi, or from the perspective of luxury, or how was it thought about from the perspective of theatre?' That was quite a nice way of allowing people to have the best of both worlds, to comfort people that they knew what was going on, but to give them something new at the same time.

DW: I particularly liked the scene [in *Guilty Pleasures*] about funerals in the Kerameikos, ancient Athens' burial ground. Classicists know that funerals were a major and contested means of 'social display' whether via a huge barrow, or a monument, or you could have a simple marker, or you could have the mass grave down there. This could have been dealt with anywhere in the programme but we held our main discussion of this back until the mass grave so that we were able to tie it back in to Pericles, Athens, Parthenon, Peloponnesian War, topics people might be familiar with. But it wasn't about the war as such; it was about how embarrassed you were about how posh you were when you went and had a funeral. Another example [in *Ancient Greece: The Greatest Show on Earth*] was using the story of Demosthenes' oratory on the Pnyx [the meeting place for the Athenian assembly] to talk about the intimate relationship between actors and orators, theatre and politics in Athens during the mid-fourth century when the city was debating its relationship with the new military power in the region, Philip II of Macedon. And Philip II of Macedon brings you within range of Alexander the Great, his son.

MS: When you talk to the executives for commissioning, what they want is a programme that says 'This is a topic you think you know about, but actually you don't know about it at all.' And they want that kind of counter-intuitive flip. TV needs to be surprising.

DW: And also they want more of the same!

MS: Yes, there is this competing need – to offer something that is in some way familiar and at the same time surprising. So in that sense the ancient Greek programmes worked, because they managed to do those two things. We took stories that people had some sense of, but actually some of them were quite uncomfortable about, and exploited that discomfort to go to some new places. But we always related it to the familiar, with the end result that people had a new version of that familiar. For example in Athens: the Parthenon, people know about that; empire, people know about that; but burying people in mass graves who died preserving/expanding the empire as a means of civic honours and the ultimate expression of democracy? They did not know about that! What does that say about ancient democracy? And what does that say about democracy today and the legacy of ancient Greece at its heart?

## THE TROUBLE WITH RUINS

DW: The other thing the commissioner will always tell you when it's about ancient worlds is 'Oh god, please don't spend all your time in ruins.' So visually, what are you going to be looking at, when the world you're representing doesn't exist?

FH: That's surprising to me, because when you look at ancient Greece programmes, so much of it is ruin-based, isn't it? You have your presenter on location, or you just have an image.[11]

DW: Ruins can be a problem. Sometimes it's not obvious what they are. And sometimes it's not obvious why we are there. The solution is – as with any other sequence – to give the ruins a narrative. You need to make sure you pass through the place so as to arrive at the key location at the point in the film where you want to say the thing you want. It's quite hard to script it, so that you don't ruin the logic by showing people something you've already talked about or vice versa. You have to dramatise your walking shots and your pieces to camera, just as cleverly as you would in any drama, because you want to hit people with the punchline when they need the punchline. A good example is the scene in *Guilty Pleasures* about the Panathenaea, Athens' most important religious festival. It was part of a larger sequence about the role of meat as a luxury in ancient Athens. But we couldn't cut straight from a modern meat market to the site of the altar of Athena on the Acropolis where animals were sacrificed and butchered, not least because the altar does not exist any more!

Figure 10.1 At the theatre in Rhamnous in *Ancient Greece: The Greatest Show on Earth*, episode 1 'Democrats' (2013). Tern Television.

We had to get Michael in there, building the tension and providing the context at the same time, holding back the pieces to camera [the punchline] until we got there. There are lots of scenes in our films where Michael goes to something, he looks at something, and he takes it up and he reads it. Now that's the first time we've seen it. For another example there's a scene in *Ancient Greece: The Greatest Show on Earth* at Rhamnous [see Figure 10.1] where Michael finds the inscription: 'Yeah, there it is, Dionysus.' And he reads it and says 'Ah, what you think is a town square is a theatre.' Bang. And then you can go on. But to get him there we had to plan the shots, getting him in there so for the viewer there was a tension about what's going on, where is he going? You have to do that all the time.

MS: This is where in doing television there's an extraordinary sense of teamwork. I may know what the story is, but David is the expert in how you tell that story through the medium of television, which is simultaneously visual and aural. How you tell that story has to be fundamentally different from the way you would tell it when it's a written paper, in a book, or even as a paper you'd give at a conference. Part of that TV storytelling style is how you edit the shots together that open up a site and a story simultaneously, so as to deliver both the site, the storyteller and the story to the right point at the right place at the right time. To bring it all together, link it all together and tie it up is an extraordinarily difficult thing to do that requires a whole set of skills and a lot of teamwork.

DW: Ruins must be telling if you are going to use them – but they can be nondescript, or unintelligible or just plain ugly sometimes. But if they are part of the narrative they will have some kind of emotional status. So you can deploy music and sound effects to help you out. Sound effects and music are all about telling you how to feel before you see it. So a guy's walking up onto the Acropolis. Is he walking up in a happy way? In a celebratory way? A proud way? Or is he rather fearful? The point is you can change the tone of that in making a film, just by changing the music or just having really crunchy footsteps (crunch, crunch), or buzzes, for flies. And of course if you've written it properly you will have shot it to make just those points in the first place.

## TALES OF THE UNEXPECTED

FH: We are starting to think about some practical issues of storyboarding, filming and editing. Before going further, could you say more about how the production process pans out?

MS: First, there'll be six to eight weeks of pre-production, developing your scripts, working out the filming schedule and getting yourself in a position where you're ready to film. Filming takes the shortest possible time because every day is a cost. And then there is a six-week editing process to fine-tune how those oral and visual and musical stories are being told at the same time. Throughout which the dialogue over the storyline goes on. The edit team will come back with some ideas, try something out. There'll be rough cuts and draft final scripts going backwards and forwards throughout the edit.

FH: Do you reshoot at all, go back and re-edit the story?

DW: We've only reshot once, and that was on the drama programme where the BBC wanted extra material. Otherwise, no. It's an anathema. You only get one go. Even, if the weather's bad, that's tough. If it's raining on the Parthenon, that's what you've got [laughing]. If the mines at Laureion are vital but completely waterlogged, that's where you stick your presenter. That's what you have to do. You make it work. You stick your presenter down there, and they say, 'Yeah, it's pretty horrible for me, but back then for them it was even worse.' You make something of it. You have to make something out of everything you do. In fact, you make an issue of it. And that means rethinking the script on the move.

MS: The script that you've worked on in those six to eight weeks is at very best a guide. There will be lots of words in the script, but actually all you're interested in fixing while you're out filming are the pieces to camera. All the words in the commentary links that you've written will change beyond belief by the time you come to an edit script. Because how can you possibly know what exactly you're going to say in the voiceover commentary until you have pictures in front of you and lined up? So you go out to film. And if you turn up at the Parthenon and it's raining, that piece to camera that you've nicely thought about what you were planning to say, you need to keep that main point because you need that point to keep the overarching framework of the argument in place. But you're going to have to find a new way to say it, so that it makes sense of the fact you're standing there in the rain, as if you had intended to stand there in the rain. Actually the whole reality about filming, particularly documentary filming which is done on a shoestring budget with a limited number of days, is that you have to roll with every punch and respond to every reality on the ground. And that can mean that it's raining, it can mean that actually the site is closed, despite the fact you've got permission, or the object you have wanted is out for restoration, or the location you are filming is right next door to a site where they have just started digging up the concrete with a piledriver, so you have to find new locations and objects at the drop of a hat. All of these things happen, and you have to respond. So fundamentally what you end up seeing on the programme, although the programme will make it look like it was a natural part of the story, are building blocks that were created out of practical possibility on the day that you happened to be there filming with the people that you were there filming with.

DW: That kind of flexibility, if you can roll with the punches, can be a huge success. When we were at Delphi I'd spent the whole of the recce [reconnaissance, or survey] and most of the shoot worrying that nobody's going to know what Delphi is, nobody's going to be able to see it for a place as a whole that you can look at. Everybody knows what the Parthenon looks like. It's an icon of ancient and modern Greece. But nobody knows what Delphi looks like. That was until finally we were having lunch with Anne Jacqeumin [an archaeologist from the University of Strasbourg who has worked extensively on the

Figure 10.2 Top shot of Delphi from *Delphi: The Bellybutton of the Ancient World* (2010). Tern Television.

site], one of our French contributors, and she told us to drive down to the port and forty minutes up this valley on the other side. So we did. We found a mobile phone mast, a craggy precipice, and there it was. And that's how we got our top shot. It was a bit of a punt, wasn't it?

MS: Yes, because if it's a one-off chance, and if you don't get any filming in the can, that's an afternoon down the drain that you don't get back.

DW: But instead what we got was utterly wonderful. So much so that we started the film with it [see Figure 10.2].

MS: That's where the flexibility works in our favour, and works in favour of having an academic as the presenter. If a site has to change, if a different object has to be used or a better location or objects are suggested and made available, then the academic can respond to that and bring their knowledge of the period to bear on working with that new site or object.

DW: Are we allowed to stand on the temple at Delphi, where the oracle was? At first they might say no, but if we keep asking and they get to know us, then perhaps yes!

MS: Or again at Delphi, you [David] were wondering what to do with all the tourists running about. We can't pay to have the site shut off, and they won't allow us to film before the tourists come in. So we have to film with the tourists. Again, it's a practical issue, because the cameraman will say, 'Well, we can probably frame them out, but then we can only look at this.' So you need to decide whether to trade off the background. But the sound person will say, 'Look, you can't not see them because you will still hear them.' If you can hear the tourists but not see them, that's always weird for viewers.

DW: So we made an issue of it. We filmed them and used the tourists as an analogue for ancient visitors coming to Delphi from all over the ancient world, and even put in a bit of dialogue from one of them.

MS: So once again the story has to change to reflect the realities on the ground.

FH: From your description, it seems that conditions on location can really set the agenda, in terms of what the viewer will eventually see and hear. How easy is it to film where you want to be?

MS: You start with this really wide longlist. Then there's the routine of thinking, 'Right, what is going to be available during the shoot? What's going to be open, what can we actually get to?' The average budget for a BBC4 one-hour documentary allows for about six days of foreign filming, so what can we get to in six days? What are you going to prioritise, if it's going to take half a day to get somewhere, versus three sites that are all close by? Right, now you get in touch with the authorities. 'Can we come and film here on this day?' 'No, but you can come two days later.' Can the schedule be reworked to be there on Wednesday, when actually we wanted to be there on Monday?

DW: And if it can't, you rewrite the script. You might just say, 'OK, we won't do a ten-minute sequence about this', and actually do a really, really hyped piece to camera, very quiet, just you and the hurricane lamp, usually in a tent somewhere. Just do it as the hard sell, boom, you're keeping the emotion going. You just wind the whole thing down, and say [whispering] 'Right, this is the point.' The thing to do is keep your eye on the prize all the time of what you're going for. Or you can find while filming that you've missed something important in the scripting by being too close to things, which is perhaps the worst danger. There was a good moment like this on the Delphi shoot. We had filmed all the way up the sanctuary, filming building after building, making our points at each one. All good stuff but then our cameraman said, 'Yes, but what was it like to be here?' Yes, they listen! He was right. So we stopped in the theatre, looking down on the sanctuary, and Michael wrote a piece to camera about the experience of being in Delphi for the festival. And it went in. So there are many ways up the mountain. As long as you know where the top is, you can get up there. It can be quite nerve-racking at the time, but actually it always works out.

## TELEVISUAL GREECE

FH: The opportunities you describe arising from the challenges of filming on location seem very much tied to the potential offered by television: to show the presenter on site, to capture it visually and aurally in its entirety, to select what the viewer will eventually see and hear. Are there other ways in which telling stories about ancient Greece benefits from the audiovisual medium, if we might regard it as another practical constraint or, perhaps better, opportunity?

DW: Michael's research speciality is space, how people move around in classical Greece.[12] How people move through monuments has been reasonably big in British archaeology for quite a long time.[13] It's actually one of the few ways modern people can use to try to understand the purpose of some of the more enigmatic monuments. So I've spent a lot of time trying to film my way around places like Avebury, trying to see them as they were meant to be seen. Ancient Greece is no different. We may know a lot more about them and the people who made them but for me a camera is really the best way to see a lot of these places. You're moving through the monument visually, you're not looking at a plan, you're not looking at a wide shot for very long, you have to get in there, and then you have to move purposefully around it. And my narrative point is actually the same as one of Michael's academic points, which is that how you went in affects the way you saw it. And every time we film a monument, that's how we think.

FH: So, when a presenter 'follows in the footsteps', it's more than a trope?[14]

DW: You know, there's a great moment [in *Delphi*] when Michael comes round the corner and says 'This is where you had to queue, this is where you waited to be let it, and finally you were allowed in here' – and he climbs up and goes in, and you go with him. That may be good telly. But also, if you didn't see it that way, you wouldn't be seeing it in an ancient way either.

MS: It goes fundamentally to the heart of 'Why should there be a programme about ancient Greece on the television? Should we all know the ins and outs of the consultation of the Delphic oracle?' No, actually, most people would be able to perfectly live their lives without knowing a thing about the Delphic oracle. But what you're trying to get across is a sense of this world, what it was like, what made it tick. And then on top of that, where that world fits in the bigger picture of human history, and as a result contributes to the way our world works today. If you say 'It's very important that you know about ancient Greece because . . .,' you'll have lost most people from the beginning. If you say, 'Check out what this was like for them, this crazy experience of going to consult an oracle', then the viewers' own questions start to form in their heads about that process and that world. It's not about giving them all the facts and all the scholarly opinions and all the background. It's getting them curious enough to ask their own questions. And you do that through giving them the experience.

DW: And teasing them, as you travel through the place. Where are they going to end up?

MS: The camera itself as a thing that moves, giving you a viewpoint, forces people to consider what it was actually like to live and breathe back then, much more so in many ways than if you read a book. So yes, the very medium of television offers a different kind of way of understanding and talking about ancient Greece.

FH: So the technology very much contributes to the story you tell.

MS: Yes. It's also what you can do with that technology. On *Delphi*, we were experimenting as well with different camera lenses. The cameraman had this wobbly glass lens.

DW: This is where you have a filter made of slightly warped thicker and thinner glass, so that when you pan across a scene the perspective of part of the scene changes as you move, in a rather trippy way [see Figure 10.3]. So if you're talking about hallucination, that's quite

# Greece in the Making 219

Figure 10.3 The 'wobble' effect in *Delphi: The Bellybutton of the Ancient World* (2010). Tern Television.

a cool thing to do. At Delphi, altered states of consciousness of one form or another were key to the oracle, so this was a way of taking the audience there. We did it a lot on *Resurrection* too [a 2004 programme on Channel 4 about Jesus].

MS: But then there are time lapses as well. So you can set a camera going, you want to give a sense of what it's like to be in a place for a day. Or we might reflect on what's happening now in terms of 3D immersive and dramatic reconstruction. We did a little bit of that in *Delphi*, rebuilding buildings. Particularly for ruins, you can use this new video technology to help reconstruct environments.[15] But I've been flabbergasted by how much it has come on in the last five years. There's a programme we just did for BBC1, *Rome's Invisible City* [broadcast in 2015], where we were working with a laser scanning team, where the laser scans that they create are now so good in quality that you can fly around within a laser scan and 3D immersive, and then seamlessly move back into camera footage. The result is a greater sense of the experience of place, or connection between different spaces, a more mobile and immersive sense of what the world was like, and a more dynamic sense of storytelling. So there is a whole new era of technology now that the ancient, no longer existing, worlds will benefit from.

FH: Given the fundamentally visual aspect of ancient Greece on television, and the way the story you tell is shaped by all these techniques, are there any topics from ancient Greece that you actually couldn't create on screen?

DW: I was going to say it would be quite hard to do a programme about philosophy. Maybe there would be a way, but it would have to be quite sparky. Television isn't really about words, you see, it's about things and feelings all the time. Words are often just explaining what you are looking at. Not that that isn't vital. Take the rock art in *Ape Man* [David Wilson's film about human evolution, broadcast on BBC2 in 2000]. Once you know what the paintings are about it's amazing to see. But if you don't, you're still getting this amazing experience in a cave with these paintings, but that's all they are, pretty pictures of animals. In the same way, if you know what the Parthenon frieze is about it is much, much more telling. It's not just art. It's art with a story, and a meaning. That's what the words do. But the art is the thing you're looking at all the time. And it's what makes you feel as you do.

MS: The more ideas-based, the less it can be related to events, people, things, places, and the harder it is for the televisual medium to tell a story. Television has difficulties in talking about stories that it can't find some way of showing. It also goes back to what television is supposed to do, and what the commissioners will commission. It is not a lecture about the pre-Socratic philosophers. Just because they're interesting, which of course they are, doesn't mean that it should – or even can – be a TV programme.

## THE ANCIENT GREEKS AND US

FH: One final question, if I may. Your programmes have been syndicated around the globe, and *Delphi* has been shown in Britain more than twenty times. What is the appeal?

DW: People love ancient Greece. That audience loves being there. And because it's difficult to be there, because you have that foreign language to read, or lots of very big books, what we can do is take them there. It keeps ancient Greece part of the culture. And I think it's a very valuable part of our culture. Historically it's undeniable that our culture derived some way or another from ancient Greece.[16] But that needs to be kept alive, that idea. Because, as

Edith Hall says in her *Guardian* article,[17] unless people are told this, they will forget. And knowing where you come from is quite important.

MS: As this book makes clear, there are particular moments in our recent past, in television's history, when ancient Greece has suddenly hit a sweet spot in terms of what people are after. And that is exactly the sort of moment that we were involved in during 2010 with the 'ancient Greece' season and then with *Luxury*, which was responding to the global crash of 2011, and which you can see coming up again now. The whole production team of the *Hunger Games* have just been fast-tracked to make a film of the *Odyssey*.[18] What's the *Odyssey* about? It's the search to reclaim identity in a world where the hero is lost.[19] Within this global, constantly evolving, high-technology world in which we now live, more and more people are writing about the difficulties for individuals, groups, communities and nations to maintain their identities. The *Odyssey* speaks directly to those concerns. And I have no doubt that ancient Greece will continue to come back to our screens at different times for a long time to come because it is, at the end of the day, such an incredible melting pot of ideas about human society and human existence. There's always going to be something there to play with and think with in relation to our modern world.

## PROGRAMMES DISCUSSED

*Delphi: The Bellybutton of the Ancient World*. Prod. and dir. David Wilson. Tern Television. BBC4. Monday 22 November 2010, 9.00–10.00pm.

*Guilty Pleasures: Luxury in Ancient Greece*. Prod. and dir. David Wilson. Tern Television. BBC4. Monday 27 July 2011, 9.00–10.00pm.

*Ancient Greece: The Greatest Show on Earth*. 3-part series. Prod. and dir. David Wilson. Tern Television. BBC4. From Tuesday 27 August 2013, 9.00–10.00pm.

## NOTES

1 For further information about Michael Scott, visit <http://michaelscottweb.com>; and for David Wilson, see <http://davidgmwilson.wix.com/david>. We are grateful to Professor Greg Woolf and Valerie James from the Institute for help in arranging this meeting and to the University of

Liverpool Postgate Trust for financial support. (All websites cited in this chapter were accessed 19 December 2016.)

2 Basic information on these programmes, plus some short clips, is available through dedicated pages on the BBC website. On *Delphi: The Bellybutton of the Ancient World*, see <http://www.bbc.co.uk/programmes/b00w4jtx>; *Guilty Pleasures: Luxury in Ancient Greece*, <http://www.bbc.co.uk/programmes/b0126vdc>; and *Ancient Greece: The Greatest Show on Earth*, <http://www.bbc.co.uk/programmes/b039gly5>. Unofficial versions regularly make their way onto YouTube, but are just as regularly removed for breaching copyright. Readers at UK educational institutions may be able to access them on demand via the subscription service Box of Broadcast (bob) provided by Learning on Screen: <http://learningonscreen.ac.uk/ondemand>.

3 A comparison might be drawn with the experiences of another presenter, Bettany Hughes, and her initial attempts to persuade a Channel 4 commissioner to support the project that eventually became *The Spartans* (2004): see Hughes (2009: 7–9). See Gray and Bell (2013: 26–51) on the motivations and decision-making of television executives regarding factual history on television more broadly.

4 On the combination of emotion and intellectual endeavour in television histories, see also Hughes (2009: 4), with Hobden (2013a: 31–4).

5 Representative of the 'affective turn' across the social sciences and humanities, studies collected in Bartsch, Eder and Fahlenbrach (2007) provide an excellent introduction to the issue of emotion in audiovisual media, albeit with a strong focus on film rather than television. Bassols, Cros and Torrent (2013) offer a good summary of the arguments around emotion and cognition in relation to television, plus their own evaluation of factual television in Spain. The interplay between emotion and cognition from a neuroscience perspective is explored by Panksepp (2004).

6 For open access resources developed by the OU around the programme, visit <http://www.open.edu/openlearn/whats-on/tv/ancient-greece-the-greatest-show-on-earth>. The OU collaborated closely on (radio and) television productions as an integral part of its distance-learning (and public engagement) package from its inception: Wrigley (2017a) examines its co-productions of theatre plays in the 1970s.

7 *Coast* has been running on BBC2 since 2005 and is co-produced by BBC Productions and the OU. See <http://www.open.edu/openlearn/whats-on/ou-on-the-bbc-coast>.

8 BBC4 Service Licence. September 2013: <http://downloads.bbc.co.uk/bbctrust/assets/files/pdf/regulatory_framework/service_licences/tv/2013/bbc_four_sep13.pdf>.

9 As observed also by Schadla-Hall and Morris (2009) in relation to factual programmes about ancient Egypt.

10 On the comparative dearth of films about ancient Greece, a 'cinematic

failure' which may partly account for the difficulties in picturing Greece, see Nisbet (2008: 7–9).
11  Hobden (2013b: 367–71) offers an interpretation of the interplay between presenter and ruins in *Delphi: The Bellybutton of the Ancient World*.
12  For example, Scott (2010, 2013).
13  See, for example, Barrett (1994).
14  For an examination of this trope, see Hobden (2017).
15  A digital technique and method discussed by Foka, Chapter 9, above.
16  Hobden, Chapter 1, above, examines this premise in television documentaries, including *Ancient Greece: The Greatest Show on Earth*.
17  Hall (2015).
18  As reported by McNary (2015).
19  For the theme of exile and identity in the reception of the *Odyssey* in previous years, see Hall (2008).

# *Bibliography*

Adler, J. (1989), 'Origins of sightseeing', *Annals of Tourism Research*, 16, 7–29.
Albrecht-Crane, C. and D. Cutchins (2010), *Adaptation Studies: New Approaches*, Madison, WI: Fairleigh Dickinson University Press.
Aldridge, M. (2012), *The Birth of British Television: A History*, Basingstoke: Palgrave Macmillan.
Althusser, L. (1971), *Lenin and Philosophy and Other Essays*, trans. B. Brewster, New York: Monthly Review Press.
Anderson, M. (2004), 'Digital spaces: Pompeii, the internet, and beyond', *Archeologia e Calcolatori*, 15, 449–64.
Andrews, H. (2014), *Television and British Cinema: Convergence and Divergence since 1990*, Basingstoke: Palgrave Macmillan.
Anon. (n.d.), 'Timeline', *The Burton Holmes Archive*, <http://www.burtonholmesarchive.com/?page_id=14> (accessed 28 December 2016).
Anon. (1943a), 'Broadcasting review', *The Manchester Guardian*, 31 March, p. 6.
Anon. (1943b), 'Greek sacrifices for liberty: an appeal to free women', *The Times*, 6 February, p. 3.
Anon. (1943c), 'In the Greek mountains', *The Times*, 19 January, p. 5.
Anon. (1958), 'Sir C. Mackenzie on Cyprus: British policy blamed', *Glasgow Herald*, 18 November.
Anon. (1979a), 'Greek tragedy challenge for make-up', *Ariel: BBC Staff Journal*, 183, 21 February.
Anon. (1979b), 'One man's myth and magic', *The Observer*, 25 February, Magazine, pp. 40–2.
Anon. (2003), 'Obituaries: Don Taylor', *The Times*, 15 December, p. 28.
Appleyard, B. (1982), 'Investing in culture', *The Times*, 21 August, p. 5.
Aspinall, T. (1961), 'Back to school with Lamb's tales – and Shakespeare', *TV Times*, 15 January, pp. 10–11.
Augoustakis, A. and M. S. Cyrino (eds) (2016), *STARZ Spartacus: Reimagining an Icon on Screen*, Edinburgh: Edinburgh University Press.
Aurell, J. (2015), 'Rethinking historical genres in the twenty-first century', *Rethinking History*, 19.2, 145–57.

Aziza, C. (ed.) (1998), *Le péplum: l'antiquité au cinéma* (CinémAction 89), Condé-sur-Noireau: Corlet and Télérama.
Bailey, M. (2007), 'Rethinking public service broadcasting: the historical limits to publicness', in R. Butsch (ed.), *Media and Public Spheres*, Basingstoke: Palgrave Macmillan, pp. 96–108.
Bainbridge, J. (2010), 'New worlds of animation: "Ulysses 31", "The mysterious cities of gold" and the cultural convergence of anime in the West', *Journal of the Oriental Society of Australia*, 42, 77–94.
Bakogianni, A. (2009a), 'Euripides on the modern stage: *The Women of Troy*', *Amphora*, 8.1, 4–5, 18.
Bakogianni, A. (2009b), 'Voices of resistance: Michael Cacoyannis' *The Trojan Women*', *Bulletin of the Institute of Classical Studies*, 52.1, 45–68.
Balfour, M. (1979), *Propaganda in War 1939–1945: Organisations, Policies and Publics in Britain and Germany*, London: Routledge & Kegan Paul.
Banks-Smith, N. (1990), 'An implausible day of judgement', *The Guardian*, 23 July, p. 37.
Barber, B. R. (1984), *Strong Democracy: Participatory Politics for a New Age*, Berkeley, Los Angeles and London: University of California Press.
Barker, D. (2005), 'Obituary: Ken Swan: pioneering cruises to the classical world', *The Guardian*, 10 October, <http://www.theguardian.com/travel/2005/oct/10/travelnews> (accessed 28 December 2016).
Barker, E., C. Bissell, L. Hardwick, A. Jones, M. Ridge and J. Wolffe (2012), 'Colloquium: digital technologies: help or hindrance for the humanities?', *Arts and Humanities in Higher Education*, 11.1–2, 185–200.
Barrett, C. (1994), *Fragments from Antiquity: An Archaeology of Social Life in Britain, 2900–1200 BC*, Oxford and Cambridge, MA: Blackwell.
Bartsch, A., J. Eder and K. Fahlenbrach (eds) (2007), *Audiovisuelle Emotionen: Emotionsdarstellung und Emotionsvermittlung durch audiovisuelle Medienagebote*, Cologne: Herbert vom Halem.
Bassols, M., A. Cros and A. M. Torrent (2013), 'Emotionalization in new television formats of science popularization', *Pragmatics*, 23.4, 605–32.
BBC (1961), 'Memorandum no. 10: television: serious programmes in peak hours', in Cmnd. 1819 *Report of the Committee on Broadcasting, 1960, Volume I Appendix E Memoranda Submitted to the Committee (Papers 1–102)*, London: HMSO, pp. 210–13.
Bell, E. and A. Gray (eds) (2010), *Televising History: Mediating the Past in Post-war Europe*, Basingstoke: Palgrave Macmillan.
Belton, J. (1992), *Widescreen Cinema*, Cambridge, MA: Harvard University Press.
Bendazzi, G. (2016), *Animation: A World History*, 3 vols, Boca Raton, FL: Taylor & Francis.
Berti, I. and M. García Morcillo (eds) (2008), *Hellas on Screen: Cinematic Receptions of Ancient History, Literature and Myth*, Stuttgart: Franz Steiner.

Bignell, J., S. Lacey and M. Macmurraugh-Kavanagh (eds) (2000), *British Television Drama: Past, Present and Future*, Basingstoke: Palgrave.

Blanshard, A. J. L. (2010), *Sex: Vice and Love from Antiquity to Modernity*, Malden and Oxford: Wiley-Blackwell.

Blanshard, A. J. L. and K. Shahabudin (2011), *Classics on Screen: Ancient Greece and Rome on Film*, London: Bristol Classical Press.

Blegen, C. W. (1963), *Troy and the Trojans*, New York: Praeger.

Boschi, A. and A. Bozzato (2005), *I greci al cinema: Dal peplum 'd'autore' alla grafica computerizzata*, Bologna: Digital University Press.

Brayfield, C. (1986), 'Riveting blend of old and new', *The Times*, 17 September, p. 19.

Briggs, A. (1970), *The History of Broadcasting in the United Kingdom*, Vol. 2: *The War of Words*, Oxford: Oxford University Press.

Briggs, A. (1995), *The History of Broadcasting in the United Kingdom*, Vol. 4: *Sound and Vision*, new edn, Oxford: Oxford University Press.

Brown, W. (2013), *Supercinema: Film-Philosophy for the Digital Age*, Oxford and New York: Berghahn Books.

Burdge, A. S. (2013), 'The professor's lessons for the Doctor: the Doctor's sub-creative journey toward Middle-earth', in A. S. Burdge, J. Burke and K. Larsen (eds), *The Mythological Dimensions of Doctor Who*, n.p.: CreateSpace Independent, pp. 65–84.

Buzard, J. (1993), *The Beaten Track: European Tourism, Literature and the Ways to Culture, 1800–1918*, Oxford: Oxford University Press.

Cain, J. and B. Wright (1994), *In a Class of its Own . . . : BBC Education, 1924–1994*, London: BBC Education.

Cannadine, D. (ed.) (2004), *History and the Media*, Basingstoke: Palgrave Macmillan.

Castello, M. G. and C. Scilabra (2015), '*Theoi* becoming *kami*: classical mythology in the anime world', in F. Carlà and I. Berti (eds), *Ancient Magic and the Supernatural in the Modern Visual and Performing Arts*, London: Bloomsbury Academic, pp. 177–96.

Caughie, J. (2000), *Television Drama: Realism, Modernism, and British Culture*, Oxford: Oxford University Press.

Chapman, A. (2016), *Digital Games as History: How Video Games Represent the Past and Offer Access to Historical Practice*, London: Routledge.

Chapman, J. (2013), *Inside the TARDIS: The Worlds of Doctor Who*, rev. edn, London and New York: I. B. Tauris.

Clements, J. (2013), *Anime: A History*, London: BFI and Palgrave Macmillan.

Cohen, J. J. (ed.) (1996), *Monster Theory: Reading Culture*, Minnesota and London: University of Minnesota.

Cole, E. (2015), 'The Method behind the madness: Katie Mitchell, Stanislavski, and the classics', *Classical Receptions Journal*, 7.3, 400–21.

Collard, C. (trans.) (2002), *Aeschylus: Oresteia*, Oxford: Oxford University Press.

Coltman, V. (2009), *Classical Sculpture and the Culture of Collecting in Britain since 1760*, Oxford: Oxford University Press.
Connelly, M. (2004), *We Can Take It! Britain and the Memory of the Second World War*, Harlow: Pearson Education.
Conrad, D. (2011), '*Femmes futures*: one hundred years of female representation in SF cinema', *Science Fiction Film and Television*, 4.1, 79–99.
Constantine, D. (1984), *Early Greek Travellers and the Hellenic Ideal*, Oxford: Oxford University Press.
Cooke, L. (2015), *British Television Drama: A History*, 2nd rev. edn, London: Palgrave and BFI.
Cornelius, M. G. (ed.) (2015), *Spartacus in the Television Arena: Essays on the STARZ Series*, Jefferson: McFarland.
Corner, J. (1995), *Television Form and Public Address*, London: Edward Arnold.
Corrigan, K. and E. Glazov-Corrigan (2004), *Plato's Dialectic at Play: Argument, Structure, and Myth in the Symposium*, University Park: Pennsylvania State University Press.
Coulton, B. (1980), *Louis MacNeice in the BBC*, London: Faber and Faber.
Crace, J. (1986), 'Classics for pleasure', *Radio Times*, 11 September, pp. 82–3, 85.
Craik, J. (1991), *Resorting to Tourism: Cultural Policies for Tourist Development in Australia*, Sydney: Allen and Unwin.
Crashaw, C. and J. Urry (1997), 'Tourism and the photographic eye', in C. Rojek and J. Urry (eds), *Touring Cultures: Transformations of Travel and Theory*, London: Routledge, pp. 176–95.
Crépon, M. (2006), *Altérités de l'Europe*, Paris: Galilée.
Crisell, A. (2002), *An Introductory History of British Broadcasting*, 2nd edn, London and New York: Routledge.
Crook, D. (2007), 'School broadcasting in the United Kingdom: an exploratory history', *Journal of Educational Administration and History*, 39.3, 217–26.
Cropper, M. (1986), 'Dubious bonuses', *The Times*, 18 September, p. 19.
Crozier, M. (1958), *Broadcasting: Sound and Television*, London and New York: Oxford University Press.
Cuddon, J. A. (2013), *A Dictionary of Literary Terms and Literary Theory*, 5th edn rev. M. A. R. Habib, Oxford: Wiley-Blackwell.
Cyrino, M. S. (2005), *Big Screen Rome*, Malden and Oxford: Blackwell.
Cyrino, M. S. (ed.) (2008), *Rome, Season One: History Makes Television*, Malden and Oxford: Blackwell.
Cyrino, M. S. (ed.) (2013), *Screening Sex and Love in the Ancient World*, New York: Palgrave Macmillan.
Cyrino, M. S. (ed.) (2015), *Rome, Season Two: Trial and Triumph*, Edinburgh: Edinburgh University Press.
Danek, G. (2007), 'The story of Troy through the centuries', in M. M.

Winkler (ed.), *Troy: From Homer's Iliad to Hollywood Epic*, Malden and Oxford: Blackwell, pp. 68–84.
Daniel, G. E. (1954), 'Archaeology and television', *Antiquity*, 28, 201–5.
Davie, J. (trans.) (2005), *Euripides: The Bacchae and Other Plays*, London: Penguin.
Davies, B. (1979), 'One man's television', *Broadcast*, 19 March, pp. 8–9.
Day-Lewis, S. (1990), 'TV highlights', *The Sunday Telegraph*, 15 July, '7 Days' supplement, p. 34.
Dillon, R. (2010), *History on British Television: Constructing Nation, Nationality and Collective Memory*, Manchester: Manchester University Press.
Dodds, E. R. (1951), *The Greeks and the Irrational*, Berkeley, Los Angeles and London: University of California Press.
Dodds, E. R. (1960), *The Bacchae*, 2nd edn, Oxford: Clarendon Press.
Dowling, L. C. (1994), *Hellenism and Homosexuality in Victorian Oxford*, Ithaca, NY, and London: Cornell University Press.
Drouin, O. (1981), 'Les bonnes affaires d'*Ulysse 31*', *Le Nouvel Economiste* (Paris), 316, 21 December.
Dunkley, C. (1986a), 'Today's television', *The Financial Times*, 16 September, p. 15.
Dunkley, C. (1986b), 'Blind faith and blinkered views', *The Financial Times*, 17 September, p. 23.
Dunkley, C. (1986c), 'Today's television', *The Financial Times*, 17 September, p. 23.
Dunkley, C. (1986d), 'Today's television', *The Financial Times*, 19 September, p. 23.
Earl, G. P. (2007), 'De/construction sites: Romans and the digital playground', in J. Bowen, S. Keene and L. MacDonald (eds), *Proceedings of the Electronic Visualisation and the Arts (EVA) Conference, London, 2007*, pp. 1–11.
Early, F. and K. Kennedy (2003), *Athena's Daughters: Television's New Women Warriors*, Syracuse, NY: Syracuse University Press.
Elleström, L. (ed.) (2010), *Media Borders, Multimodality and Intermediality*, Basingstoke: Palgrave Macmillan.
Elliott, A. B. R. (2013a), '"And all is real": historical spaces and special f/x in HBO's *Rome*', *Critical Studies in Television*, 8.3, 65–77.
Elliott, A. B. R. (2013b), 'Rewriting European history: national and transnational identities in *Rome*', *Historical Journal of Film, Radio and Television*, 33.4, 576–93.
Ellis, J. (1982), *Visible Fictions: Cinema, Television, Video*, London: Routledge & Kegan Paul.
Ellis, J. (2008), 'What did Channel 4 do for us? Reassessing the early years', *Screen*, 49.3, 331–42.
Ellis, R. (1998), *Imagining Atlantis*, New York: Alfred A. Knopf.
Etlin, R. A. (2005), 'The Parthenon in the modern era', in J. Neils (ed.),

*The Parthenon: From Antiquity to the Present*, Cambridge: Cambridge University Press, pp. 363–95.
Faviez, P. (1996), 'Interview de Yoko', <http://www.citesdor.com/presentation/deyries_2.html> (accessed 6 July 2016).
Fenwick, H. (1979), 'House of horror', *Radio Times*, 3 March, pp. 72–5.
Fiske, J. (1987), *Television Culture*, London and New York: Methuen.
Flower, M. A. (2012), *Xenophon's Anabasis, or The Expedition of Cyrus*, Oxford: Oxford University Press.
Foka, A. and V. Arvidsson (2016), 'Experiential analogies: a sonic digital *ekphrasis* as a digital humanities project', *Digital Humanities Quarterly*, 10.2, <http://www.digitalhumanities.org/dhq/vol/10/2/000246/000246.html> (accessed 20 March 2017).
Ford, P. (2007), *Eye of the Gorgon: The Sarah Jane Adventures, from the Makers of Doctor Who*, London: Penguin.
Forte, M. (ed.) (2010), *Cyber-Archaeology*, BAR International Series 2177, Oxford: Archaeopress.
Forte, M. and A. Siliotti (eds) (1997), *Virtual Archaeology: Re-Creating Ancient Worlds*, New York: H. N. Abrams.
Friedberg, A. (1993), *Window Shopping: Cinema and the Postmodern*, Berkeley and Los Angeles: University of California Press.
Friedrich, W. L. (2000), *Fire in the Sea. The Santorini Volcano: Natural History and the Legend of Atlantis*, trans. A. R. McBirney, Cambridge: Cambridge University Press.
Friendly, A. (1970), 'What became of Atlantis?', *The Guardian*, 3 October, p. 9.
Gamel, M.-K. (2013), 'Can "democratic" modern stagings of ancient drama be "authentic"?', in L. Hardwick and S. Harrison (eds), *Classics in the Modern World: A 'Democratic Turn'?*, Oxford: Oxford University Press, pp. 183–95.
Geraghty, C. (2008), *Now a Major Motion Picture: Film Adaptations of Literature and Drama*, Lanham, MD: Rowman & Littlefield.
Giaccardi, E. (ed.) (2012), *Heritage and Social Media: Understanding Heritage in a Participatory Culture*, London and New York: Routledge.
Golphin, P. (2012), '"Ephemeral work?": Louis MacNeice, broadcasting and poetry', PhD thesis, Open University.
Gransden, K. W. (1959), 'Lighting up the past', *The Listener*, 9 April, p. 644.
Graves, R. (1981), *Greek Myths: Illustrated Edition*, 3rd edn (condensed version of the 1955 1st edn), London: Cassell.
Gray, A. and E. Bell (2013), *History on Television*, London and New York: Routledge.
Griffith, M. (2007), 'Gilbert Murray on Greek literature: the great/Greek man's burden', in C. Stray (ed.), *Gilbert Murray Re-Assessed: Hellenism, Theatre, and International Politics*, Oxford: Oxford University Press, pp. 51–80.

de Groot, J. (2009), *Consuming History: Historians and Heritage in Contemporary Popular Culture*, London and New York: Routledge.

Hajkowski, T. (2010), *The BBC and National Identity in Britain, 1922–53*, Manchester and New York: Manchester University Press.

Hales, S. (2011), 'Cities of the dead', in S. Hales and J. Paul (eds), *Pompeii and the Public Imagination from its Rediscovery to Today*, Oxford: Oxford University Press, pp. 153–70.

Hall, E. (2004), 'Introduction: why Greek tragedy in the late twentieth century?', in E. Hall, F. Macintosh and A. Wrigley (eds), *Dionysus Since 69: Greek Tragedy at the Dawn of the Third Millennium*, Oxford: Oxford University Press, pp. 1–46.

Hall, E. (2008), *The Return of Ulysses: A Cultural History of Homer's Odyssey*, London: I. B. Tauris.

Hall, E. (2015), 'Classics for the people: why we should all learn from the ancient Greeks', *The Guardian*, 20 June, <https://www.theguardian.com/books/2015/jun/20/classics-for-the-people-ancient-greeks> (accessed 19 December 2016).

Hall, E. and F. Macintosh (2005), *Greek Tragedy and the British Theatre, 1660–1914*, Oxford: Oxford University Press.

Hammond, N. (1969), 'Fresh thinking on Atlantis favours a Cretan location', *The Times*, 15 September, p. 12.

Hanna, E. (2009), *The Great War on the Small Screen: Representing the First World War in Contemporary Britain*, Edinburgh: Edinburgh University Press.

Harlan, D. (2009), 'Travel, pictures, and a Victorian gentleman in Greece', *Hesperia*, 78.3, 421–53.

Harrisson, J. G. (2017), '*I, Claudius* and ancient Rome as televised period drama', in A. J. Pomeroy (ed.), *A Companion to Ancient Greece and Rome on Screen*, Malden: Wiley-Blackwell, pp. 271–91.

Hartog, F. (2005), *Anciens, modernes, sauvages*, Paris: Galaade Éditions.

Harvey, C. B. (2013), 'Canon, myth, and memory in *Doctor Who*', in A. S. Burdge, J. Burke and K. Larsen (eds), *The Mythological Dimensions of Doctor Who*, n.p.: CreateSpace Independent, pp. 22–36.

Hastings, M. (2011), *All Hell Let Loose: The World at War 1939–1945*, London: HarperPress.

Hayles, N. K. (1999), *How We Became Posthuman: Virtual Bodies in Cybernetics, Literature, and Informatics*, Chicago: University of Chicago Press.

Hayward, A. (2003), 'Obituaries. Don Taylor: exponent of live television and theatre', *The Independent*, 22 November, p. 26.

Heaney, S. (2004), *The Burial at Thebes: Sophocles' Antigone*, London: Faber and Faber.

Hebert, H. (1986), 'Televising the Thebans', *The Guardian*, 17 September, p. 9.

Hills, M. (2010), *Triumph of a Time Lord: Regenerating Doctor Who in the Twenty-First Century*, London and New York: I. B. Tauris.

Hobden, F. (2009), 'History meets fiction in *Doctor Who*, "The Fires of Pompeii": a BBC reception of ancient Rome on screen and online', *Greece & Rome*, 56.2, 147–63.

Hobden, F. (2013a), 'The archaeological aesthetic in ancient world documentary', *Media, Culture & Society*, 35.3, 366–81.

Hobden, F. (2013b), 'Presenting the past: authenticity and authority in *Athens: The Truth about Democracy* (Lion TV, 2007)', *Classical Receptions Journal*, 5.1, 1–37.

Hobden, F. (2016), 'Between media and genres: Pompeii and the construction of historical knowledge on British television today', in S. Jaki and A. Sabban (eds), *Wissensformate in den Medien: Analysen aus Medienlinguistik und Medienwissenschaft*, Berlin: Frank & Timme, pp. 119–38.

Hobden, F. (2017), 'Ancient world documentaries', in A. J. Pomeroy (ed.), *A Companion to Ancient Greece and Rome on Screen*, Malden and Oxford: Wiley-Blackwell, pp. 491–514.

Hodder, I. and S. Hutson (2003), *Reading the Past: Current Approaches to Interpretation in Archaeology*, 3rd edn, Cambridge: Cambridge University Press.

Hodge, B. (R. I. V.) and D. Tripp (1986), *Children and Television: A Semiotic Approach*, Cambridge: Polity.

Hodgson, C. and J. Wyver (1979), 'Classics for pleasure', *Time Out*, 2–8 March.

Holmes, B. (1901), *The Burton Holmes Lectures with Illustrations from Photographs by the Author*, Vol. III, Battle Creek: Little-Preston.

Home, A. (1993), *Into the Box of Delights: A History of Children's Television*, London: BBC Books.

Home, A. (2011), 'The struggle for quality children's television in the UK', *Journal of Children and Media*, 5.1, 102–6.

Horner, R. (1979), 'A classic case of violence', *The Daily Express*, 8 March, p. 27.

Howatson, M. C. (ed.) (2011), *The Oxford Companion to Classical Literature*, 3rd edn, Oxford: Oxford University Press.

Hughes, B. (2005), *Helen of Troy: Goddess, Princess, Whore*, London: Jonathan Cape.

Hughes, B. (2009), '"Terrible, excruciating, wrong-headed and ineffectual": the perils and pleasures of presenting antiquity to a television audience', in D. Lowe and K. Shahabudin (eds), *Classics for All: Reworking Antiquity in Mass Culture*, Newcastle upon Tyne: Cambridge Scholars, pp. 2–16.

Hughes, B. (2012), 'TV: modern father of history?', *The Historian*, Summer, pp. 6–10.

Hughes-Warrington, M. (2009), 'Introduction. History on film: theory, production, reception', in M. Hughes-Warrington (ed.), *The History on Film Reader*, London and New York: Routledge, pp. 1–12.

Huhtamo, E. (2013), *Illusions in Motion: Media Archaeology of the*

*Moving Panorama and Related Spectacles*, Cambridge, MA: MIT Press.

Irwin, M. (2011), 'Monitor: the creation of the television arts documentary', *Journal of British Cinema and Television*, 8.3, 322–36.

Jacobs, J. (1998), 'No respect: shot and scene in early television drama', in J. Ridgman (ed.), *Boxed Sets: Television Representations of Theatre*, Luton: John Libbey Media, pp. 39–61.

Jacobs, J. (2000), *The Intimate Screen: Early British Television Drama*, Oxford: Oxford University Press.

James, C. (1979), 'Belfast dreamer', *The Observer*, 11 March, p. 20.

Jenkins, T. E. (2015), *Antiquity Now: The Classical World in the Contemporary American Imagination*, Cambridge: Cambridge University Press.

Jenkyns, R. (1980), *The Victorians and Ancient Greece*, Oxford: Blackwell.

Jenkyns, R. (2007), 'United Kingdom', in C. W. Kallendorf (ed.), *A Companion to the Classical Tradition*, Malden and Oxford: Blackwell, pp. 265–78.

Jones, D. A. N. (1979), 'Here be monsters', *The Listener*, 26 July.

Joshel, S. R. (2001), '*I, Claudius*: projection and imperial soap opera', in S. R. Joshel, M. Malamud and D. T. McGuire (eds), *Imperial Projections: Ancient Rome in Modern Popular Culture*, Baltimore: Johns Hopkins University Press, pp. 119–61.

Joshel, S. R., M. Malamud and M. Wyke (2001), 'Introduction', in S. R. Joshel, M. Malamud and D. T. McGuire (eds), *Imperial Projections: Ancient Rome in Modern Popular Culture*, Baltimore: Johns Hopkins University Press, pp. 1–22.

Judt, T. (2005), *Postwar: A History of Europe since 1945*, London: Heinemann.

Kallendorf, C. W. (ed.) (2007), *A Companion to the Classical Tradition*, Malden and Oxford: Blackwell.

Keen, A. G. (2008), 'Katie Mitchell's *Trojan Women*', *Memorabilia Antonina*, 12 January, <http://tonykeen.blogspot.co.uk/2008/01/katie-mitchells-trojan-women.html> (accessed 18 August 2017).

Keen, A. G. (2010a), 'Sideways Pompeii! The use of a historical period to question the Doctor's role in history', in R. P. Garner, M. Beattie and U. McCormack (eds), *Impossible Worlds, Impossible Things: Cultural Perspectives on Doctor Who, Torchwood and The Sarah Jane Adventures*, Newcastle upon Tyne: Cambridge Scholars, pp. 94–117.

Keen, A. G. (2010b), 'It's about Tempus: Greece and Rome in "classic" *Doctor Who*', in D. C. Wright and A. W. Austin (eds), *Space and Time: Essays on Visions of History in Science Fiction and Fantasy Television*, Jefferson: McFarland, pp. 100–15.

Kempton, M. (n.d.), 'An unreliable and wholly unofficial history of BBC Television Centre ... ', *An Incomplete History of London's Television*

Studios, <http://www.tvstudiohistory.co.uk/tv%20centre%20history.htm> (accessed 18 August 2017).

Kennedy, G. A. (2003), *Progymnasmata: Greek Textbooks of Prose Composition and Rhetoric*, Atlanta: Society of Biblical Literature.

Kershaw, B. (1992), *The Politics of Performance: Radical Theatre as Cultural Intervention*, London: Routledge.

Kilburn, M. (2007), 'Bargains of necessity? *Doctor Who, Culloden* and fictionalising history at the BBC in the 1960s', in D. Butler (ed.), *Time and Relative Dissertations in Space: Critical Perspectives on Doctor Who*, Manchester: Manchester University Press, pp. 68–85.

King, G. and T. Krzywinska (2000), *Science Fiction Cinema: From Outerspace to Cyberspace*, London and New York: Wallflower Press.

Klaniczay, G., M. Werner and O. Gecser (eds) (2011), *Multiple Antiquities – Multiple Modernities: Ancient Histories in Nineteenth Century European Cultures*, Frankfurt and New York: Campus.

Knight, P. (1986a), 'Tuesday guide', *The Daily Telegraph*, 16 September 1986, p. 29.

Knight, P. (1986b), 'Wednesday guide', *The Daily Telegraph*, 17 September 1986, p. 35.

Korfmann, M. O. (2007), 'Was there a Trojan War? Troy between fiction and archaeological evidence', in M. M. Winkler (ed.), *Troy: From Homer's Iliad to Hollywood Epic*, Malden and Oxford: Blackwell, pp. 20–6.

Kovacs, D. (ed. and trans.) (2003a), *Euripides: Bacchae, Iphigenia at Aulis, Rhesus*, Cambridge, MA: Harvard University Press.

Kovacs, D. (2003b), 'Towards a reconstruction of *Iphigenia Aulidensis*', *Journal of Hellenic Studies*, 123, 77–103.

Krémer, P. (2002), 'Succès retentissant pour les soirées "Gloubiboulga" dédiées aux 25–35 ans nostalgiques de leur enfance', *Le Monde*, 3 June, p. 10.

Landeschi, G., N. Dell'Unto, K. Lundqvist, D. Ferdani, D. M. Campanaro and A.-M. Leander Touati (2016), '3D-GIS as a platform for visual analysis: investigating a Pompeian house', *Journal of Archaeological Science*, 65, 103–13.

Landesman, O. (2008), 'In and out of this world: digital video and the aesthetics of realism in the new hybrid documentary', *Studies in Documentary Film*, 2.1, 33–45.

Lane Fox, R. (2005), *The Classical World: An Epic History of Greece and Rome*, London: Allen Lane.

Langlands, R. (1999), 'Britishness or Englishness? The historical problem of national identity in Britain', *Nations and Nationalism*, 5.1, 53–69.

Last, R. (1990), 'Don't cry for me, Iphigenia', *The Daily Telegraph*, 23 July, p. 14.

Leab, D. J. (2007), *Orwell Subverted: The CIA and the Filming of Animal Farm*, University Park: Pennsylvania State University Press.

Ledoux, T. and D. Ranney (1997), *The Complete Anime Guide: Japanese*

*Animation Film Directory & Resource Guide*, ed. F. Patten, 2nd edn, Issaquah: Tiger Mountain Press.

LeMahieu, D. L. (1988), *A Culture for Democracy: Mass Communication and the Cultivated Mind in Britain Between the Wars*, Oxford: Clarendon Press.

Lennon, P. (1986), 'You wus framed!', *The Listener*, 25 September, pp. 34–5.

Lindhé, C. (2013), '"A visual sense is born in the fingertips": towards a digital *ekphrasis*', *Digital Humanities Quarterly*, 7.1, <http://www.digitalhumanities.org/dhq/vol/7/1/000161/000161.html> (accessed 24 August 2017).

Lindner, M. (2008), 'Colourful heroes: ancient Greece and the children's animation film', in I. Berti and M. García Morcillo (eds), *Hellas on Screen: Cinematic Receptions of Ancient History, Literature and Myth*, Stuttgart: Franz Steiner, pp. 39–55.

Lindner, M. (2017), 'Mythology for the young at heart', in A. J. Pomeroy (ed.), *A Companion to Ancient Greece and Rome on Screen*, Oxford: Wiley-Blackwell, pp. 515–34.

Lloyd-Jones, H. (1970a), *Aeschylus: Agamemnon*, Englewood Cliffs, NJ: Prentice Hall.

Lloyd-Jones, H. (1970b), *Aeschylus: The Libation Bearers*, Englewood Cliffs, NJ: Prentice Hall.

Lloyd-Jones, H. (1970c), *Aeschylus: Eumenides*, Englewood Cliffs, NJ: Prentice Hall.

Lloyd-Jones, H. (1979a), *Aeschylus: Oresteia. Agamemnon*, London: Duckworth.

Lloyd-Jones, H. (1979b), *Aeschylus: Oresteia. The Libation Bearers*, London: Duckworth.

Lloyd-Jones, H. (1979c), *Aeschylus: Oresteia. Eumenides*, London: Duckworth.

Lowe, D. and K. Shahabudin (eds) (2009), *Classics for All: Reworking Antiquity in Mass Culture*, Newcastle upon Tyne: Cambridge Scholars.

Lowe, R. (1988), *Education in the Post-War Years: A Social History*, London: Routledge.

Lyons, C. L. (2005), 'The art and science of antiquity in nineteenth-century photography', in C. L. Lyons, J. K. Papadopoulos, L. S. Stewart and A. Szegedy-Maszak (eds), *Antiquity & Photography: Early Views of Ancient Mediterranean Sites*, Los Angeles: Getty, pp. 22–65.

McCloud, S. (2006), *Making Comics: Storytelling Secrets of Comics, Manga and Graphic Novels*, New York: Harper.

McDonald, P. (1998), '"With eyes turned down on the past": MacNeice's classicism', in K. Devine and A. J. Peacock (eds), *Louis MacNeice and his Influence*, Gerrards Cross: Colin Smythe, pp. 34–51.

Macintosh, F., P. Michelakis, E. Hall and O. Taplin (eds) (2005), *Agamemnon in Performance 458 BC to AD 2004*, Oxford: Oxford University Press.

McIntosh, J. (2004), 'Wheeler, Sir (Robert Eric) Mortimer (1890–1976)',

*Oxford Dictionary of National Biography*, Oxford: Oxford University Press, online edn, September 2012, <http://dx.doi.org/10.1093/ref:odnb/31825> (accessed 28 December 2016).

MacKinnon, K. (1986), *Greek Tragedy into Film*, London: Croom Helm.

Macmurraugh-Kavanagh, M. and S. Lacey (1999), 'Who framed theatre? The "moment of change" in British TV drama', *New Theatre Quarterly*, 15.1, 58–74.

McNary, D. (2015), '"Hunger Games" team developing multiple "Odyssey" movies for Lionsgate', *Variety*, 22 May, <http://variety.com/2015/film/news/hunger-games-team-multiple-odyssey-movies-lionsgate-1201503572> (accessed 19 December 2016).

MacNeice, L. (2007), *Louis MacNeice: Collected Poems*, ed. P. McDonald, London: Faber and Faber.

Maerz, A. J. and M. R. Paul (1930), *A Dictionary of Color*, New York: McGraw-Hill.

Mahony, S. and G. Bodard (eds) (2010), *Digital Research in the Study of Classical Antiquity*, Burlington and Farnham: Ashgate.

Makrinos, A. (2013), 'In search of ancient myths: documentaries and the quest for the Homeric world', in L. Hardwick and S. J. Harrison (eds), *Classics in the Modern World: A 'Democratic Turn'?*, Oxford: Oxford University Press, pp. 365–79.

Manovich, L. (2001), *The Language of New Media*, Cambridge, MA: MIT Press.

Manovich, L. and A. Kratky (2005), *Soft Cinema: Navigating the Database*, Cambridge, MA: MIT Press. [DVD, with booklet]

Marciniak, K. (ed.) (2016), *Our Mythical Childhood ... The Classics and Literature for Children and Young Adults*, Leiden: Brill.

Marland, M. (1992), 'Appreciations: Ronald Eyre', *The Times*, 23 April, p. 15.

Martindale, M. (1993), *Redeeming the Text: Latin Poetry and the Hermeneutics of Reception*, Cambridge: Cambridge University Press.

Mee, L. and J. Walker (eds) (2014), *Cinema, Television and History: New Approaches*, Newcastle upon Tyne: Cambridge Scholars.

Messenger Davies, M. (1986), 'Children's TV', *The Listener*, 6 November 1986, p. 30.

Messenger Davies, M. (1989), *Television is Good for your Kids*, London: Hilary Shipman.

Messenger Davies, M. (2001), *'Dear BBC': Children, Television Storytelling, and the Public Sphere*, Cambridge: Cambridge University Press.

Messenger Davies, M. (2010), *Children, Media and Culture*, Maidenhead: McGraw-Hill and Open University.

Michelakis, P. (2013), *Greek Tragedy on Screen*, Oxford: Oxford University Press.

Michelakis, P. and M. Wyke (eds) (2013), *The Ancient World in Silent Cinema*, Cambridge and New York: Cambridge University Press.

Miller, J. (1965), 'The Drinking Party', *Radio Times*, 11 November, p. 13.
Monoson, S. S. (2011), 'The making of a democratic symbol: the case of Socrates in North-American popular media, 1941–56', *Classical Receptions Journal*, 3.1, 46–76.
Monrós-Gaspar, L. (2015), *Victorian Classical Burlesques: A Critical Anthology*, London: Bloomsbury.
Morgan, K. A. (1998), 'Designer history: Plato's Atlantis story and fourth-century ideology', *Journal of Hellenic Studies*, 118, 101–18.
Moseley, R. (2007), 'Teenagers and television drama in Britain, 1968–1982', in H. Wheatley (ed.), *Re-Viewing Television History: Critical Issues in Television Historiography*, London: I. B. Tauris, pp. 184–97.
Moseley, R. (2016), *Hand-Made Television: Stop-Frame Animation for Children in Britain, 1961–1974*, Basingstoke: Palgrave Macmillan.
Mulhallen, J. (2010), *The Theatre of Shelley*, Cambridge: Open Book.
Müller, J. E. (2010), 'Intermediality revisited: some reflections about basic principles of this *axe de pertinence*', in L. Elleström (ed.), *Media Borders, Multimodality and Intermediality*, Basingstoke: Palgrave Macmillan, pp. 237–52.
Murnaghan, S. (2011), 'Classics for cool kids: popular and unpopular versions of antiquity for children', *The Classical World*, 104.3, 339–53.
Murray, G. (1921), 'The value of Greece to the future of the world', in R. W. Livingstone (ed.), *The Legacy of Greece*, Oxford: Clarendon Press, pp. 1–23.
Murray, G. (2013) [1947], 'Greece and her tradition', in H. Krabbe (ed.), *Voices from Britain: Broadcasts from the BBC 1939–45*, Stroud: Fonthill, pp. 80–3.
Murray, J. H. (1998), *Hamlet on the Holodeck: The Future of Narrative in Cyberspace*, Cambridge, MA: MIT Press.
Musser, C. (1990), 'The travel genre in 1903–1904: moving towards fictional narrative', in T. Elsaesser with A. Barker (eds), *Early Cinema: Space, Frame, Narrative*, London: BFI, pp. 123–32.
Neville, J. (1960), 'Exploring the theatre of today', *Radio Times*, 29 January, 'Junior Radio Times' supplement, p. 1.
Newman, S. (1982), 'Letters to the Editor. The producer system', *The Times*, 22 October, p. 13.
Nicholas, S. (1996), *The Echo of War: Home Front Propaganda and the Wartime BBC, 1939–1945*, Manchester: Manchester University Press.
Nicholas, S. (2006), 'The good servant: the origins and development of BBC Listener Research, 1936–1950', in *BBC Audience Research Reports. Part 1: BBC Listener Research Department, 1937–c. 1950. A Guide to the Microfilm Edition*, Wakefield: Microform Academic, <https://microform.digital/boa/collections/16/bbc-listener-research-department-reports-1937–c1950/detailed-description> (accessed 24 August 2017).
Nichols, K. (2015), *Greece and Rome at the Crystal Palace: Classical*

*Sculpture and Modern Britain, 1854–1936*, Oxford: Oxford University Press.
Nisbet, G. (2008), *Ancient Greece in Film and Popular Culture*, 2nd edn, Exeter: Bristol Phoenix Press.
Nygren, T., A. Foka and P. Buckland (2014), 'The status quo of digital humanities in Sweden: past, present and future of digital history', in H-Soz-Kult (eds), *The Status Quo of Digital Humanities in Europe*, <http://hsozkult.geschichte.hu-berlin.de/index.asp?id=2402&view=pdf&pn=forum&type=diskussionen> (accessed 20 March 2017).
O'Ferrall, G. M. (1937), 'The televising of drama demands a special technique', *Radio Times*, 19 March, 'Television Supplement', pp. 4–5.
O'Mahony, D. (2007), '"Now how is that wolf able to impersonate a grandmother?": history, pseudo-history and genre in *Doctor Who*', in D. Butler (ed.), *Time and Relative Dissertations in Space: Critical Perspectives on Doctor Who*, Manchester: Manchester University Press, pp. 56–67.
Open University (2011), 'The Burial at Thebes. Part 2', *AA100 The Arts Past and Present*, Milton Keynes: Open University. [CD]
Örnebring, H. (2007), 'Writing the history of television audiences: the Coronation in the Mass-Observation Archive', in H. Wheatley (ed.), *Re-Viewing Television History: Critical Issues in Television Historiography*, London: I. B. Tauris, pp. 170–83.
Osborne, R. (2009), *Greece in the Making, 1200–479 BC*, 2nd edn, London and New York: Routledge.
Page, D. L. (ed.) (1972), *Aeschyli: Septem Quae Supersunt Tragoedia*, Oxford: Clarendon Press.
Panksepp, J. (2004), *Affective Neuroscience: The Foundations of Human and Animal Emotions*, new edn, Oxford: Oxford University Press.
Panos, L. (2013), 'Stylised worlds: colour separation overlay in BBC television plays of the 1970s', *Critical Studies in Television*, 8.3, 1–17.
Paul, J. (2010), 'Oliver Stone's *Alexander* and the cinematic epic tradition', in P. Cartledge and F. Rose Greenland (eds), *Responses to Oliver Stone's Alexander: Film, History, and Cultural Studies*, Madison: University of Wisconsin Press, pp. 15–35.
Paul, J. (2013a), *Film and the Classical Epic Tradition*, Oxford: Oxford University Press.
Paul, J. (2013b), '"Madonna and whore": the many faces of Penelope in *Ulisse* (1954)', in P. K. P. Nikoloutsos (ed.), *Ancient Greek Women in Film*, Oxford: Oxford University Press, pp. 139–62.
Pellegrino, C. (1991), *Unearthing Atlantis: An Archaeological Odyssey*, New York: Random House.
Pemble, J. (2009), *The Mediterranean Passion: Victorians and Edwardians in the South*, London: Faber and Faber.
Peterson, J. (2005), 'Travelogues', in R. Abel (ed.), *Encyclopaedia of Early Cinema*, London and New York: Routledge, pp. 640–3.
Peterson, J. (2013), *Education in the School of Dreams: Travelogues and*

*Early Nonfiction Film*, Durham, NC, and London: Duke University Press.

Pomeroy, A. J. (2008), *'Then It Was Destroyed by the Volcano': The Ancient World in Film and on Television*, London: Duckworth.

Pomeroy, A. J. (ed.) (2017), *A Companion to Ancient Greece and Rome on Screen*, Malden and Oxford: Wiley-Blackwell.

Porter, L. (2012), *The Doctor Who Franchise: American Influence, Fan Culture and the Spinoffs*, Jefferson: McFarland.

Postgate, R. and J. Weltman (1966), 'The present pattern in television and radio: national and regional organisations', in J. Robinson (ed.), *Educational Television and Radio in Britain: Present Provision and Future Possibilities*, London: BBC, pp. 55–86.

Potter, A. (2009), 'Hell hath no fury like a dissatisfied viewer: audience responses to the presentation of the Furies in *Xena: Warrior Princess* and *Charmed*', in D. Lowe and K. Shahabudin (eds), *Classics for All: Reworking Antiquity in Mass Culture*, Newcastle upon Tyne: Cambridge Scholars, pp. 217–36.

Potter, A. (2010), 'Beware of geeks appropriating Greeks: viewer reception of the myth of Philoctetes in *Torchwood*', in R. P. Garner, M. Beattie and U. McCormack (eds), *Impossible Worlds, Impossible Things: Cultural Perspectives on Doctor Who, Torchwood and The Sarah Jane Adventures*, Newcastle upon Tyne: Cambridge Scholars, pp. 79–93.

Potter, A. (2014), 'Viewer reception of classical myth in *Xena: Warrior Princess* and *Charmed*', PhD thesis, Open University.

Potter, A. (2016), 'Classical monsters in new *Doctor Who* fan fiction', *Transformative Works and Cultures*, 21, <http://journal.transformativeworks.org/index.php/twc/article/view/676> (accessed 9 January 2017).

Potter, J. (1989), *Independent Television in Britain*, Vol. 3: *Politics and Control, 1968–80*, London: Macmillan.

Potter, J. (1990), *Independent Television in Britain*, Vol. 4: *Companies and Programmes, 1968–80*, London: Macmillan.

Puchner, M. (2010), *The Drama of Ideas: Platonic Provocations in Theatre and Philosophy*, Oxford and New York: Oxford University Press.

Purser, P. (1986), 'Cash and classics', *The Sunday Telegraph*, 21 September, p. 16.

Purser, P. (2007), 'Taylor, Donald Victor [Don] (1936–2003)', *Oxford Dictionary of National Biography*, Oxford: Oxford University Press, online edn, May 2008, <http://dx.doi.org/10.1093/ref:odnb/92954> (accessed 22 August 2017).

Purser, P. and M. Billington (2003), 'Don Taylor', *The Guardian*, 20 November, p. 29.

Rafer, D. (2007), 'Mythic identity in *Doctor Who*', in D. Butler (ed.), *Time and Relative Dissertations in Space: Critical Perspectives on Doctor Who*, Manchester: Manchester University Press, pp. 123–37.

Raphael, F. (2015), *Going Up: To Cambridge and Beyond – A Writer's Memoir*, London: Robson Press.

Raphael, F. and K. McLeish (1979), *The Serpent Son. Aeschylus: Oresteia*, Cambridge: Cambridge University Press.

Reith, J. C. W. (1924) *Broadcast over Britain*, London: Hodder and Stoughton.

Renger, A. B. and J. Solomon (eds) (2013), *Ancient Worlds in Film and Television: Gender and Politics*, Leiden: Brill.

Ridgman, J. (1998a), 'Producing *Performance*: an interview with Simon Curtis', in J. Ridgman (ed.), *Boxed Sets: Television Representations of Theatre*, Luton: John Libbey Media, pp. 199–208.

Rieu, E. V. (trans.) (1991), *Homer: The Odyssey*, rev. D. C. H. Rieu, London: Penguin.

Robinson, T. (1986), 'Ways of telling', *Books for Keeps: The Children's Book Magazine Online*, 40, September, <http://booksforkeeps.co.uk/issue/40/childrens-books/articles/other-articles/ways-of-telling> (accessed 6 July 2016).

Robinson, T. and R. Curtis (1986), *Odysseus: The Greatest Hero of Them All*, London: BBC and Knight Books.

Robinson, T. and R. Curtis (1987), *Odysseus II: The Journey Through Hell*, London: BBC and Knight Books.

Robson, M. (2008), 'An other Europe', *Paragraph*, 31.3, 375–88.

Romain, M. (1992), *A Profile of Jonathan Miller*, Cambridge: Cambridge University Press.

Rose, C. B. (1998), 'Troy and the historical imagination', *The Classical World*, 91.5, 405–13.

Rose, S. O. (2003), *Which People's War? National Identity and Citizenship in Wartime Britain 1939–1945*, Oxford: Oxford University Press.

Rosen, P. (2001), *Change Mummified: Cinema, Historicity, Theory*, Minneapolis: University of Minnesota Press.

Ruoff, J. (2006), 'Introduction: the filmic fourth dimension', in J. Ruoff (ed.), *Virtual Voyages: Cinema and Travel*, Durham, NC, and London: Duke University Press, pp. 1–21.

Rusbridger, A. (1986), 'Oedipus schmoedipus', *The Observer*, 21 September, p. 32.

Safran, M. (2017), 'Greek tragedy as theater in screen-media', in A. J. Pomeroy (ed.), *A Companion to Ancient Greece and Rome on Screen*, Malden and Oxford: Wiley-Blackwell, pp. 187–207.

Saïd, S. (2011), *Homer and the Odyssey*, Oxford: Oxford University Press.

Say, R. (1986), 'Drama week', *The Sunday Telegraph*, 14 September, p. 16.

Schadla-Hall, T. and G. Morris (2009), 'Ancient Egypt on the small screen: from fact to fiction in the UK', in S. Macdonald and M. Rice (eds), *Consuming Ancient Egypt*, London and New York: Routledge, pp. 195–214.

Schreibman, S., R. Siemens and J. Unsworth (eds) (2004), *A Companion to Digital Humanities*, Malden and Oxford: Blackwell.

Scott, M. (2010), *Delphi and Olympia: The Spatial Politics of Panhellenism in the Archaic and Classical Periods*, Cambridge: Cambridge University Press.

Scott, M. (2013), *Space and Society in the Greek and Roman Worlds*, Cambridge: Cambridge University Press.

Scupham, J. (1961), 'Back to school', *Radio Times*, 14 September, p. 20.

Selway, J. (1986), 'Week in view', *The Observer*, 14 September, p. 30.

Sendall, B. (1982), *Independent Television in Britain*, Vol. 1: *Origin and Foundation, 1946–62*, London: Macmillan.

Sendall, B. (1983), *Independent Television in Britain*, Vol. 2: *Expansion and Change, 1958–68*, London: Macmillan.

Senter, A. (1986), 'Encounter group', *The Listener*, 11 September, pp. 29–30.

Shahabudin, K. (2006), 'Ancient Greece in popular cinema', PhD thesis, University of Reading.

Sharp, S. (2008), 'Star Maidens: gender and science fiction in the 1970s', *Science Fiction Film and Television*, 1, 275–87.

Silk, M., I. Gildenhard and R. Barrow (2014), *The Classical Tradition: Art, Literature, Thought*, Malden and Oxford: Wiley-Blackwell.

Smart, B. (2016), 'Two Edwardian dramas 2: *Play of the Month*: Waste (BBC1, 4 December 1977)', 17 January <https://forgottentelevisiondrama.wordpress.com/2016/01/17two-edwardian-dramas-2-play-of-the-month-waste-bbc1-4-december-1977> (accessed 25 August 2017).

Smith, A. (ed.) (1998), *Television: An International History*, 2nd edn, Oxford: Oxford University Press.

Smithies, J. (2014), 'Digital humanities, postfoundationalism, postindustrial culture', *Digital Humanities Quarterly*, 8.1, <http://www.digitalhumanities.org/dhq/vol/8/1/000172/000172.html> (accessed 20 March 2017).

Solomon, J. (2007), 'The vacillations of the Trojan Myth: popularization & classicization, variation & codification', *International Journal of the Classical Tradition*, 14.3/4, 482–534.

Stallworthy, J. (1995), *Louis MacNeice*, London: Faber and Faber.

Steemers, J. (2004), *Selling Television: British Television in the Global Marketplace*, London: BFI.

Steemers, J. (2010), *Creating Preschool Television: A Story of Commerce, Creativity and Curriculum*, Basingstoke: Palgrave Macmillan.

Steemers, J. (2013), 'Children's television culture', in D. Lemish (ed.), *The Routledge International Handbook of Children, Adolescents and Media*, London and New York: Routledge, pp. 103–10.

Steemers, J. (2016), 'Production studies, transformations in children's television and the global turn', *Journal of Children and Media*, 10.1, 123–31.

Stephens, S. A. and P. Vasunia (eds) (2010), *Classics and National Cultures*, Oxford: Oxford University Press.

Stiegler, B. (2005), *Constituer l'Europe*, 2 vols, Paris: Galilée.

Stone, C. (n.d.), 'Swan Hellenic refines the art of discovery cruising', *Prow's Edge Cruise Magazine*, <http://www.prowsedge.com/views-colin-stone.html> (accessed 28 December 2016).
Stray, C. (1998), *Classics Transformed: Schools, Universities, and Society in England, 1830–1960*, Oxford: Clarendon Press.
Stringer, R. (1986a), 'Oedipus the King', *The Daily Telegraph*, 17 September, p. 10.
Stringer, R. (1986b), 'Focus on cruelty', *The Daily Telegraph*, 18 September, p. 10.
Sweeney, M. (2011), 'Doctor Who BBC Worldwide's biggest-selling TV show internationally', *The Guardian*, 12 July, <https://www.theguardian.com/media/2011/jul/12/doctor-who-bbc-worldwide> (accessed 10 February 2017).
Szegedy-Maszak, A. (2005), 'Introduction', in C. L. Lyons, J. K. Papadopoulos, L. S. Stewart and A. Szegedy-Maszak (eds), *Antiquity & Photography: Early Views of Ancient Mediterranean Sites*, Los Angeles: Getty, pp. 2–21.
Taplin, O. (1989), *Greek Fire*, London: Jonathan Cape.
Taplin, O. (2005), 'The Harrison version: "so long ago that it's become a song?"', in F. Macintosh, P. Michelakis, E. Hall and O. Taplin (eds), *Agamemnon in Performance 458 BC to AD 2004*, Oxford: Oxford University Press, pp. 235–51.
Taylor, D. (1964), 'The Gorboduc stage', *Contrast*, 3.3, 151–3, 204–8.
Taylor, D. (1981), 'A time to speak', *New Statesman*, 30 October, pp. 32–3.
Taylor, D. (1990a), *Days of Vision. Working with David Mercer: Television Drama Then and Now*, London: Methuen.
Taylor, D. (trans.) (1990b), *Euripides: The War Plays. Iphigenia at Aulis, The Women of Troy, Helen*, London: Methuen.
Taylor, D. (1996), *Directing Plays*, London: Black.
Taylor, D. (1998a) [1986], 'Translator's introduction: Sophocles, our contemporary', in J. M. Walton (ed.), *Sophocles: Plays I*, London: Methuen, pp. xiv–lix.
Taylor, D. (1998b), 'Pure imagination, poetry's lyricism, Titian's colours: whatever happened to the studio play on British TV?', *New Statesman*, 6 March, pp. 38–9.
Taylor, N. (1998), 'A history of the stage play on BBC television', in J. Ridgman (ed.), *Boxed Sets: Television Representations of Theatre*, Luton: John Libbey Media, pp. 23–37.
'Television Critic' (1958), 'Television notes: *Armchair Voyage* too short', *The Manchester Guardian*, 22 July, p. 14.
Thompson, D. P. (2004), *The Trojan War: Literature and Legends from the Bronze Age to the Present*, Jefferson: McFarland.
Thomson, G. D. (ed.) (1938), *The Oresteia of Aeschylus*, 2 vols, Cambridge: Cambridge University Press.
Treacey, M. E. M. (2016), *Reframing the Past: History, Film and Television*, London and New York: Routledge.

Tulloch, J. and M. Alvarado (1983), *Doctor Who: The Unfolding Text*, New York: St Martin's.

Tziovas, D. (2014), *Re-Imagining the Past: Greek Antiquity and Modern Greek Culture*, Oxford: Oxford University Press.

Unwin, S. (1997), 'Obituary: Kenneth McLeish', *The Independent*, 11 December, <http://www.independent.co.uk/news/obituaries/obituary-kenneth-mcleish-1288109.html> (accessed 16 August 2017).

Vellacott, P. (trans.) (1956), *Aeschylus: The Oresteian Trilogy. Agamemnon, The Choephori, The Eumenides*, Harmondsworth: Penguin.

Verreth, H. (2008), 'Odysseus' journey through film', in I. Berti and M. García Morcillo (eds), *Hellas on Screen: Cinematic Receptions of Ancient History, Literature and Myth*, Stuttgart: Franz Steiner, pp. 65–73.

Vidal-Naquet, P. (2005), *L'Atlantide: petite histoire d'un mythe platonicien*, Paris: Les Belles Lettres.

Vidal-Naquet, P. and J. Lloyd (1992), 'Atlantis and the nations', *Critical Inquiry*, 18.2, 300–26.

Wake, O. (2014), 'Don Taylor', February, rev. version of article first published on the *British Television Drama* blog in 2010, <http://www.britishtelevisiondrama.org.uk/?p=461> (accessed 22 August 2017).

Wakeman, R. (2012), 'Veblen redivivus: leisure and excess in Europe', in D. Stone (ed.), *The Oxford Handbook of Postwar European History*, Oxford: Oxford University Press, pp. 423–42.

Wallace, G. (2004), 'Mackenzie, Sir (Edward Montague Anthony) Compton (1883–1972)', *Oxford Dictionary of National Biography*, Oxford: Oxford University Press, online edn, January 2011, <http://dx.doi.org/10.1093/ref:odnb/31392> (accessed 28 December 2016).

Ward, P. (2005), *Documentary: The Margins of Reality*, London: Wallflower Press.

Warren, B. W. (2000), 'After Arnold: narratives of the posthuman cinema', in V. Sobchack (ed.), *Meta-Morphing: Visual Transformation and the Culture of Quick Change*, Minneapolis: University of Minnesota Press, pp. 159–79.

Waymark, P. (1986a), 'Self-made man and the ministry', *The Times*, 13 September, p. 17.

Waymark, P. (1986b), 'Choice: *The Theban Plays* of Sophocles', *The Times*, 16 September, p. 55.

Webb, R. (2009), *Ekphrasis, Imagination and Persuasion in Ancient Rhetorical Theory and Practice*, Burlington and Farnham: Ashgate.

Wellings, B. (2002), 'Empire-nation: national and imperial discourses in England', *Nations and Nationalism*, 8.1, 95–109.

Wells, P. (1998), *Understanding Animation*, London and New York: Routledge.

Wells, P. (2007), 'Classic literature and animation: all adaptations are equal, but some are more equal than others', in D. Cartmell and I. Whelehan (eds), *The Cambridge Companion to Literature on Screen*, Cambridge: Cambridge University Press, pp. 199–211.

Westin, J. (2012), *Negotiating 'Culture', Assembling a Past: The Visual, the Non-Visual and the Voice of the Silent Actant*, Gothenburg: University of Gothenburg Press.

Wheatley, H. (ed.) (2007), *Re-Viewing Television History: Critical Issues in Television Historiography*, London: I. B. Tauris.

Winkler, M. M. (ed.) (2004), *Gladiator: Film and History*, Malden and Oxford: Blackwell.

Wood, M. (1985), *In Search of the Trojan War*, Oxford and New York: Facts on File.

Wood, M. (2001), *In Search of the Trojan War*, rev. edn, London: BBC.

Wright, P. (2005), 'British television science fiction', in D. Seed (ed.), *A Companion to Science Fiction*, Malden: Blackwell, pp. 289–305.

Wrigley, A. (2006), 'Aeschylus' *Agamemnon* on BBC Radio, 1946–1976', *International Journal of the Classical Tradition*, 12.2, 216–44.

Wrigley, A. (2011a), 'Greek plays: *Women of Troy* (BBC, 1958)', 6 June, <http://screenplaystv.wordpress.com/2011/06/21/women-of-troy-bbc-1958/> (accessed 19 August 2017).

Wrigley, A. (2011b), 'Greek plays: Sophocles' *Electra* (A-R for ITV, 1962)', 10 August, <http://screenplaystv.wordpress.com/2011/08/10/greek-plays-sophocles-electra-itv-1962/> (accessed 19 August 2017).

Wrigley, A. (2011c), 'Greek plays: *King Oedipus* (BBC, 1972)', 17 August, <https://screenplaystv.wordpress.com/2011/08/17/king-oedipus-bbc-1972/> (accessed 19 August 2017).

Wrigley, A. (2011d), 'Greek plays: Sophocles' *Electra* (BBC, 1974)', 26 August, <https://screenplaystv.wordpress.com/2011/08/26/sophocles-electra-bbc-1974/> (accessed 19 August 2017).

Wrigley, A. (2011e), 'Greek plays: *Oedipus the King* (BBC/The Open University, 1977)', 2 September, <https://screenplaystv.wordpress.com/2011/09/02/oedipus-the-king-bbc-ou-1977/> (accessed 19 August 2017).

Wrigley, A. (2011f), 'Greek plays: *The Serpent Son* (BBC, 1979)', 5 November, <https://screenplaystv.wordpress.com/2011/11/05/serpent-son-bbc-1979> (accessed 18 August 2017).

Wrigley, A. (2011g), *Performing Greek Drama in Oxford and on Tour with the Balliol Players*, Exeter: University of Exeter Press.

Wrigley, A. (2012a), 'Greek plays: *Oedipus the King*, part 1 of *The Theban Plays* (BBC, 1986)', 9 March, <https://screenplaystv.wordpress.com/2012/03/09/oedipus-the-king-bbc-1986> (accessed 22 August 2017).

Wrigley, A. (2012b), 'Greek plays: *Oedipus at Colonus*, part 2 of *The Theban Plays* (BBC, 1986)', 20 March, <https://screenplaystv.wordpress.com/2012/03/20/oedipus-at-colonus-bbc-1986> (accessed 22 August 2017).

Wrigley, A. (2012c), 'Greek plays: *Antigone*, part 3 of *The Theban Plays* (BBC, 1986)', 6 April, <https://screenplaystv.wordpress.com/2012/04/06/antigone-bbc-1986> (accessed 22 August 2017).

Wrigley, A. (2012d), 'Greek plays: *Iphigenia at Aulis* (BBC, 1990)', 26 April, <https://screenplaystv.wordpress.com/2012/04/26/iphigenia-at-aulis-bbc-1990> (accessed 22 August 2017).
Wrigley, A. (2012e), 'Greek plays: the National Theatre's *The Oresteia* (Channel 4, 1983)', 23 January, <https://screenplaystv.wordpress.com/2012/01/23/oresteia-channel-4-1983> (accessed 12 September 2016).
Wrigley, A. (2013), 'Introduction. Louis MacNeice, classical antiquity, and BBC Radio: from wartime propaganda to radio plays', in A. Wrigley and S. Harrison (eds), *Louis MacNeice: The Classical Radio Plays*, Oxford: Oxford University Press, pp. 1–30.
Wrigley, A. (2014a), 'Aristophanes at the BBC, 1940s–1960s', in S. D. Olson (ed.), *Ancient Comedy and Reception: Essays in Honor of Jeffrey Henderson*, Berlin: de Gruyter, pp. 849–70.
Wrigley, A. (2014b), 'The Edwardians: J. M. Synge's *Riders to the Sea* (BBC, 1960)', 30 April, <https://screenplaystv.wordpress.com/2014/04/30/riders-to-the-sea-bbc-1960> (accessed 25 November 2016).
Wrigley, A. (2015a), *Greece on Air: Engagements with Ancient Greece on BBC Radio, 1920s–1960s*, Oxford: Oxford University Press.
Wrigley, A. (2015b), 'Sophoclean television: *Electra* without subtitles on ITV in 1962', in J. Vatain-Corfdir (ed.), *La scène en version originale*, Paris: Presses de l'Université Paris-Sorbonne (PUPS), pp. 55–65.
Wrigley, A. (2015c), 'The spaces of medieval mystery plays on British television', *Shakespeare Bulletin*, 33.4, 569–93.
Wrigley, A. (2017a), 'Higher education and public engagement: Open University and BBC drama co-productions on BBC2 in the 1970s', *Journal of British Cinema and Television*, 14.3, 377–93.
Wrigley, A. (2017b), 'Aeschylus' *Oresteia* on British television', in R. Kennedy (ed.), *The Brill Companion to the Reception of Aeschylus*, Leiden: Brill, pp. 430–54.
Wrigley, A. (forthcoming), *Greece on Screen: Greek Plays on British Television*, Oxford: Oxford 221
ersity Press.
Wrigley, A. and S. J. Harrison (eds) (2013), *Louis MacNeice: The Classical Radio Plays*, Oxford: Oxford University Press.
Wyver, J. (2007), *Vision On: Film, Television and the Arts in Britain*, London: Wallflower Press.
Wyver, J. (2011), '100 television stage plays: [10] 2001–2011', 31 October, <https://screenplaystv.wordpress.com/2011/10/31/100-television-stage-plays-10-2001-2011> (accessed 22 August 2017).
Wyver, J. (2012a), '*For Schools: Hamlet* (A-R for ITV Schools, 1961)', 5 July, <https://screenplaystv.wordpress.com/2012/07/05/for-schools-hamlet-a-r-for-itv-schools-1961> (accessed 22 November 2016).
Wyver, J. (2012b), '*Julius Caesar* (BBC Schools, 1960)', 29 May, <https://screenplaystv.wordpress.com/2012/05/29/julius-caesar-bbc-schools-

1960> (accessed 22 November 2016).
Wyver, J. (2014a), '"All the trimmings?" The transfer of theatre to television in adaptations of Shakespeare stagings', *Adaptation*, 7.2, 104–20.
Wyver, J. (2014b), 'The Edwardians: *Play of the Month*: *Waste* (BBC, 1977)', 18 May, <https://screenplaystv.wordpress.com/2014/05/18/the-edwardians-play-of-the-month-waste-bbc-1977> (accessed 25 August 2017).
Wyver, J. (2014c), '*Serjeant Musgrave's Dance* and the politics of possibility in two television adaptations', *Critical Studies in Television*, 9.3, 89–99.
Wyver, J. (2016), '"A profound commentary on kingship": the monarchy and Shakespeare's Histories on television, 1957–1965', in I. Morra and R. Gossedge (eds), *The New Elizabethan Age: Culture, Society and National Identity after World War II*, London and New York: I. B. Tauris, pp. 267–88.
Wyver, J. and C. Stevens (2018), 'Intermedial relationships of radio features with Denis Mitchell's and Philip Donnellan's early television documentaries', in A. Lodhi and A. Wrigley (eds), *Radio Modernisms: Features, Cultures and the BBC* [= *Media History*, 24.2].
Žižek, S. (1989), *The Sublime Object of Ideology*, London and New York: Verso.
Žižek, S. (2005), *Interrogating the Real*, ed. R. Butler and S. Stephens, London and New York: Continuum.

# Index

Page references in *italics* refer to illustrations.

*300* (film, dir. Snyder, 2006), 195, 208
*2001: A Space Odyssey* (film, dir. Kubrick, 1968), 152

*About the Theatre* (BBC, 1960), 105n8
*Adventure Story* (BBC, 1950), 8
*Aeneid*, Virgil, 171, 172, 179
Aeschylus *see individual plays*; *Oresteia*
*Agamemnon see Oresteia*
*Alistair Cooke's America* (BBC, 1972), 81
*Anabasis*, Xenophon, 12, 48–9
*Ancient Greece: The Greatest Show on Earth* (BBC, 2013), 17, 27–8, 29, 32, 39, 41, 203, 206–7, 210, 212, 212, 221
*Ancient Worlds* (BBC, 2010), 28–9, 30, 31, 32, 41
*The Angry Gods see Oresteia*
*Animal, Vegetable, Mineral?* (BBC, 1952–9), 76
*Animal Farm* (cartoon film, dir. Batchelor and Halas, 1954), 18n3
animation, 14, 17, 18n3, 147–9, 150–7, 163, 164n6, 166n22
anime (Japanese animation), 147, 150–7, 163, 164n6, 166n27, 167n28
*Antigone*, Sophocles, 28
 *Antigone* (BBC, 1962), 86, 94
 *Antigone* (Thames, 1969), 87
 *Antigone at the Barbican* (BBC, 2015), 14, 23n45, 122n47, 144n2
 *see also The Theban Plays*
*Ape Man* (BBC, 2000), 220
archaeology, 74, 75, 76, 78, 174, 188, 189, 190, 195–8, 204, 211, 217; *see also* digital technologies: cyber-archaeology; Greece, ancient: archaeological sites
Aristophanes *see individual plays*
Aristotle, 70
*Armchair Voyage: Hellenic Cruise* (BBC, 1958), 9, 12, 24–5, 35, 40, 64–81
Associated-Rediffusion, 13, 84, 85, 86, 88, 94–105, 106n11
Association of Cinematograph Technicians, 75
Atlantis, 16, 173–5, 187–202
*Atlantis: End of a World, Birth of a Legend* (BBC, 2011), 188, 192–4, 199
'Atlantis: The Evidence' (*Timewatch* episode, BBC, 2010), 16, 187–202, *194*, *197*
audiences
 evidence for, 5, 25, 68, 85, 87, 88–92, 101, 103, 110, 116, 136–8, 142–3, 154, 172, 174, 175, 181–3
 for radio pre-WWII, 44–5, 85
 for schools television, 84–5, 91–2, 101
 *see also* BBC; education
Aylen, Leo, 1
Ayrton, Michael, 110, 121n32

*Bacchae*, Euripides
 *Bacchae*, extract (Associated-Rediffusion, 1961), 96
 *Bacchae* (BBC, 1961), 86, 92–4, 105
 *Bacchae*, scenes (*In Rehearsal*, BBC, 1969), 87
back projection, 67, 80
Baker, Pat, 95

Ball, Joanna, 113
Bates, Barbara, 95
BBC (British Broadcasting Corporation)
  archives, 87–8
  Children's Department, 157, 160
  Drama Department, 125–6
  Features Department, 44–63, 126
  and national identity, 22n30
  paternalism, charges of, 10
  propaganda, wartime, 44–63
  public service broadcaster, 13, 65, 68, 72, 149, 165n8, 205–6, 207
  schools television, 84–94, 102–4
  Talks Department, 76
  see also audiences; *individual programmes*; radio
Beard, Mary, 201n22
Beeching, Angela, 159–60
Bell, Harry, 205, 206
Bennett, Alan, 4
Beveridge Report (1942), 56
*The Black Adder* (BBC, 1983), 158
*Blake's 7* (BBC, 1978–81), 113, 115
*Britain's Bloodiest Dynasty* (Channel 5, 2014), 207–8
British Film Institute (BFI), 87
*Buffy the Vampire Slayer* (The WB 1997–2000, UPN 2001–3), 180
*Buried Treasure* (BBC, 1954–9), 76
Burstall, Christopher, 25

Cacoyannis, Michael, 27, 117, 118
Cavander, Kenneth, 88, 106n13
Central School of Speech and Drama, 95
CGI (computer-generated imagery) *see* digital technologies
Channel 4, 10, 26, 32, 35, 100, 160, 219, 222n3
*Characters*, Theophrastus, 28
*Charmed* (The WB, 1998–2006), 20n22, 180
Children's BBC (1985–), 147–67
Children's ITV (1983–), 148, 160
*Civilisation* (BBC, 1969), 80–1
Clark, Kenneth, 80–1
*Clash of the Titans* (film, dir. Davis, 1981), 164n6
*Clash of the Titans* (film, dir. Letterier, 2010), 184
classical education *see* education
Classical Reception Studies, 2, 6
*Clouds*, Aristophanes (OU/BBC, 1971), 87

colour separation overlay (CSO), 115, 121n30
Cornwall, 149, 158, 160, *161*
Cotton, Donald, 169–71
*Critias*, Plato, 174, 187, 189, 190-9
Curtis, Richard, 15, 157–63
Curtis, Simon, 127
cyber-archaeology *see* digital technologies

Davies, Russell T., 178, 180
*The Death of Socrates* (BBC, 1966), 19n14
'The Death of Socrates' (*You Are There* episode, 1953–71), 21n28
Delphi, 34, 204–5, 209–10, 214, 215–16
*Delphi: The Bellybutton of the Ancient World* (BBC, 2010), 17, 203–5, 209–10, 215, 214–19, 219, 220, 221
democracy
  Athenian, 24, 46, 48–9, 50, 53–7, 96, 208, 211
  modern, 36, 38, 49, 53–7
design (set, costume, etc), 14, 30, 100, 109–19, 122n46, 128–32, 138, 154–5
*Dialogues*, Plato, 189, 190-9
digital technologies, 16–17, 187–202, 219
  CGI (computer-generated imagery), 16, 187–8, 190–5, *196*, 198, 201n32
  cyber-archaeology, 16, 188, 189, 195–8
*Divine Women* (BBC, 2012), 38, 41
documentaries, television, on ancient Greek topics, 10, 20n22, 24–43, 64–83, 187–202, 203–23; *see also individual programmes*
*Doctor Who* (BBC, 1963–89; 2005–), 14, 15–16, 110–19, 168–86, *171*
Dodds, E. R., 92
Doumas, Christos, 191–2
*The Drinking Party* (BBC, 1965), 1, 2–7, *3*, 18, 116

education
  aspirations (post-war, middle-class), 65, 69
  classical, 2, 6, 10, 11, 69, 88, 89, 109, 111, 157, 172, 204
  Education Act (1944), 7, 69, 106n19, 125

education (cont.)
  further education programmes, 87, 91
  higher education programmes, 17, 87, 117, 206–7
  informal impact of broadcasting on, 65, 68–9, 72, 149, 168, 188, 206
  public school, 2–4, 6, 125
  schools programmes: broadcasters' printed materials for, 84, 85–6, 88–92, 94, 98–101; on radio, 85, 88, 102, 105n5; teachers, role of, 88–9, 92; on television, 13, 84–108, 206
  see also Open University; School Broadcasting Council
Egypt, 60, 121n34, 193, 208
Electra, Sophocles
Electra (Associated-Rediffusion, 1962), 14, 84, 100, 117
Electra (BBC, 1974), front cover, 13, 87, 117
The Empire Strikes Back (film, dir. Kershner, 1980), 152
Euripides see individual plays
Eyre, Ronald, 89, 106n11

Fat Tulip (BBC, 1985), 160
The Fate of the City (BBC, 1951), 8
features (radio form), 45; see also BBC: Features Department; individual works
fidelity discourse, 18n5
film
  ancient world on, 20n24, 21n26, 162, 164n6, 166n21, 172, 185n3, 192
  clips, 93–4, 190, 195
  travelogues ('scenics'), 65, 72–4
football crowds, 29, 30
Fortune, John, 3, 4
The Four Freedoms (BBC, 1943), 53–7, 62

gaming software, 197, 200n5
Gladiator (film, dir. Scott, 2000), 21n26, 192
The Glory that is Greece (BBC, 1941), 49–51, 53, 61, 96
The Glory that was Greece (Stobart's book, 1911), 66
The Glory that was Greece (BBC, 1959), 12, 64–81

The Gods of the Greeks (Kerényi's book, 1951), 69
Goldie, Grace Wyndham, 68, 72, 77, 83n41
The Grand Tour see travel
The Grandeur that was Rome (BBC, 1960), 65, 80, 81
Graves, Robert, 158, 162
Greece, ancient
  archaeological sites, 11, 64–5, 71, 73, 74, 211–14, 219; see also Delphi; Parthenon
  art, 37, 69–70
  drama see individual plays
  Hellenic ideal, 69–60
  'legacy', assertions of, 8, 11–12, 24–40, 211, 220–1
  as propaganda in WWII, 44–63
  on radio, 1, 9–10, 44–63, 65, 74, 88, 165n7, 169–70, 172, 185n3
  women in, 38, 55, 67
Greece, modern
  Athens, 29
  civil war, 65, 78–9
  football crowds in, 29, 30
  independence, war of, 52, 56, 58, 77, 78, 79
  National Organisation of Greek Women, 51–2
  post-WWII condition of, 8–9
  as tourist destination, 13, 24–5, 64–83
  women in, 51–2
  in WWII, 44–63, 79
  see also Armchair Voyage: Hellenic Cruise
Greece Fights On see Long Live Greece
Greek drama see individual plays
Greek Fire (Channel 4, 1989), 10, 26, 32–6, 38, 39, 40–1
The Greeks (RSC, 1980), 106n13
The Greeks: A Journey in Space and Time (BBC, 1980), 25, 40
Guilty Pleasures: Luxury in Ancient Greece (BBC, 2011), 17, 203, 209–10, 211–12, 221, 222n2

Half the World Away (BBC, 1957), 75
Hall, Peter, 110, 117
Hamlet, Shakespeare, 104, 106n11
Hardiman, Terrence, 114, 117
Harrison, Tony, 110
Harvey, Tim, 113, 115
The Haunted House see Mostellaria

Hays, Bill, 110, 116, 117, 144
Hearst, Stephen, 68, 75, 76–7
*Hellenic Cruise* see *Armchair Voyage: Hellenic Cruise*
The Hellenic Travellers' Club, 65, 70
*Hellenic Voyage* (BBC Radio, 1936), 74–5
*Heritage* (Thames), 87
'The Heritage of Greece' (BBC Radio, 1924), 74
Herodotus, 49
history, on television, 20n21
Holmes, Burton, 73
Homer, 79, 162, 169–72; see also individual works
Howard, Alan, 89, 90
Hughes, Bettany, 38, 188, 189–93, 196–8, 222n3

*I, Claudius* (BBC, 1976), 21n28, 110, 115, 117, 121n27
*Iliad*, Homer, 10, 162, 169–71
*In Rehearsal* (BBC), 87
*In Search of the Trojan War* (BBC, 1985), 10
independent television (ITV), 75
 schools television, 84–5
 see also Associated-Rediffusion
*Iphigenia in Aulis*, Euripides
 abridged, as prologue to *The Theban Plays* (BBC, 1986), 121n31
 *Iphigenia at Aulis* (Associated-Rediffusion, 1961), 94, 95, 96–7
 *Iphigenia at Aulis* (BBC, 1990), 13–14, 123–46, *130*, *131*
Italy, in WWII, 51, 52

*Jackanory* (BBC, 1965–96), 15, 147, 157, 158, 160, 163, 167n48
Jacqeumin, Anne, 214
*Julius Caesar*, Shakespeare, 86, 106n11, 106n16

Kidd, Barbara, 113, 115

Lawrence, Charles, 89
Lewis, Geoffrey, 128
*Long Live Greece* (BBC, 1943), 56, 62
Love, Enid, 98
*Lysistrata*, Aristophanes, 28
 *Lysistrata* (BBC, 1964), 20n22

*Macbeth*, Shakespeare, 104
McCoy, Floyd, 191

Mackenzie, Compton, 13, 46, 50, 64–83
McLeish, Kenneth, 109–10, 114, 115
MacNaughton, Alan, 89
MacNeice, Louis, 44–63
 *Autumn Journal*, 46–7, 49, 55
 writing for radio see individual works
magic lantern slides, 72–3
Mair, A. W., 74
manga (Japanese comics), 154–5
*The March of the 10,000* (BBC, 1941), 48–9, 50, 55, 61
*Medea*, Euripides
 *Medea* (Associated-Rediffusion, 1963), 86–7, 100–2, *101*, 105
 *Medea* (ABC, 1968), 87
 *Medea* (film, dir. Pasolini, 1969), 117
Menander, 28
*Metamorphoses*, Ovid, 180
Metaxas, Ioannis, 49
Miles, Richard, 28–9
Miller, Jonathan, 1, 2, 4
Moffat, Steven, 180–2
*Monitor* (BBC, 1958–65), 4
*Mostellaria*, Plautus, 86
Murray, Gilbert, 25–6, 46
'The Myth Makers' see *Doctor Who*

National Organisation of Cypriot Fighters (EOKA), 78
National Popular Liberation Army (ELAS), 79
National Theatre, London, 110, 118
Nazism, 37, 44–63
neoclassical architecture, 2, 6, 34
Newman, Sydney, 125–6

*Odysseus: The Greatest Hero of Them All* (BBC, 1986), 14–15, 147–9, 157–63, *161*, 164
*Odyssey*, Homer, 66, 79, 147–67, 181, 221; see also *Odysseus: The Greatest Hero of Them All*; *Ulysses* 31
*Oedipus at Colonus*, Sophocles see *The Theban Plays*
*Oedipus Tyrannus*, Sophocles
 *King Oedipus* (BBC, 1972), 87, 117
 *Oedipus the King* (OU/BBC, 1977), 87, 117
 *Oedipus* (Sky Arts 2, 2013), 14, 23n45, 122n47, 144n2
 see also *The Theban Plays*
*Of Mycenae and Men* (BBC, 1979), 115

Open University, co-productions with BBC, 17, 87, 117, 206–7; *see also* education
*Oresteia*, Aeschylus
  *The Angry Gods* (Associated-Rediffusion, 1961), 86, 94–100, 99, 104
  *The Serpent Son* (BBC, 1979), 13, 14, 87, 109–22, *111*, *114*
  *Oresteia* (stage, dir. Hall, NT, 1981; Channel 4, 1983), 110, 117
*Out of the Ruins* (BBC, 1947), 8

Page, Denys, 109–10
Palyvou, Clairy, 197–8
*pankration* (martial art), 30
panoramas, 65, 72–3, 81
Parthenon, 31, 38, 210, 211, 213, 214, 220
Pasco, Richard, 89, *90*
Pasolini, Pier Paolo, 117
*Patterns of Love* (Associated-Rediffusion, 1962), 86
Paulin, Tom, 122n52
*Peace*, Aristophanes (Thames, 1969), 87
Peiraïkon Theatron, 14, 84
Penguin Classics, 10, 74, 109
*Percy Jackson* novels, 184
'Performance' (BBC anthology series), 127
'Pericles' *see The Four Freedoms*
Pericles' funeral oration, Thucydides, 12, 50, 52, 53–6, 96
*Persians*, Aeschylus, 27, 49
*Philoctetes*, Sophocles (BBC, 1961), 86, 88–92, *90*, 105
photography, 65, 72, 73, 190, 195
Pilkington Report (1962), 68–9, 86, 102
Pinter, Harold, 5, 86, 100
Plato, 16, 66, 70, 174, 187–99; *see also* Critias; *The Death of Socrates*; *Dialogues*; *The Drinking Party*; *Symposium*; *Timaeus*
Plautus *see Mostellaria*
Pompeii, 178, 185, 191, 201n22
*Pompeii: Life and Death in a Roman Town* (Lion TV, 2010), 201n22
Postgate, Richmond, 84–5
posthumanism, 16, 189, 192–3, 195, 198–9
*Producing Macbeth* (ITV, 1958), 104

*Prometheus Bound*, Aeschylus *see Seize the Fire*
propaganda, wartime *see* BBC
public service broadcasting *see* BBC

radio (BBC)
  and ancient Greece, 1, 9–12, 44–63, 65, 74, 106n13, 109
  as informally educational, 65, 68–9
  listeners *see* audiences
  *see also* BBC: Features Department; individual works
*Radio Times*, 2, 8, 58, *59*, 66, 74, 84, 104, 110, *111*, 112, 116, 125, 126, 129, 138, 158–9
Raphael, Frederic, 109–10, 114, 115
re-enactment, historical, 16, 20n21, 30–1
Reith, John, 5, 126, 144n18
*Resurrection* (Channel 4, 2004), 219
*Return from the Valley* (BBC, 1952), 8
Rigg, Diana, 110, *111*
Robinson, Tony, 15, 149, 157–63, *161*
*Rome* (HBO/BBC, 2005–7), 20n23, 20n24, 192
Rome, ancient, 27, 80, 185n3, 208, 219
*Rome's Invisible City* (BBC, 2015), 219

*The Sacred Band* (BBC, 1944), 58–61, *59*, 62
Salamis, battle of, 27, 49
*Salutation to Greece* (BBC, 1942), 52–3, 61
*Salute to Greece* (BBC, 1942), 52–3, 62
*The Sarah Jane Adventures* (BBC, 2007–11), 15, 168, 176, 178–80, 184
*Scene* (BBC, 1968–2007), 105n8
School Broadcasting Council, 13, 85, 91–2
schools programmes *see* education
science fiction, 111–19, 149, 151, 152, 155, 165n14; *see also Doctor Who*
Scott, Michael, 16–17, 25, 27–31, 203–23, *215*
scripts, 13, 45, 95–6, 109, 205, 207, 210, 211, 213–14, 216
*Seize the Fire* (OU/BBC, 1989), 122n52
*The Serpent Son see Oresteia*
Shakespeare, on television, 19n8, 85, 86, 104, 117, 122n44, 127; *see also individual plays*
Shelley, Percy Bysshe, 25

sightseeing *see* travel
Sigurdsson, Haraldur, 191
Society for the Promotion of Hellenic Studies, 70
Sooke, Alastair, 37
Sophocles, 70; *see also individual plays; The Theban Plays*
*Space: 1999* (ITV, 1975–7), 113
Sparta, Greece, 30, 33–4, 47, 53, 66
Sparta, Wisconsin, 33–4, *33*
*Spartacus* (STARZ, 2010–13), 20n23, 20n24, 195
*The Spartans* (Channel 4, 2002), 20n22
Stanford, William Bedell, 66
*Star Wars* (film, dir. Lucas, 1977), 131, 152
Stobart, J. C. *see The Glory that was Greece*
*Survivors* (BBC, 1975–7), 113
Swan Hellenic Cruises, 70
Swan's Tours, 76
Swan's Travel Bureau, 70
*Symposium*, Plato, 1, 2–7, 18, 116; *see also The Drinking Party*

*Take It from the Top* (Rediffusion, 1965), 87
Taplin, Oliver, 10, 32
Taylor, Don, 14, 87, 123–46; *see also Iphigenia in Aulis; The Theban Plays*
television
  as informally educational, 65, 68–9
  pre-WWII BBC, 44, 75
  *see also* Associated-Rediffusion; BBC; Channel 4
*Tempo*, 87
Tern Television, 41, 204–5, 221
*Theatres and Temples: The Greeks* (Associated-Rediffusion, 1963), 86–7, 100–1, *101*, 105
*The Theban Plays* (BBC, 1986), 13–14, 87, 120n10, 123–46, *131*, *134*, *142*; for other productions see also *Antigone*; *Oedipus Tyrannus*
Theophrastus *see under Characters*
*Theseus the Hero* (BBC, 1985), 158–60, 163
*The Thracian Horses* (BBC, 1946), 8
Thucydides, 46, 70; *see also* Pericles' funeral oration
*Timaeus*, Plato, 174, 189, 190
*Timewatch* (BBC, 1982–) *see* 'Atlantis: The Evidence'

*The Tomorrow People* (ITV, 1973–9), 113
*Torchwood* (BBC, 2006–11), 15, 168, 178–82, 184
tourism *see* travel
travel, 13, 64–5, 69–81
  The Grand Tour, 64, 69–71, 80
  virtual, 65, 72–4, 80
travelogues *see* film
*Treasures of Ancient Greece* (BBC, 2015), 37–8, 41
*Troilus and Cressida*, Shakespeare, 171–2, 186n12
*Trojan Women*, Euripides
  *Women of Troy* (BBC, 1958), 8–9, 13, 86, 117, 118
  *Trojan Women* (Rediffusion, 1965), 87
  *Trojan Women* (film, dir. Cacoyannis, 1971), 27, 118
  *Women of Troy* (stage, dir. Mitchell, NT, 2007), 118
Turkey, 25, 58, 65, 77–9, 169
*TV Times*, 98, 104

*Ulisse* (film, dir. Camerini, 1954), 153, 166n21
*Ulysses 31* (DiC Entertainment/ Tokyo Movie Shinsha, 1981; BBC broadcast, 1985–6), 14–15, 147–57, *150*, 161, 163, 164
United States of America, 33–5, 48, 53, 81

Vellacott, Philip, 100, 109
video tape, 112, 115, 132, 137
viewers *see* audiences
Virgil *see Aeneid*

'What Now?' *see The Four Freedoms*
Wheeler, Mortimer, 13, 24–5, 46, 50, 64–83, *67*
Whitehouse, Mary, 116
*Who were the Greeks?* (BBC, 2013), 25, 29–31, 32, 41
Wilde, Oscar, 19n7
Williams, Bernard, 89, 91, 92–3, *93*
Wilson, David, 16–17, 39, 203–23
*The Winter's Tale*, Shakespeare, 86, 95, 98
Wolfenden, John, 24, 66
*Women of Troy see Trojan Women*

Wood, Michael, 10
Worth, Martin, 95
*The World of Odysseus* (Finley's book, 1956), 69
Wyles, Rosie, 27

*Xena: Warrior Princess* (Renaissance Pictures, 1995–2001), 20n22, 154
Xenophon *see Anabasis*

Yentob, Alan, 127

EU representative:
Easy Access System Europe
Mustamäe tee 50, 10621 Tallinn, Estonia
Gpsr.requests@easproject.com

www.ingramcontent.com/pod-product-compliance
Lightning Source LLC
Chambersburg PA
CBHW061709300426
44115CB00014B/2615